Once and Future Partners:
The United States, Russia and Nuclear Non-proliferation

Edited by

William C. Potter and Sarah Bidgood

Once and Future Partners:
The United States, Russia and Nuclear Non-proliferation

Edited by

William C. Potter and Sarah Bidgood

IISS The International Institute for Strategic Studies

The International Institute for Strategic Studies

Arundel House | 6 Temple Place | London | WC2R 2PG | UK

First published July 2018 **Routledge**
4 Park Square, Milton Park, Abingdon, Oxon, OX14 4RN

for **The International Institute for Strategic Studies**
Arundel House, 6 Temple Place, London, WC2R 2PG, UK
www.iiss.org

Simultaneously published in the USA and Canada by **Routledge**
711 Third Avenue, New York, NY 10017

Routledge is an imprint of Taylor & Francis, an Informa Business

DIRECTOR-GENERAL AND CHIEF EXECUTIVE Dr John Chipman
EDITOR Dr Nicholas Redman
ASSOCIATE EDITOR Nicholas Payne
EDITORIAL Jill Lally, Gaynor Roberts, Sam Stocker
COVER/PRODUCTION John Buck, Kelly Verity
COVER IMAGE: Top: US President Lyndon B. Johnson (far right) watches Secretary
of State Dean Rusk sign the Treaty on the Non-Proliferation of Nuclear Weapons,
1 July 1968 (Corbis via Getty Images)

The International Institute for Strategic Studies is an independent centre for research, information and debate on the problems of conflict, however caused, that have, or potentially have, an important military content. The Council and Staff of the Institute are international and its membership is drawn from almost 100 countries. The Institute is independent and it alone decides what activities to conduct. It owes no allegiance to any government, any group of governments or any political or other organisation. The IISS stresses rigorous research with a forward-looking policy orientation and places particular emphasis on bringing new perspectives to the strategic debate.

The Institute's publications are designed to meet the needs of a wider audience than its own membership and are available on subscription, by mail order and in good bookshops. Further details at www.iiss.org.

British Library Cataloguing in Publication Data
A catalogue record for this book is available from the British Library

Library of Congress Cataloging in Publication Data

ADELPHI series
ISSN 1944-5571

ADELPHI 464–465
ISBN 978-1-138-36636-7

Contents

ACKNOWLEDGEMENTS

This volume is the product of research conducted under a collaborative project with the Centre Russe d'Etudes Politiques on reinforcing and sustaining US–Russia cooperation for non-proliferation. The editors wish to express their sincere gratitude to the John D. and Catherine T. MacArthur Foundation for its support of this project and for recognising the need to build a new cadre of US and Russian experts equipped to address present and future nuclear challenges.

As part of this project, the authors presented the case studies in this volume at a series of Track 1.5 workshops on US–Russia cooperation for non-proliferation in 2016 and 2017. These meetings brought together practitioners, experts and graduate students from both countries to examine how and why the superpowers collaborated on nuclear issues during the Cold War and the two decades following the collapse of the Soviet Union and to explore prospects for resuming joint work in this domain. The editors are very grateful to the workshop participants for sharing their insights, comments and suggestions – derived in many instances from their first-hand experiences. In addition, they wish to thank the many former US and Soviet/Russian government officials who gave their time and advice on this project.

The case studies presented in this volume capture significant – and often overlooked – examples of the rich history of US–Soviet cooperation for non-proliferation. It is hoped that they will lead to greater recognition in Washington and Moscow of the prospects for future collaboration on non-proliferation issues even when the political environment is severely strained.

Finally, the editors wish to express their thanks to Annelise Plooster for her editorial assistance.

GLOSSARY

ACDA   US Arms Control and Disarmament Agency

AEC   US Atomic Energy Commission

BWC   Biological Weapons Convention

CCD   UN Conference of the Committee on Disarmament

CD   UN Conference on Disarmament

COCOM   US Coordinating Committee for Multilateral Export Controls

CTBT   Comprehensive Nuclear-Test-Ban Treaty

CWC   Chemical Weapons Convention

ENDC   Eighteen-Nation Disarmament Committee

ERW   enhanced radiation weapon

EURATOM   European Atomic Energy Community

IADA   International Atomic Development Authority

IAEA   International Atomic Energy Agency

INFCE   International Nuclear Fuel Cycle Evaluation

IPNDV   International Partnership for Nuclear Disarmament Verification

LTBT   Limited Test-Ban Treaty

MAPI   Soviet Ministry of Atomic Power and Industry

MLF   Multilateral Nuclear Force

MW   megawatt

MWe   megawatt electric

NAM	Non-Aligned Movement
NGO	non-governmental organisation
NNWS	non-nuclear-weapons states
NPT	Treaty on the Non-Proliferation of Nuclear Weapons (Non-Proliferation Treaty)
NSG	Nuclear Suppliers Group
NWS	nuclear-weapons states
PNE	peaceful nuclear explosion
PNET	Peaceful Nuclear Explosions Treaty
PRC	People's Republic of China
R&D	research and development
RW	radiological weapons
RWC	Radiological Weapons Convention
SALT	Strategic Arms Limitation Talks
SLBM	submarine-launched ballistic missile
START	Strategic Arms Reduction Treaty
TPNW	Treaty on the Prohibition of Nuclear Weapons
TTBT	Threshold Test-Ban Treaty
UNGA	United Nations General Assembly
WMD	weapons of mass destruction

CONTRIBUTORS

Dr William C. Potter directs the James Martin Center for Nonproliferation Studies and is the Sam Nunn and Richard Lugar Professor of Nonproliferation Studies at the Middlebury Institute of International Studies at Monterey. Trained as a Sovietologist, he has participated as a delegate at every NPT meeting since 1995.

Sarah Bidgood is a senior research associate and project manager at the James Martin Center for Nonproliferation Studies at the Middlebury Institute of International Studies at Monterey. Her research interests include US–Russia relations and the international non-proliferation regime.

Dr Lewis A. Dunn is a retired US ambassador and former senior vice-president at Science Applications International Corporation (SAIC). He was Assistant Director to the US Arms Control and Disarmament Agency during the Reagan administration and US ambassador to the 1985 NPT Review Conference.

Lesley Kucharski received her master's degree in Nonproliferation and Terrorism Studies from the Middlebury Institute of International Studies at Monterey. She worked at the UN Office for Disarmament Affairs in 2017 during the negotiations on the Treaty on the Prohibition of Nuclear Weapons.

Dr Nikolai Sokov is a senior fellow at the James Martin Center for Nonproliferation Studies at the Middlebury Institute of International Studies at Monterey. From 1987 to 1992, he worked at the Ministry of Foreign Affairs of the Soviet Union and later Russia, where he participated in the START I and START II negotiations.

Paul Warnke is a graduate research assistant at the James Martin Center for Nonproliferation Studies and a master's degree candidate at the Middlebury Institute of International Studies at Monterey. In 2017, he worked at the Weapons of Mass Destruction Branch of the UN Office for Disarmament Affairs.

Relations between Moscow and Washington are worse today than they have been at any point since the Cuban Missile Crisis in October 1962. Russia and the United States have radically different positions on almost every international problem, be it Ukraine, Syria or the Iran nuclear deal. Even more dangerous is the total absence of mutual respect or trust between the parties, a tendency on both sides to regard every action by the other with deep suspicion if not outright hostility, intensive information warfare, and the collapse of virtually all modes of routine bilateral interaction and dialogue. At the same time, both countries shun further nuclear-arms reduction negotiations, question the value of existing ones and have embarked on significant weapons-modernisation programmes. A new arms race looms on the horizon just as the New Strategic Arms Reduction Treaty (New START) approaches its end date.

Despite these circumstances, and, in many ways, because of them, Russia and the US are, as Sig Hecker, former Director of the Los Alamos National Laboratory, termed it 'doomed to cooperate' in reducing nuclear risks or together suffer severe and potentially catastrophic consequences.

The logic of collaboration is especially clear with respect to preventing nuclear proliferation, where there is a rich, if often underappreciated, Cold War history of US–Soviet cooperation on nuclear-weapons threat reduction and a strong emphasis on ensuring strategic stability. That cooperation was based on shared existential interests and the recognition that the spread of nuclear weapons would undermine regional and global security, and increase the risk of nuclear-weapons use.

This timely book explores a number of important episodes of Soviet and US non-proliferation cooperation. Its case studies provide an important reminder and key insights into how and why collaboration between the two rivals was possible in spite of prevailing Cold War acrimony. They also demonstrate how the routine dialogue, personal relationships and trust established through these joint efforts in a relatively narrow domain helped prevent a nuclear holocaust and contributed to a better understanding more generally of each side's perspectives on foreign-policy issues. Perhaps most importantly, the historical research points to areas where non-proliferation cooperation between Moscow and Washington might be possible today even as tensions rise. These case studies serve as a critical reminder both of the sober responsibilities the two nuclear powers continue to share and of the tremendous benefits that can be derived from addressing them together. They also point to the need to rise above current tensions and appreciate that history did not start yesterday and will not end tomorrow – at least as long as we keep in mind that we will all either perish or survive together.

Alexei Arbatov
Sam Nunn

Today we confront a world in deep crisis and disarray with more disorder on the horizon. It is a world beset by growing populism and extremism, including in mature democracies, and political dysfunction at the national and international level. According to one observer, we are experiencing nothing less than the breakdown of the 400-year-old Westphalian system of international relations, the core of which is respect for sovereign nation-states.[1] It is a world that brings to mind the universe described vividly in the poem 'The Second Coming' by William Butler Yeats: 'Things fall apart; the center cannot hold.'

Not surprisingly, the general international malaise discerned is also manifest in the realm of non-proliferation, and it involves a growing set of challenges to the international non-proliferation regime. Two of the most critical dangers are the erosion of support for multilateral non-proliferation treaties and institutions and the demise of US–Russia cooperation to curtail the spread of nuclear weapons.

The cornerstone of the non-proliferation regime is the 1970 Treaty on the Non-Proliferation of Nuclear Weapons, or

Non-Proliferation Treaty (NPT), as it is better known. Since its indefinite extension in 1995, the treaty has been subjected to a series of body blows, which has led many non-proliferation experts, policymakers and pundits to prophesise an impending cascade of nuclear-weapons spread and the possible demise of the NPT as we currently know it. Among the most pressing challenges are:

- North Korean nuclear brinkmanship, following its withdrawal from the NPT;
- uncertainty about the durability of the Joint Comprehensive Plan of Action with respect to Iran;
- increased risk of nuclear accidents and weapons use as a result of command-and-control vulnerabilities and potential cyber attacks;
- increased reliance on nuclear weapons by nuclear-weapons possessors and the slow pace of disarmament;
- diminished interest in and support for multilateral processes and international institutions by the US;
- a crisis in US leadership and diminished confidence among US allies in the credibility of security assurances
- a nuclear-arms race in South Asia;
- the rise of non-state actors as nuclear suppliers, middlemen and end users;
- the subordination of global non-proliferation objectives to other domestic and regional economic and political considerations by states party to the NPT;
- a growing gulf between nuclear-weapons states (NWS) and non-nuclear-weapons states (NNWS), the absence of effective 'bridge-builders' across the divide, and little prospect of their emergence;
- significant acrimony between proponents and critics of the Treaty on the Prohibition of Nuclear Weapons

and its potentially negative impact on the NPT review process;

- an uncritical embrace of nuclear power by most states without adequate attention to the full range of economic, safety, terrorism and opportunity costs;
- complacency and ignorance about issues of disarmament and non-proliferation by otherwise well-educated citizens and their elected officials;
- inadequate adherence to and implementation of NPT provisions by states party to the treaty, compounded by the absence of an effective enforcement mechanism;
- the conflict between the inalienable right to peaceful nuclear use and the prudent exercise of that right;
- the politicisation of the International Atomic Energy Agency;
- the re-evaluation by a number of NPT states of the value of the NPT for their security, raising the prospect of additional NPT withdrawals.

All of the aforementioned challenges are significant and merit sustained attention and collective action, and their remediation in many instances will require cooperative engagement by Moscow and Washington. The potential for such collaboration, however, appears dim given the continuing downward spiral in US–Russia relations. Indeed, looking forward, arguably the most acute nuclear danger arises from the total absence of trust between the two largest nuclear-armed states. As wise statespeople and analysts have noted, the US–Russia bilateral relationship is at its lowest point in the post-Cold War era and, in some respects, is more dangerous than during the Cold War.[2]

At this moment of heightened danger, Moscow and Washington are largely disengaged in areas of significant importance to both parties, including, notably, on matters of nuclear non-proliferation. This devolution of interactions and interruption of routine consultations did not occur overnight, and can be traced to a number of factors, many of which do not pertain directly to nuclear issues and occurred before the crisis in US–Russia relations over Crimea in 2014. They include: lingering Russian anger over NATO expansion; scepticism over rationales provided by the US regarding missile-defence deployments in Eastern Europe; US accusations about Russian violations of the Intermediate-Range Nuclear Forces (INF) Treaty; Russian concern about possible future 'colour revolutions' orchestrated by the West; domestic politics in both countries that cater to nationalist policies; diverging Russian and US threat perceptions and preferred approaches for dealing with proliferation problems and problem countries; and ill-considered policies poorly informed by past practices.

As a result of these and other developments, both countries scaled back, and in some instances cut off altogether, important joint programmes. Russia, for example, decided not to extend the Nunn–Lugar Cooperative Threat Reduction Program – one of the most important and long-standing cooperative activities involving Russian and US scientists and defence officials – ostensibly because it no longer had a need for US financial and technical assistance, and also due to a growing priority attached to protecting national-security information.[3] It also pulled out of the last round of the Nuclear Security Summit process in 2016, one of US President Barack Obama's signature non-proliferation initiatives and an area that previously had highlighted Russian and US cooperation. More recently, in 2017, Russia suspended implementation of the joint Plutonium Management and Disposition Agreement. For its part, the US also contributed to the near standstill in routine interactions by suspending its participation in the work of the US–Russia Bilateral Presidential Commission, which included working groups on nuclear energy and nuclear security, foreign policy and fighting terrorism, and arms control and international security. The US government also greatly restricted participation by scientists from its national laboratories in international meetings held in Russia and curtailed their engagement in other bilateral activities. Even in the traditionally collaborative environment among NWS in NPT Review Conference meetings, the last such meeting in 2015 featured major US–Russia disputes and ended without a consensus final document, in large part due to the inability of Moscow and Washington to resolve their differences over the Middle East.

Ironically, one of the very few areas in which Russian and US nuclear perspectives appear to coincide today involves denunciation of the recently concluded Treaty on the Prohibition of Nuclear Weapons. While this rare convergence of views is unlikely to cement their cooperation at the next NPT Review Conference, it may well produce a backlash among the overwhelming majority of NNWS, especially if Moscow and Washington are unable to put forward a viable alternative disarmament or nuclear-risk-reduction initiative.

The paucity of high- and mid-level governmental interaction in the nuclear-arms-control space does not augur well for crisis prevention and management, nuclear-risk reduction, bilateral nuclear-arms control, reinforcement of a frayed NPT regime and prevention of the spread of nuclear weapons to third parties, including non-state actors. The greatest risk of nuclear catastrophe is likely to result from a fateful error, rather than intentional action, and yet both countries are proceeding in a fashion that makes such mistakes more likely.[4]

Reversing this trend will require concerted and deliberate effort. History illustrates, however, that it is possible for Moscow and Washington to collaborate on nuclear non-proliferation even when relations in other areas are poor. Beginning in the 1960s, policymakers and diplomats in the Soviet Union and the US began to cooperate closely on non-proliferation issues, leading to the negotiation of the NPT. Subsequently, as illustrated in Table 1, this cooperation intensified and expanded, and by the mid-1970s frequent and often close coordination of Soviet and US policies to address challenges to the inchoate non-proliferation regime, often with great success, could be observed. This partnership was rarely the subject of contemporary commentary or subsequent historical study. Nevertheless, it is noteworthy that the two superpowers were able to forge common ground on many nuclear issues despite being military and ideological adversaries.

How was this cooperation possible and why did it succeed? More specifically, what were the origins of US–Soviet cooperation in the non-proliferation realm? What enabled cooperation to persist and prosper in this sensitive policy sphere at a time when there was little cooperation in other issue areas? What mechanisms did Soviet and US policymakers utilise to overcome differences in their positions? To what degree did domestic and bureaucratic politics intrude? What role did personal relations among US and Soviet diplomats and policymakers play in facilitating cooperation? And how important were previous examples of non-proliferation cooperation as templates for subsequent cooperation?

This *Adelphi* examines a number of important episodes in Soviet and US non-proliferation cooperation in order to answer these questions. These case studies draw extensively on recently declassified and digitised primary source material, as well as interviews with many former Soviet and US officials, several of whom are chapter authors. In doing so, they elucidate new details of important instances of past cooperation between the two superpowers.

The findings in this volume, while interesting in their own right, also are important for the lessons they suggest for the

Table 1. **Fora for US–Soviet consultations on non-proliferation issues during the Ford, Carter and Reagan administrations, 1974–89**

Forum	Administration	Frequency	Focus	Remarks
Zangger Committee	• Ford • Carter • Reagan	1/yr*	Export guidelines	• Set up in 1970. • Relatively dormant between 1977 and 1981. • Continues to meet annually today.
London/Nuclear Suppliers Group	• Ford (1975–76) • Carter (1977–78)		Export guidelines	• First met in 1975. • Did not meet between 1978 and 1991.
International Nuclear Fuel Cycle Evaluation	Carter (1977–80)	Three plenary conference meetings and 61 working-group meetings	Nuclear-fuel cycle	
Threshold Test-Ban and Underground Nuclear Explosions for Peaceful Purposes (PNE) Negotiations	Ford (1974–76)		Nuclear-test limitations	
Comprehensive Test-Ban	Carter (1977–80)		Nuclear-test limitations	
International Atomic Energy Agency (IAEA) Board of Governors	• Ford (1974–76) • Carter (1977–80) • Reagan (1981–89)	4/yr		Usually involves lower-level representation than General Conference.
IAEA General Conference	• Ford (1974–76) • Carter (1977–80) • Reagan (1981–89)	1/yr		• Very important forum for US–Soviet consultation. • Usually involved lengthy reviews of a wide range of proliferation issues.
IAEA Expert Consultant Groups**				
1. International Spent Fuel Management	• June 1979–July 1982			
2. International Plutonium Storage	• First convened September 1978; concluded end of 1982			
3. Committee for Assurances of Supply	• First convened June 1980			
Scientific Advisory Committee of the Director General of IAEA	• Ford (1974–76) • Carter (1977–80) • Reagan (1981–83)		Discussion of technical issues	

Table 1. **Fora for US–Soviet consultations on non-proliferation issues during the Ford, Carter and Reagan administrations, 1974–89 (continued)**

Forum	Administration	Frequency	Focus	Remarks
Joint Committee established by the US–Soviet Agreement for Cooperation on Atomic Energy	• Carter (1977–79) • Reagan (1983–84)			
United Nations General Assembly and First Committee of the UN (Political and Security)				
NPT Review Conference	• Ford (May 1975) • Carter (August 1980) • Reagan (1985)			
Ad hoc	Ford (autumn 1974)		Export controls/ safeguards	Stoessel (US) and Morokhov (USSR) chaired bilateral discussions on coordinating nuclear supply preceding first meeting of London Club.
Ad hoc	Carter (March 1977)			Vance discussed holding meetings with Soviets when he presented Carter's comprehensive arms-control proposals.
Ad hoc	Carter (June 1977)			• First meeting held to follow up March 1977 proposal. • Chaired by Warnke and Nye (US) and Morokhov (USSR).
Ad hoc	Carter (August and September 1977)		South Africa	• Exchange of intelligence information regarding South African nuclear-test site. • Discussions at ambassadorial level.
Ad hoc	Carter (May 1978)		South Africa	Nye and Timerbaev met in Geneva.
Ad hoc	Reagan (December 1982, June 1983, February 1984)		IAEA, export controls, NPT Review Conference	• Kennedy and Morozov met in Washington DC (1982). • Kennedy and Petrosyants met in Moscow (1983) and Vienna (1984).
Embassy-to-embassy (in some Nth countries)				

*Chairman may call additional meetings and has done so in the past.
**The US ceased to participate in these meetings following the International Atomic Energy Agency vote to withdraw Israel's credentials at the September 1982 IAEA General Conference. In February 1983, after a five-month reassessment of its participation, the US announced its intention to resume participation at an 'early, appropriate date'. It resumed participation that same month.

current environment in which preciously little US–Russia cooperation can be found. While the parallels between the Cold War and the present should not be overdrawn, the threats posed by the spread of nuclear weapons remain remarkably constant and negatively affect both Russian and US core national interests, as well as international security more broadly. It therefore is imperative for policymakers in both countries to refresh their institutional memory and recall why they were doomed to cooperate in the past and must continue to do so.

CHAPTER ONE

The origins of US–Soviet non-proliferation cooperation[1]

William C. Potter

The impetus for extended US–Soviet cooperation in nuclear-arms control, including non-proliferation, is traceable directly to the Cuban Missile Crisis in October 1962 or, as it was known in the Soviet Union, the 'Caribbean Crisis'. As many studies have concluded, the crisis was the closest the two superpowers came to nuclear conflict and prompted reconsideration in both the Soviet Union and the US about the risks of nuclear weapons and the need for their control.[2]

A shared recognition of these dangers and the urgency of mitigating them did not diminish the fundamental nature of their Cold War ideological or military rivalry. It did, however, lead both states to recognise that non-proliferation cooperation served each country's interests and could usefully be pursued through a variety of formal and informal means, including treaty negotiations, parallel export-control policies, routine bilateral consultations and, on occasion, intelligence sharing and high-level coordinated diplomacy.

Evolution of non-proliferation policy

The word 'evolution' is perhaps a misnomer for the development of Soviet or US non-proliferation policy, as it implies a process of continuous and unidirectional change toward a more complex or sophisticated and desirable state of affairs. That description does not accurately capture the dynamics of Soviet and US non-proliferation policy between 1945 and 1992. However, at least four different periods in the development of both countries' non-proliferation policies and perspectives since the beginning of the nuclear age can be discerned.[3] Although the dates in some periods are rough approximations, as the change in policies sometimes occurred gradually and was not always linear, each period had distinctive characteristics and dominant tendencies.[4] Both countries followed the same sequence and general trajectory, but at difference paces. As such, there were significant parallels in the development of Soviet and US non-proliferation policies, but the formative events and learning experiences were not always the same.

Secrecy and denial
United States

The initial US response to the splitting of the atom and the recognition of its dual potential for military and peaceful purposes was to try to keep information about atomic energy secret. Characteristic of this secrecy and denial approach to non-proliferation was the Atomic Energy Act of 1946 that prohibited the international exchange of scientific information about the peaceful uses of nuclear energy. This restriction applied even to the closest allies of the US, Canada and the United Kingdom, both of which had contributed to the Manhattan Project.

At the same time that the US was drafting legislation to control nuclear-information sharing, at the international level it proceeded to give priority to preventing the spread of nuclear weapons by promoting what became known as the Baruch Plan. Based on an internal US governmental report directed by Undersecretary of State Dean Acheson and Tennessee Valley

Authority Chairman David Lilienthal, the Baruch Plan called for the creation of an International Atomic Development Authority (IADA), to which would be entrusted all phases of development and use of atomic energy. More specifically, the IADA was to have 'managerial control or ownership of all atomic activities potentially dangerous to world security', 'power to control, inspect and license all other atomic activities' and 'the duty of fostering the beneficial uses of atomic energy'.[5] The Baruch Plan also called for the cessation of the manufacture of atomic bombs and the disposal of existing atomic stockpiles. These latter steps, however, were conditioned on the prior establishment and operation of the IADA and an adequate system for control of atomic energy. Finally, the Baruch Plan specified that punishment for violations of the plan was not subject to veto in the United Nations Security Council.

The passage of the Atomic Energy Act of 1946 following the Soviet Union's negative response to the Baruch Plan marked the height of US efforts to prevent by 'secrecy/denial' the spread of nuclear technology. By the end of 1953, however, it was apparent that this approach had failed. The Soviet Union had joined the US as an atomic-weapons state and both countries had tested hydrogen bombs. In addition to the development of more sophisticated nuclear weapons, research also had progressed on the peaceful uses of nuclear power, especially in the commercial applications of nuclear reactors for the generation of electricity. Moreover, it was no longer clear whether a US policy of strict secrecy would encourage or discourage indigenous nuclear-development programmes in other states. As Secretary of State John Foster Dulles noted during testimony before the Joint Committee on Atomic Energy, knowledge about atomic energy was growing in so much of the world that it was impossible for the US to 'effectively dam ... the flow of information'. Even if we did try to do it, he observed, 'we [would] only dam our own influence and others [would] move into the field with the bargaining power that that involves'.[6]

Soviet Union

From the American perspective, the Baruch Plan was a magnanimous proposal involving the promised surrender of the US nuclear monopoly in the interests of world peace. The plan was viewed very differently, however, from the Soviet vantage point.

The Baruch Plan's proposed elimination of the veto power of Security Council members, rather than guaranteeing swift and sure punishment for guilty parties, was seen by Moscow as an attempt by the US to facilitate mobilisation of the Western-dominated UN against the Soviet Union. The plan's proposal for international control over atomic energy, similarly, was seen in the Kremlin as a manoeuvre by which the West might gain control over the Soviet economy, at least to the extent that it became dependent upon nuclear power.[7] Inspection procedures called for by the Baruch Plan also probably raised in Joseph Stalin's mind the spectre of Western intelligence operations within the Soviet Union and possible espionage directed at military-industrial facilities. Since the Soviet Union had yet to test a nuclear explosive, it also had some reason to regard the Baruch Plan as a strategy to perpetuate Soviet nuclear inferiority.[8] In short, from the Soviet perspective, to have accepted the Baruch Plan's approach to place the development of atomic energy under UN control would have been tantamount to placing it under the control of the US.

Given these reservations by the Soviet leadership about the Baruch Plan, it is not surprising that their response was a counter-proposal that reversed the sequence of control and disarmament. Whereas the US proposal envisioned first the creation of inspection-and-control machinery and then disarmament, the Soviets insisted that the destruction of all atomic weapons precede introduction of an international control system. This meant, in practice, nuclear disarmament by the US alone. Although discussions over the alternative proposals continued for several years, fundamental differences between the Soviet and US approaches to the control of atomic energy made agreement impossible.

Throughout the period 1945–54, Soviet concerns with the issue of nuclear non-proliferation were clearly peripheral to the major problem of countering the US nuclear-weapons superiority. Soviet research-and-development (R&D) efforts in the nuclear field, therefore, were primarily oriented to military purposes and conducted in great secrecy and in isolation from other countries. However, this policy of secrecy did not preclude the Soviet Union from exploiting the uranium deposits of Soviet-bloc states in Eastern Europe. It also did not interfere with the enthusiastic, if imprecise, media depiction of the enormous domestic economic potential of nuclear power.

Atoms for Peace

United States

The change in US policy from secrecy/denial to active promotion of peaceful applications of atomic energy was clearly signalled in President Dwight Eisenhower's famous 'Atoms for Peace' speech before the UN in December 1953. Eisenhower acknowledged in his address that the secret of the atom eventually would be acquired by other states, and he emphasised the need to exploit those properties in the atom that were good rather than evil. More specifically, he proposed that the governments principally involved in nuclear R&D make joint contributions from their stockpiles of fissionable materials to an International Atomic Energy Agency (IAEA). The agency was to be set up under the jurisdiction of the UN and would be responsible for the storage and protection of contributed fissionable materials. The IAEA also was to have the important responsibility for devising methods to distribute fissionable material for peaceful purposes, especially electrical energy production.

It took nearly four years before Eisenhower's Atoms for Peace proposals found fruition in the establishment of the IAEA. Not only did opposition to the proposals from the Soviet Union need to be overcome, but substantial revisions had to be made in the very restrictive 1946 US Atomic Energy Act. These changes were incorporated in the Atomic Energy Act of 1954 and included the removal of most controls on the classification of information regarding nuclear research, approval of private ownership of nuclear facilities and fissionable material by private industry, and authorisation of the government to enter into agreements for cooperation with other nations on the peaceful uses of nuclear energy. Although these agreements required guarantees by the recipient of nuclear materials or equipment to forswear their use for military purposes, the 1954 Act clearly signalled a basic reordering of US nuclear non-proliferation and export-control priorities. As one observer of the change in US policy pointed out: 'While the idea of safeguards and protective requirements was by no means forsaken, it now took a backseat to the promotion of atomic energy domestically and internationally.'[9]

One of the ironies of the period of relaxed control over nuclear information ushered in by Eisenhower's Atoms for Peace programme was the development of a US–Soviet peaceful nuclear-energy and -prestige race in tandem with the superpower arms race. One aspect of the former competition was the rush by both the Soviet Union and the US to declassify and disseminate a large volume of technical nuclear information. By 1958, this competition had resulted in the adoption of new guidelines for information declassification in the US that made it possible for any nation to gain access to almost all basic scientific information on research, development and the operation of plants and equipment in the field of nuclear fission.[10] During the same period in the 1950s, the US moved to the forefront in the international nuclear-export race, exploiting its lead in the field of enriched-uranium research reactors to capture the market abroad. The US position as the only supplier of enriched uranium for these reactors gave it an invaluable political as well as commercial advantage and enabled it 'to require that the reactors be used only for peaceful purposes, and be inspected first by Americans and then by the IAEA'.[11]

The administrations of Eisenhower, Kennedy, Johnson and Nixon differed widely in their commitment to nuclear-test limitations and other negotiated non-proliferation restrictions. However, until 1974, both Democratic and Republican administrations were inclined to discount – or at least minimise – the relationship between the worldwide growth of nuclear power and the risk of nuclear-weapons proliferation. As such, they tended to subordinate the military implications of nuclear exports to those of commercial advantage. It is telling, for example, that even the major non-proliferation accomplishment of that period, the 1968 Treaty on the Non-Proliferation of Nuclear Weapons (Non-Proliferation Treaty, or NPT), was promoted by both superpowers as a grand nuclear bargain in which the nuclear powers would provide non-nuclear-weapons states with civilian nuclear technology for peaceful purposes in exchange for the latter's pledge to forgo a military capability. This ambiguous division between peaceful and military nuclear activity was reinforced by language in the treaty that distinguished between peaceful and military nuclear-explosive capability. Benefits from the former, it was promised, would be made available to non-nuclear parties to the treaty at a low cost.

If the defining characteristic or tendency of the second phase in the evolution of Soviet and US non-proliferation policy was promotion of the peaceful use of the atom, another very important feature of this period was maintaining alliance relations. During the Eisenhower administration, this meant giving priority to the retention of flexibility in the employment of nuclear weapons over that of the 'non-dissemination' or 'non-diffusion' of nuclear weapons, as non-proliferation typically was referred to at the time. According to one former US government official, this meant, among other things, placing 'a higher premium on nuclear weapons cooperation with [US] allies – even at the price of encouraging and stimulating independent atomic-weapons programs – than … seeking international agreements retarding the spread of nuclear weapons'.[12] Pentagon officials, for example, made the case that the spread of nuclear weapons 'would work to the advantage of the United States because the Soviet Union would not allow its unreliable Eastern European allies to acquire nuclear weapons', while weapons spread to allies such as France and Japan 'would add to the Western advantage in nuclear weapons'.[13]

To be sure, US nuclear policy was not constant during the Atoms for Peace period, and the priority given to non-proliferation rose following the 1960 presidential election. Nevertheless, US nuclear policy during the early 1960s continued to reflect an effort to balance alliance nuclear sharing and cohesion and the promotion of global non-proliferation norms.[14] An important aspect of this balancing act involved the constraints imposed by the overall political relationship between the two superpowers and military rivals. Although oversimplified, the basic mechanism at work appeared to be the phenomenon in which the more hostile the superpower environment, the greater the perceived need in Washington (and Moscow) to maintain alliance solidarity, even if that meant forgoing efforts to curtail the spread of nuclear weapons. Conversely, as prospects for detente increased, there was greater perceived room to promote non-proliferation objectives in both capitals. In this respect, the Cuban Missile Crisis and the subsequent rapprochement in US–Soviet relations convinced President John F. Kennedy and Soviet Premier Nikita Khrushchev of the urgent need to pursue nuclear-arms control and also reduced their sensitivity to the demands of some alliance partners that previously had impaired non-proliferation cooperation.[15]

Soviet Union

Prior to 1954, the Soviet nuclear non-proliferation and export policy resembled that of the US in its emphasis on secrecy and denial. Although the initial Soviet reaction to Eisenhower's 1953 speech reportedly was 'skeptical, but not dismissive',[16] it did not take long for the Soviet Union to launch its own international crusade for peaceful nuclear energy.[17] One of the first steps in the campaign was sponsorship of a series of meetings during 1954 in the Soviet Union and Eastern Europe to which were invited physicists and engineers from Western Europe as well as the developing world. When in December 1954 the US Atomic Energy Commission decided to declassify information on the Argonne (Illinois) atomic reactor, the Soviet Union responded in January 1955 by announcing its own readiness to share the technical data it had collected during the operation of its first atomic power plant.[18] Shortly thereafter, the Soviet Union extended an invitation to scientists from 41 nations to attend a conference in Moscow in July 1955 on the peaceful uses of atomic energy. This conference preceded by one month another international nuclear-energy conference in Geneva and marked the escalation of a nuclear-information export race in which 'the nuclear giants lifted their skirts of secrecy, each challenging the other to reveal more evidence of dedication to the peaceful atom'.[19]

By the mid-1950s, this race had taken the form of exporting not only nuclear-power information and technical experts, but also research reactors. The first recipients of Soviet nuclear exports were the Eastern European states and the People's Republic of China (PRC). Each of these countries in 1955 was offered small research reactors and a small amount of uranium enriched to 10%.[20] Czechoslovakia was also promised a 150-megawatt (MW) natural-uranium-fuelled heavy-water-moderated reactor, while Hungary and East Germany were promised small power reactors.[21] Nuclear R&D in the socialist countries was also encouraged by means of a series of bilateral agreements with the Soviet Union and the creation in 1956 of the Joint Institute for Nuclear Research, at Dubna (near Moscow), whose facilities were made available to scientists from China and Eastern Europe.[22] These intra-bloc arrangements were followed in early 1956 by a nuclear-cooperation agreement with Yugoslavia and an offer to set up a nuclear-research laboratory in Egypt.[23] Significantly, the Soviets failed to apply safeguards to any of these nuclear exports, perhaps because of their confidence in being able to control the nuclear programmes of their allies, but more likely due to a lack of awareness of the ease with which they could be used for military purposes.[24] An alternative explanation is that Khrushchev was prepared to accept the nuclear-proliferation risks in exchange for anticipated political benefits.[25] The latter explanation appears to be most relevant with respect to Soviet nuclear relations with the PRC.

By far the most extensive and significant nuclear assistance provided by the Soviet Union in the mid-1950s was to the PRC. Between 1955 and 1958, the Soviet Union concluded at least six different agreements to assist China in the development of its nuclear programmes, including in the military sector.[26] This assistance included aid in constructing a chemical-separation plant in Xinjiang, delivery of a 6.5-MW heavy-water research reactor (over three times as powerful as the research reactors provided to the East European countries) and the preliminary design of a gaseous-diffusion uranium-enrichment plant at Lanzhou.[27] In Khrushchev's own words: 'Before the rupture in our relations, we'd given the Chinese almost everything they asked for. We kept no secrets from them.'[28] Indeed, the Soviet Union came very close to providing China with a prototype atomic bomb, which had been packed on a train, but at the last moment Khrushchev reversed the decision to send the train to China.[29]

Sino-Soviet nuclear cooperation reconsidered

A number of recent analyses and publicly accessible archival documents require reconsideration of conventional explanations regarding Sino-Soviet nuclear cooperation. In particular, compelling evidence now suggests that while Khrushchev may initially have entertained some idealistic notions that nuclear aid was part and parcel of promoting socialist solidarity and a robust Sino-Soviet alliance – not to mention Soviet demand for Chinese natural uranium – the fluctuations in Sino-Soviet nuclear relations in the period between 1954 and 1960 appear to have been primarily affected by a combination of external events (including a major challenge to alliance solidarity) and domestic Kremlin politics. In other words, although a prominent characteristic or dominant tendency in Soviet nuclear exports and non-proliferation during this relatively short time span was active promotion of Atoms for Peace, this tendency as it applied to China also was significantly driven by domestic and international political considerations.

Although Khrushchev was wary from the outset about Mao Zedong's views on nuclear war and feared that China might drag the Soviet Union into a nuclear conflict with the

US, his readiness to meet Chinese requests for both peaceful and military nuclear assistance noticeably increased following the Hungarian uprising in October 1956. According to the memoirs of People's Liberation Army Marshal Nie Rongzhen, who oversaw China's nuclear-weapons programme in the 1950s, the more accommodating Russian attitude was linked directly to anti-Soviet developments in Eastern Europe and Khrushchev's need to shore up support in the socialist camp.[30] Moscow seized the opportunity to negotiate a new 'Defence Technical Accord' in 1957, which committed the Soviet Union to assist in developing Chinese nuclear missiles.

Khrushchev's political problems had domestic roots linked to the post-Stalin struggle for power within the Kremlin, which were acute during 1957 when Khrushchev sought to expel a number of his powerful adversaries from the Central Committee of the Communist Party. In July 1957, Khrushchev dispatched his fellow Politburo member Anastas Mikoyan to Beijing to solicit Mao's support in his struggle to consolidate power within the Party leadership. Reportedly, Mao gave his support and was rewarded with a promise to assist China in developing atomic weapons and their delivery systems.[31]

It is evident from both Khrushchev's and Nie Rongzhen's memoirs that each side was distrustful of the other, regarded the other as unreliable, and was wary of the other party's political and strategic intentions. Although it remains unclear precisely what led to the Soviet Union's decision to renege on its secret pledge to provide nuclear-weapons assistance to China, it appears that a number of events collectively contributed to the decision, which some believe was reached in early 1958 – about the same time as the public announcement that China intended to produce its own nuclear weapons.[32] The events included both quarrels over very narrow issues, such as Chinese lack of responsiveness to Soviet requests to view a US-designed *Sidewinder* air-to-air missile that China had recovered after it failed to explode following its launch by the Taiwan Air Force, and much broader disputes involving growing divergence in Soviet and Chinese views about nuclear-arms control, non-proliferation and the dangers of superpower nuclear confrontation.[33] The two Communist parties disagreed fundamentally on the wisdom of nuclear-arms-control negotiations, and a comprehensive nuclear-test-ban treaty (CTBT) in particular – an issue that took on prominence with the initiation of negotiations between the Soviet Union and the US on a CTBT in 1958. In fact, the test-ban issue was used as a pretext by Moscow in its formal notification to China on 20 June 1959 that it would not supply a prototype bomb or nuclear-weapons technical data.[34] By the end of August 1960, Moscow had withdrawn all of its nuclear advisers and technicians from China. Not coincidentally, by 1959 Khrushchev also had consolidated his position as leader of the USSR, and no longer required assistance from Mao to shore up his political base.

Technology control
United States

If China in 1958 provided the Soviet Union with cause to re-evaluate its nuclear-export and non-proliferation policy, the comparable learning experience for the US occurred in May 1974, when India exploded a 'nuclear device'. The Indian test, coming as it did after the entry into force of the NPT, was particularly dramatic as it demonstrated that even a relatively poor, developing country could, with sufficient political will and preparation, circumvent the proliferation barriers imposed by the NPT and leapfrog into the ranks of the nuclear-weapons club. The deficiencies of the existing US nuclear-export policy and the international non-proliferation regime were further highlighted by the benign public responses of the nuclear-weapons states to the explosion and by India's insistence that the detonation was a 'peaceful nuclear explosion', a claim facilitated by the NPT's unfortunate affirmation of the distinction between peaceful and non-peaceful nuclear explosions.[35]

Although Washington's public rebuke of India was mild, the Indian explosion served as a catalyst for a major revision in US thinking about nuclear exports and non-proliferation.[36] It also had the effect of moving non-proliferation from the periphery toward the centre stage of Washington's foreign-policy agenda. The practical consequence of this change in priority was the intensification of US diplomatic efforts to establish strict guidelines for the major nuclear-exporting states, covering the transfer of nuclear fuel and sensitive technology and facilities. Two multinational bodies meeting in secret – the Nuclear Exporters Committee and the London Suppliers Group – were mobilised for this purpose.

The Nuclear Exporters Committee, better known as the Zangger Committee after its first chairman, Claude Zangger, was set up in 1970 to interpret the safeguards clause of the NPT (i.e. the provision of Article III designed to prevent the unsafeguarded transfer of nuclear supplies). However, it was not until June 1974, one month after the Indian detonation, that a formal decision was reached to adopt a nuclear-export trigger list. This list specified those items whose export would trigger the application of IAEA safeguards to the facility for which items were supplied. Items on the trigger list, in other words, were not supposed to be exported to non-signatories of the NPT unless the recipient state accepted IAEA safeguards designed to detect the diversion of nuclear material from peaceful to military purposes.

Despite the adoption of the major components of its programmes by the Zangger Committee, there was concern in Washington that a more comprehensive trigger list and more stringent safeguards were necessary to reduce the risk of nuclear material and technology being used for military purposes. Consequently, in late 1974, the US moved to organise a new multilateral body for the purpose of regulating international nuclear commerce. This body, which started meeting in London in 1975, was known as the London Club or the London Suppliers Group, and initially consisted of the seven major suppliers of nuclear materials and equipment: Canada, the Federal Republic of Germany, France, Japan, the Soviet Union, the UK and the US.[37] In January 1976, these seven states exchanged letters endorsing a uniform code of conduct for international nuclear exports. The major provision of the code, which is essentially an unofficial agreement rather than a legally binding treaty, requires that before sensitive nuclear materials, equipment or technology are transferred, the recipient state must:

1) 'Pledge not to use the transferred materials, equipment or technology in the manufacture of nuclear explosives;
2) accept, with no provision for termination, international safeguards on all transferred materials and facilities employing transferred equipment or technology, including any facility that replicates or otherwise employs transferred technology;
3) provide adequate physical security for transferred nuclear facilities and materials to prevent theft and sabotage; and
4) agree not to retransfer the materials, equipment or technology to third countries unless they too accept the constraints on use, replication, security and transfer, and unless the original supplier concurs in the transactions.'[38]

In addition to its diplomatic efforts to establish stricter international nuclear-export guidelines, after 1974 the US moved unilaterally to tighten nuclear-export controls. Particularly significant was President Gerald Ford's policy statement on 28 October 1976 that declared the US would no longer regard the reprocessing of spent nuclear fuel as a 'necessary and inevitable step in the nuclear fuel cycle', and that 'the reprocessing and recycling of plutonium should not proceed unless there is sound reason to conclude that the world community can effectively overcome the associated risks of proliferation'.[39] Ford also directed the Energy Research and Development Administration to seek new means to meet US energy needs that did not require the separation of plutonium from spent fuel, and proposed an international three-year moratorium on the sale or purchase of enrichment and reprocessing facilities.

If Ford's administration initiated the trend in US non-proliferation policy away from reliance upon the efficacy of the NPT and the existing non-proliferation regime, the Carter administration completed the return to an earlier US approach to non-proliferation that emphasised technology denial. The Carter approach, however, departed from past policy in advocating not only denial of nuclear technology to others but self-denial. This dual-denial posture was most clearly expressed in the seven-point nuclear programme announced by President Jimmy Carter in April 1977. The programme entailed:

1) Indefinite deferral of the commercial reprocessing and recycling of plutonium produced in the US on the grounds that reprocessing and recycling were not essential for a viable and economic nuclear programme;

2) deferral of the date of introduction of breeder reactors into commercial use and restructuring of the US breeder-reactor programme to give greater priority to alternative designs;

3) refocusing of US nuclear R&D programmes to accelerate research into alternative nuclear-fuel cycles that do not involve direct access to materials usable in nuclear weapons;

4) expansion of US production capacity for enriched uranium to provide adequate and timely supply of nuclear fuels to other states in order to reduce their incentives to develop indigenous enrichment facilities;

5) revision of the nuclear-export-licensing process to permit the US to conclude nuclear-fuel-supply contracts with other countries and to guarantee delivery of such fuels in order to reduce pressure for the reprocessing of nuclear fuels by other states;

6) continuation of the embargo of US uranium-enrichment and chemical-reprocessing equipment and technology; and

7) continuation of discussions with supplier and recipient states on means to achieve mutual energy objectives without contributing to the proliferation of nuclear weapons.

The most significant and controversial measure taken by the US to implement Carter's non-proliferation programme was the Nuclear Non-Proliferation Act passed in 1978. This legislation, based on the faulty premise that other states would remain dependent on US nuclear assistance, required a cut-off, after 24 months, of all US nuclear exports to non-nuclear-weapons states lacking full-scope safeguards. It also prohibited the reprocessing or retransfer of US-exported material without prior US approval; called for the cut-off of nuclear exports to non-nuclear-weapons states that detonate a nuclear device or engage in activities 'having direct significance for the manufacture or acquisition of a nuclear explosive device' and obliged the president to renegotiate existing agreements to meet the new criteria.[40]

Soviet Union

The termination of Soviet nuclear assistance to China marked a major shift in Soviet nuclear-export and non-proliferation policy, away from reliance on political (as opposed to techno-logical) controls. Having provided a major boost to China's nuclear-weapons development programme, after 1958 the Soviet Union noticeably revamped its nuclear-export poli-cies. The earlier promise to Hungary of a 100-MW reactor, for example, was not fulfilled, nor was the pledge to assist the Czechs in bringing into operation their natural-uranium (and high-plutonium-producing) power plant.

Moscow also adopted a new policy of restricting nuclear-reactor exports to the light-water-reactor variety and, significantly, instituted a serious safeguards system, well in advance of any comparable safeguards adopted by other nuclear suppliers.[41] It also insisted that all recipients of its nuclear reactors obtain the nuclear fuel for their operation from the Soviet Union and return the spent fuel rods to the USSR. In addition, the Soviet Union acted to restrict its allies in Eastern Europe from developing their own uranium-enrichment and plutonium-reprocessing facilities.[42]

Soviet efforts to impose more stringent controls on nuclear exports coincided with the rise of nuclear non-proliferation in the hierarchy of foreign-policy objectives. This develop-ment was reflected in the negotiations undertaken by Moscow with London and Washington over a nuclear-test-ban treaty.[43] Following the successful conclusion of the Limited Test-Ban Treaty (LTBT) in 1963, Soviet foreign-policy efforts in the nuclear-arms-control field were directed primarily at prevent-ing West German acquisition of nuclear weapons.[44] The major vehicle for promoting this policy objective was an international non-proliferation treaty, the first Soviet draft of which was submitted in September 1965.[45] Nearly three more years of intensive negotiations were required before the NPT was endorsed by the UN General Assembly and opened for signature in July 1968.

Although US–Soviet relations were often strained during this period, policymakers' views about the underlying logic of non-proliferation increasingly converged. Therefore, while Moscow's interest in non-proliferation cooperation included a desire to enhance its international standing as a global power and Washington's diplomatic equal, it also involved a sincere recognition of the risks to regional and international stability posed by the spread of nuclear weapons. Although West Germany was the paramount concern, Soviet policymakers also recognised the broader nature of the problem. Long-time Soviet ambassador to the United States Anatoly Dobrynin, for example, observed in 1964 that Moscow now 'had not only Germany in view' regarding proliferation, 'but ten or fifteen other powers capable of making the bomb in the coming years'.[46]

Similar views were expressed by Soviet Minister of Foreign Affairs Andrei Gromyko, who acknowledged that 'an increase in the number of nuclear countries producing and possessing nuclear weapons is accompanied by a growing danger of the outbreak of a war using such weapons'.[47] As noted in one of the few comparative analyses of US and Soviet non-proliferation policy, the Soviet-controlled press also echoed the concern that proliferation would be damaging to Moscow's interests.[48]

Symbolically, the NPT was a milestone in US–Soviet relations and proved that superpower cooperation in the non-proliferation and nuclear-export sphere was possible. The NPT was also significant in creating a bureaucratic group with a vested interest in continuing such superpower cooperation.[49]

The basis for this cooperative effort in the nuclear-export realm, however, was put to the test following India's May 1974 'peaceful nuclear explosion'.

Both the Soviet and the US reaction to the Indian nuclear test were inconsistent with the countries' stated commitments to a strong non-proliferation regime. However, while the public reaction in Washington could be at least characterised as mildly disapproving, that in Moscow was, at most, politely noncommittal. According to a report by the Soviet state news agency TASS on the day of the explosion, India had conducted 'a peaceful explosion of a nuclear device' and had 'reaffirmed its strong opposition to the use of nuclear explosions for military purposes'.[50] Subsequent reports in the Soviet press generally reiterated this position, although on occasion reference to an Indian bomb could be found.[51]

The initial Soviet public response to the Indian explosion, while seemingly at odds with Moscow's stance on non-proliferation, could in part be explained in terms of the high political costs Moscow would probably have incurred had it adopted a more disapproving posture. The uncritical Soviet response may also have been influenced by Moscow's continuing support domestically for peaceful nuclear explosions as a significant economic resource, notwithstanding the fact that by 1974 Moscow recognised that 'there was no essential difference between … nuclear explosive devices which serve military or peaceful purposes'.[52] Finally, the Soviet Union could point to the fact that its nuclear-export policy, unlike those of Canada and the US, had not contributed directly to the Indian atomic explosion.

More difficult to reconcile with the Soviet Union's post-1958 policy of tightened nuclear-export controls was news in late 1976 that Moscow planned to provide India with a large supply of heavy water. Heavy water supplied by Canada and the US had been used by India to produce plutonium for its first atomic explosion, and US observers were fearful that the Soviet Union had agreed to the heavy-water sale without assurances from India that it would not explode another nuclear device. This fear was reinforced by information that Moscow had violated the nuclear-export guidelines endorsed by the London Suppliers Group in 1976 by not requiring India to accept, as a precondition for the heavy-water sale, international safeguards on the transferred material as well as on all facilities in which the material was to be used.[53] The sale was especially disturbing and confusing to US non-proliferation advocates who had cooperated with the Soviet Union during the London Group deliberations, in which Soviet representatives had regularly aligned themselves with supplier-state proponents of strict nuclear-export controls.[54]

This apparent inconsistency in post-1974 Soviet nuclear non-proliferation and export policy was lessened when the terms were announced for the nuclear-safeguards agreement India had concluded with the IAEA in September 1977 in connection with the Soviet supply of heavy water. Despite Moscow's keen interest in promoting better relations with India, it refused to ship more than one-quarter of the order of heavy water until India agreed to accept substantial nuclear safeguards. The Soviet Union also reportedly pressed the Indians to abandon their long-time opposition to 'full-scope' or 'comprehensive' safeguards.[55] Although the 1977 IAEA agreement that was ultimately concluded fell short of this objective, Moscow succeeded in securing Indian agreement to accept the then-novel safeguards concept of 'pursuit'.[56] In other words, safeguards were to follow the Soviet-origin heavy water wherever it might be introduced. In addition, the agreement encompassed important safeguards principles of 'perpetuity' and 'no peaceful nuclear-explosion use'.[57]

The full details of Indo-Soviet nuclear dealings following the 1974 detonation remain obscure, although important materials relevant to the issue have become available since the author conducted his primary field research on the topic in New Delhi, Vienna and Washington DC in 1983.[58] In particular, documents in the Hungarian National Archives offer new interpretations of Indo-Soviet nuclear relations, and the relative impact of non-proliferation and regional political considerations.[59] These point to a major tension in Soviet policy between support for the NPT as a general foreign-policy tenet and a temptation to relax the application of its non-proliferation standards when it came to India.

The lack of perfect consistency in Soviet implementation of its stated non-proliferation objectives when it came to Indo-Soviet nuclear relations is certainly clear, as is Indian appreciation for Moscow's 'expressive silence' following the 1974 test,[60] as well as for Soviet readiness to strike major nuclear-trade arrangements with India in the late 1970s and 1980s. What is less well reflected in analyses of the Hungarian archival information is the deep resentment on the part of both senior Indian diplomats and working-level government officials over what they perceived to be extraordinarily stringent and onerous conditions related to Soviet nuclear exports.[61] In addition, it should be recalled that at the time of the Soviet sale of heavy water to India in 1976, only Canada, among all the nuclear-supplier states, made full-scope safeguards a precondition for the supply of materials on the Zangger list, and it did so in reaction to its own unwitting contribution to India's nuclear-explosive programme. Moreover, although the Soviet Union was in technical violation of the guidelines of the Zangger Committee 'trigger list', as well as those of the non-binding London Suppliers Group, the safeguards it ultimately insisted upon (perpetuity, pursuit and 'no peaceful nuclear-explosion' use) were much more stringent than any previously applied to India. They also represented the first instance in which a separate safeguards agreement had been negotiated for the international sale of heavy water.

The primacy of politics

United States

One of the corollaries of an emphasis on technology control as a proliferation-preventive measure was the belief that proliferation developments could be predicted based on the state of a country's technical prowess. In other words, it was assumed that countries with the technical capability to acquire nuclear weapons would exercise those capabilities. This fallacy gave rise to many inaccurate forecasts by national intelligence agencies as well as scholars. Most memorably, it also was reflected in President Kennedy's prediction at a press conference in March 1963 that the world could see between 15 and 25 new nuclear-weapons states by the 1970s.

By the end of the 1970s, there was a growing appreciation in Washington that technical capability was but one of a number of proliferation drivers and that stringent export controls in and of themselves were unlikely to prevent the spread of nuclear weapons. Indeed, the Carter administration's punitive efforts to prevent Brazil from importing sensitive nuclear technology contributed to the development of the country's indigenous nuclear production and aversion to multilateral controls.[62] By the early 1980s, therefore, one could discern a growing readiness in Washington to elevate political and economic considerations in the crafting of non-proliferation policy.

In some instances, this led to the politicisation of non-proliferation policy. For example, in autumn 1982, the US walked out of the IAEA General Conference and undertook a reassessment of its participation in the Agency after the conference voted to withdraw Israel's credentials following the Israeli airstrike on the Osirak research reactor in Iraq the preceding year. Non-proliferation policy also was not immune from the escalation of polemics between the superpowers in the aftermath of the Soviet Union's invasion of Afghanistan and, especially, following President Ronald Reagan's 1983 'Evil Empire' speech. In January 1984, for example, the Soviet Union explicitly charged the US with failing to honour its Article VI NPT disarmament obligations.[63] US policy during this period also turned a blind eye to Pakistani military nuclear activities, due in part to the crucial role Pakistan was seen as playing in assisting the mujahideen in fighting Soviet troops in Afghanistan.

It is noteworthy, therefore, that in December 1982, after a hiatus of over three years, the Reagan administration resumed high-level, ad hoc consultations on non-proliferation issues with the Soviet Union, comparable to those undertaken during the Carter administration in 1977 and 1978. These consultations, held approximately every six months, continued through the first half of the 1980s and enabled both sides to discuss in a largely pragmatic and non-polemical fashion a wide range of both technical issues and more politically sensitive matters with regard to 'problem countries'. Significantly, during this same period and beyond, the US continued to collaborate routinely in a number of non-proliferation fora, including at the IAEA, meetings of the Nuclear Suppliers Group and during the NPT review process. For example, the two sides at the 1985 NPT Review Conference were able to adopt a 'no polemics' approach, in which political pragmatism prevailed over other considerations (see Chapter Four). As such, although the two superpowers had major substantive and procedural disagreements, especially over how to characterise the negotiation of a CTBT, both parties found it possible to subordinate those differences in the interest of forging a consensus final document.

Although there was no fundamental reordering of US non-proliferation policy with the advent of the Reagan administration in 1981, during the 1980s technology control continued to diminish as a cornerstone of US policy. Correspondingly, a strategy was embraced in which politics increasingly had primacy and regional security and international economic objectives trumped those of non-proliferation. In addition, the prevailing view in Washington began to shift from emphasising global non-proliferation objectives to a more selective approach that distinguished between responsible proliferators, who more often than not were US friends or allies, and those whose behaviour was inimical to US interests. Accompanying this change in perspective was a tendency to accept the fact that nuclear proliferation might be inevitable and the best that could realistically be achieved was its management – a policy that was most starkly realised many years later in the July 2005 India–US Joint Statement.[64]

Soviet Union
It is difficult to pinpoint the date on which Soviet non-proliferation policy moved from an emphasis on technology control to what in the American context is described as the 'primacy of politics'. Indeed, it could be argued that an important strand of Soviet nuclear non-proliferation and export policy always has exhibited the primacy of domestic and international political considerations. Still, since its experience with China in the mid-1960s, the Soviet Union was remarkably constant in pursuing an overall non-proliferation policy that embraced prudent nuclear-export controls, the non-proliferation tenets of the NPT, and the view that its military and political interests were best served if the spread of nuclear weapons to other states was prevented.

Ironically, given Cold War history and Western stereotypes about Soviet misbehaviour, the long-standing experience of

US–Soviet cooperation on non-proliferation in the 1970s and 1980s contributed to the lack of attentiveness by US policy-makers to signs of change in Soviet nuclear non-proliferation policy, which began to emerge in the late 1980s. Indications of change were most apparent in the area of nuclear-export behaviour.

Under Mikhail Gorbachev, the Soviet Union in the late 1980s and early 1990s undertook a number of nuclear-export initiatives that signalled a less prudent approach to non-proliferation. These initiatives included efforts to market nuclear goods and services to non-NPT parties (e.g. Argentina, India, Israel and Pakistan) without requiring the application of international safeguards on all the recipient state's nuclear facilities. During the same period, Moscow adopted a more lax nuclear-export policy toward NPT states and expressed a readiness, for example, to sell South Korea sensitive nuclear technology, including that related to uranium enrichment and fast-breeder reactors. Although none of these export initiatives was prohibited by the NPT, they implied that even long-time supporters of non-proliferation were, for the right price, prepared to sell nuclear equipment, technology and services to potential proliferators.

Significantly, these less prudent nuclear initiatives coincided with the decline of the Soviet Ministry of Foreign Affairs' influence on nuclear-export decisions and the corresponding rise in power of the Ministry of Atomic Power and Industry (MAPI). MAPI's export policy seemed to be driven primarily by hard-currency considerations, with little regard for the foreign- or defence-policy implications of exports of sensitive technology. MAPI's ability to pursue an export policy that emphasised profit considerations was facilitated by the absence in the Soviet Union of any domestic legislation governing nuclear exports. It also benefited from the absence of public scrutiny because of the lack of Soviet journalists or independent experts knowledgeable about non-proliferation issues.

Points of divergence

Most of the preceding review has highlighted parallels in, and areas of convergence between, US and Soviet nuclear non-proliferation policy. These elements of cooperation were a dominant feature in US–Soviet relations in the non-proliferation sphere, especially from the mid-1960s. This tendency, however, should not obscure a number of points of divergence in US and Soviet non-proliferation perspectives and approaches. Two significant differences, which persist into the post-Soviet period, involve perceptions about the dangers posed by current and prospective nuclear-weapons possessors, and the role of plutonium in the civilian nuclear-energy fuel cycle.

Although both the Soviet Union and US subscribed to the NPT principle of universality and endorsed the restrictive NPT definition of what constituted a nuclear-weapons state, Moscow and Washington have often not shared common proliferation threat perceptions. Usually this difference of perspective is reported to have been most pronounced with respect to the nuclear risks posed by the Federal Republic of Germany prior to its ratification of the NPT. In marked contrast to Washington's relatively relaxed view of the Federal Republic's nuclear aspirations, Moscow's non-proliferation efforts in the 1960s are depicted as having been driven in large part by the objective of preventing German acquisition of nuclear weapons.[65] There is no doubt that Soviet policy-makers were more consistently and acutely worried about West German nuclear intentions than their US counterparts. However, an increasing body of evidence, including recently released archival material, reveals that key post-war US policy-makers, including President Kennedy, were far from sanguine about the prospect of a nuclear-armed Germany, routinely conducted internal reviews of the danger and also frequently raised the matter with close allies.[66]

Regardless of the relative dangers ascribed by the USSR and the US to West German nuclear behaviour, major differences in Soviet and US assessments of the proliferation risks posed by a number of other countries at various points in time, especially after the entry into force of the NPT in 1970, can be identified. These countries include India, Iran, Iraq, Israel, Libya, North Korea and Pakistan. In addition, even when the two superpowers were more or less in agreement about the dangers of nuclear-weapons diffusion, they often disagreed on the appropriate means to mitigate the threat, including the use of sanctions, UN Security Council resolutions, multilateral diplomacy, unilateral political measures and the threat of use of force.

Soviet and US policy also was often at odds about the dangers of plutonium in the civilian nuclear-fuel cycle and how to safely and securely dispose of the material. These differences were especially pronounced during the second half of the 1970s, when the Carter administration sought to promote international acceptance of its revamped non-proliferation policy by launching an International Nuclear Fuel Cycle Evaluation (INFCE). As described by Joseph Nye, one of the architects of the new look in US policy, the idea was 'to have both the supplier countries and the consumer countries come together to study the technical and institutional problems of organising the nuclear-fuel cycle in ways which provide energy without providing weaponry'.[67] INFCE officially was defined as a 'technical and analytical study', not a negotiation, but disputes reflecting political stands often dominated the discussions of the eight working groups in the 61 meetings held in Vienna between 1977 and 1979. Although American and Soviet experts shared similar views on many technical issues, the governments disagreed fundamentally on the need for plutonium reprocessing and recycling. The US, therefore, welcomed the INFCE findings that: (1) recycling in thermal reactors was not apt to promote substantial economic savings, and (2) safe storage or disposal of spent fuel did not require reprocessing, while the Soviet Union dissented from this conclusion.[68] Although this disagreement would resurface in a significant fashion in the post-Soviet period, the differences temporarily narrowed when the Reagan administration assumed office and decided to reverse US policy on these issues.

Conclusion

Table 2 provides a summary of the major episodes in US and Soviet nuclear non-proliferation and export-control policy. It is apparent that both countries nurtured for an extended period of time the misleading idea that there exist clearly distinguishable good 'atoms for peace' and bad 'atoms for war'. In this regard, both US and Soviet nuclear policies during the Atoms for Peace period actively promoted the development of civilian, and presumably safe, nuclear activities abroad with little regard for their military or dangerous implications. Both nations also had to experience unpleasant incidents in which their own nuclear assistance contributed to the expansion of the nuclear-explosives club before they recognised fully the risks associated with the spread of nuclear technology and imposed stringent export controls.[69]

Table 2. **Evolution of US and Soviet nuclear non-proliferation policy, 1945–92**

	United States	Soviet Union
Secrecy and denial	1945–53	1945–54
Atoms for Peace	1953–74	1954–58
Technology control	1974–80	1959–86
Primacy of politics	1981–92	1986–92

If the US and the Soviet Union chose to understate the degree of collaboration and synchronisation of their nuclear non-proliferation policies, their cooperation and parallel efforts in the nuclear export and non-proliferation sphere did not go unnoticed by the non-nuclear-weapons states (NNWS). From the NNWS perspective (as well as from the Chinese vantage point), the nuclear policies of Moscow and Washington were – and remain – remarkably convergent, cynical and discriminatory. In particular, the NNWS resented US and Soviet efforts to strengthen IAEA safeguards while, in their view, ignoring their obligations under the NPT to provide assistance in developing the peaceful applications of nuclear energy. To many of the NNWS, especially those with a developed civil nuclear industry, the NPT and subsequent nuclear-supplier-state agreements also appeared to be designed mainly to confer commercial advantage on the nuclear-weapons states. The failure of the superpowers to make more progress in curtailing vertical proliferation (i.e. the nuclear-arms race) further inclined the NNWS to perceive both US and Soviet efforts to restrict nuclear exports and to halt horizontal proliferation as self-serving and unjustifiably discriminatory. Such charges were routinely expressed at all NPT review conferences during the period under study and, in fact, continue to be voiced to this day.

Soviet and US non-proliferation policies were responsive to a number of domestic and international factors, including, not surprisingly, commercial and security considerations. However, the evolution of these policies also highlights the significant manner in which both domestic and international politics intruded on the formulation of policymaking and how the pursuit of mutually beneficial non-proliferation objectives, while not dependent on good bilateral relations, certainly benefited from them. Historically, it would appear that detente has both facilitated and been strengthened by US–Soviet non-proliferation cooperation.

CHAPTER TWO

The 1977 South Africa nuclear crisis

Sarah Bidgood

The atomic history of South Africa is unique for many reasons, perhaps none more significant than the fact that it remains, to this day, the only country to have completely dismantled its nuclear arsenal. Although Pretoria did not publicly acknowledge the six nuclear weapons it developed until two years after it joined the Treaty on the Non-Proliferation of Nuclear Weapons (Non-Proliferation Treaty, or NPT) in 1991,[1] indications that the country's civil nuclear programme may have acquired a military dimension began to present themselves as early as the 1970s. Both Soviet and US leaders were quick to recognise South Africa's nuclear ambitions as antithetical to their own foreign-policy interests, as well as to the greater objectives of international peace and security. In spite of the many ways in which they were ideologically at odds following the height of the Cold War, policymakers in Moscow and Washington soon realised that this threat would be better mitigated through cooperation rather than by isolated, individual efforts.

A particularly vivid example of this approach followed the discovery of South Africa's preparations to conduct a nuclear test in the Kalahari Desert in summer 1977. The background and circumstances of this incident have been well documented over the past three decades,[2] but the availability of new accounts of this story from former officials in South Africa's nuclear programme, as well as declassified cables and documents from US government sources, have brought additional important details to light.[3] While some earlier publications focused on the significance of this case as an example of US–Soviet non-proliferation cooperation,[4] the availability of additional sources allows for a deeper exploration of the motivations behind Moscow's and Washington's responses to Pretoria's activities. These include not only a commitment to the burgeoning non-proliferation regime but also self-interest and a desire to promote Soviet and US foreign-policy objectives in the region.

South Africa's nuclear-weapons programme: a brief history

South Africa began to pursue a civil nuclear-energy programme in the late 1950s: it possessed vast uranium resources on its territory[5] and, as a result of the Atoms for Peace programme pioneered by the US, ready access to nuclear-reactor technology and fuel.[6] By 1960, South Africa's Department of Foreign Affairs had expressed its intention to request 'special nuclear material', that is, U-235 enriched to 90% and plutonium, from the US under a bilateral agreement between Pretoria and Washington.[7] By 1965, it had commissioned Safari-1, a 20-megawatt electric (MWe) nuclear-research reactor of US origin,[8] and, as early as 1967, South Africa's leadership had begun to pursue the use of peaceful nuclear explosions for mining and other civil projects.[9] Within two years, investigations into the feasibility of this initiative were being undertaken by the country's Atomic Energy Board,[10] and by 1971, a peaceful nuclear explosions (PNE) programme was well under way.[11] Although the nuclear-explosion programme was developed for civil uses, it was kept secret owing to a burgeoning international norm against this deployment of nuclear devices. Furthermore, international backlash to India's 'peaceful' explosion in 1974[12] signalled that diverting nuclear imports toward these kinds of detonations was soon to become more difficult under evolving export-control regimes.[13]

In parallel with the initiation of its PNE programme, construction of South Africa's pilot enrichment plant using indigenous enrichment technology and processes began in 1971, allegedly with the objective of increasing the value of uranium exports coming from South Africa.[14] Although the US halted its supply of nuclear fuel to the Safari-1 reactor in 1976,[15] the centrifuges in the so-called Y-plant began to operate together in an arrangement known as a cascade for the first time in 1977. This breakthrough allowed the South Africans to enrich uranium from its natural concentration of approximately 0.7% U-235 to the higher concentrations required for reactor fuel or nuclear weapons, and the Y-plant yielded a small quantity of highly enriched uranium the following year.[16] While the plant would be used to produce fuel for the Safari reactor and, later, the Koeberg nuclear-power station,[17] the pilot plant's functionality also enabled a change in the focus of South Africa's PNE programme, which, according to Waldo Stumpf, former CEO of South Africa's Atomic Energy Board, had been exclusively civil until this time.[18]

While sources are conflicted on the exact moment when South Africa's nuclear programme officially took on a military dimension, this transition certainly occurred prior to 1976.[19] Funds were allotted toward identifying and securing a nuclear-test site in a remote location in Upington in the Kalahari Desert, which was named Vastrap, and a cold device (a full-scale explosive device with a depleted-uranium core for testing) was developed in August 1977.[20] Two test shafts of 385 and 216 metres were dug beneath the military testing facility in 1976 and 1977,[21] which have subsequently been geolocated using declassified information and information from the International Atomic Energy Agency's (IAEA's) later reports on the area.[22] By 1978, an official military nuclear posture developed by the staff of South Africa's then-prime minister John Vorster had been approved and adopted.[23]

Nuclear motivations

The motivations behind South Africa's decision to convert its PNE programme into a military programme are firmly linked to the country's domestic policy of apartheid and the political unrest in the surrounding region at the time. Indeed, in the period preceding the planned nuclear test in the Kalahari, South Africa was neighbour to conflicts in the former Portuguese colonies of Angola and Mozambique;[24] additional conflicts were on the rise in Namibia and Rhodesia.[25] A number of national-liberation movements supported by South Africa and the US,[26] and separately by Cuba and the Soviet Union,[27] were vying for power in southern Africa and actively seeking to overthrow the region's colonial governments. Concerned about invasion by forces backed by the nuclear-armed Soviet Union, as well as an alleged 50,000 Cuban troops amassed at its border, the South African government appears to have begun pursuing an indigenous nuclear deterrent in an effort to keep such an attack at bay.[28]

Contributing to Pretoria's threat perception was the fact that the US appeared increasingly unwilling to defend South Africa against the spread of communism in southern Africa. US intelligence reports from the time noted that the South African government 'perceives that it is facing the Communist threat alone – that the United States is no longer willing to confront

Soviet expansionism'.[29] In the estimation of some former participants in South Africa's nuclear programme, this shift in policy became apparent when the US failed to support South Africa in preventing Cuban troops from entering Angola in 1975. According to those who were involved in the conversion of South Africa's civil nuclear programme into a military one, this event marked a turning point in US–South Africa relations, which, they claim, motivated South Africa to develop its own nuclear arsenal.[30] In this light, not only were South Africa's nuclear weapons being designed to deter Soviet aggression, they also may have been intended to compel the US to support South Africa in case of an attack.[31]

Discovery of the test

By 1975 or 1976,[32] South Africa was involved in preparations for the test of its cold nuclear device. Although officials had taken precautions to conceal the test facilities at Vastrap, including by scheduling simultaneous military exercises utilising a newly developed mobile multiple-rocket launcher, their activities quickly came to the attention of the Soviet Union.[33] Perhaps following a tip from Soviet spy Dieter Felix Gerhardt, a high-ranking official embedded in the South African Navy who would have been aware of the test preparations,[34] Soviet reconnaissance satellite *Cosmos* 922 passed over the Kalahari test site on 3 and 4 July 1977. When it detected some unusual activity in this remote location, a second satellite, *Cosmos* 932, went into orbit on 20 July for a closer look. By 2 August, the images from this satellite would likely have been with the Soviet Main Intelligence Directorate for analysis, according to research published by US National Security Archive Senior Fellow Jeffrey Richelson in his comprehensive analysis of declassified primary source documents relating to this incident.[35] These photographs would have offered

Soviet officials evidence of South Africa's progress on its test preparations and confirmation of the claims of any human-intelligence sources.

Days later, on 6 August, Vladelin Vasev, who was serving as acting chief secretary of the Soviet embassy in Washington, brought a message from Soviet Premier Leonid Brezhnev to US President Jimmy Carter via William Hyland, acting assistant to the president for National Security Affairs. This message shared the Soviet finding that South Africa was preparing to conduct a nuclear test with 'serious and far-reaching after-maths for international peace and security'.[36] Brezhnev asked the US for assistance in preventing the test, while noting that he would also appeal to the leaders of France, West Germany and the UK for aid in this matter.[37] TASS then published a public announcement of these assertions on 8 August.

Brezhnev's communiqué was at once an olive branch and an admonition. In a cabled transcription of the letter, Brezhnev is shown to have stated:

> Between the Soviet Union and the United States cooperation is developing along the line of strengthening the Treaty of Nuclear Non-proliferation … now a situation has arisen when it is urgently necessary, even at once, to undertake energetic efforts toward the goals of preventing the emergence of new nuclear states and barring the proliferation of nuclear danger.[38]

Nevertheless, he is quick to point out:

> It is also known that the USA [Union of South Africa] was given access to the latest research in the nuclear field, that it received and continues to receive nuclear equipment and materials … The 'London Agreements'

demand, as is known, the observance of a number of
conditions aimed at the banning of the use of those
materials, equipment and technology received for the
creation of nuclear explosive devices. World opinion
will rightly ask: since these agreements have failed
to prevent the emergence of nuclear weapons in the
USA [Union of South Africa], then what value do they
have?[39]

Framing the issue in this way, Brezhnev managed at once
to appeal to the US as a partner in supporting the burgeoning non-proliferation regime while reminding Washington
that it could be perceived by the international community as
an abettor of South Africa's nuclear-weapons programme. This
accusation was repeated frequently by Moscow during August
1977 and beyond. For example, the Soviet démarche to West
Germany regarding the test preparations in Upington similarly
suggested that Western assistance had facilitated South Africa's
nuclear-weapons programme.[40] Its implications did not escape
the US Department of State, which, according to recently
declassified cables, also anticipated receiving questions from
Congress on the United States' potential involvement in South
Africa's nuclear-weapons programme.[41]

Motivated by both the specificity of the intelligence provided
by the USSR, as well as the fact that Soviet representatives
shared this information with the US government first before
discussing it publicly,[42] Deputy Secretary of State Warren
Christopher drafted a response to Brezhnev on 10 August
offering assistance. In his draft correspondence, Christopher
indicates that the US was

looking closely into [the existence of a nuclear test site
in the Kalahari], and it would be very helpful to us

if the Soviet Union would provide as many details as possible about this test site. For example, it would be helpful if we could be informed of the geographic coordinates, size, configuration and exact nature of the facility and any other information which would provide a basis for forming an independent judgment as to the probability of a test explosion.[43]

Christopher conveys the United States' willingness to 'exchange views and to band our efforts to halt the spread of nuclear weapons wherever the problem may arise' in the belief that 'such an approach can contribute to the development of confidence between us and the Soviet Union on this important subject'.[44]

At the same time, the US quickly began the process of verifying the Soviet claims independently: following Vasev's visit and Brezhnev's message, an unmarked light aircraft flew over the test site in early August,[45] which was later found to have belonged to the US military-attaché office in Pretoria.[46] Shortly thereafter, a US reconnaissance satellite was also directed to examine the test site. On the morning of 15 August, the representatives of the then National Foreign Intelligence Board took part in an urgent meeting at the Central Intelligence Agency's (CIA's) headquarters in Langley, Virginia, where they were encouraged to provide oral contributions to a forthcoming report on the 'Political Aspects of South Africa's Consideration of a Nuclear Test Device'.[47] This report was to be compiled in such short order that it left no time for participants to provide their contributions in writing.

Later that day, and only nine days after Brezhnev's initial communiqué, Carter felt he could confirm to his Soviet counterpart that US intelligence findings matched those of the USSR.[48] On the basis of this conclusion, William Bowdler, US ambassador to South Africa, appears to have confronted South African Minister of Foreign Affairs Pik Botha on 18 August about the test preparations at Vastrap. A UK memo cites Bowdler as having conveyed that 'the US government had substantial evidence which appeared to be contrary to previous South African assurances that their nuclear programme was devoted exclusively to peaceful purposes'.[49] He reportedly stated that he

> had been instructed to make clear that the detonation of a nuclear device, or any further steps to acquire or develop a nuclear explosive capability, would have the most serious consequences for US/South African relations and would be considered a serious threat to the peace. He added that South Africa would not be able to count on help from the Western Powers and the issue might arise in the Security Council at short notice with unforeseeable results. Bowdler asked that the South African Government 'should [illegible] to prove, in a publicly persuasive way, that you are not developing a Kalahari facility as a nuclear test site and that your pilot enrichment plant is not and will not be used to produce enriched uranium for any explosive purpose'.[50]

By 19 August, US Secretary of State Cyrus Vance had followed up on Bowdler's conversation with Botha, providing a list of suspicious areas in question at the site at the request of South African representatives. These included:

- a drill rig and associated facilities;
- a square lattice tower in a cleared area enclosed by a wall, about 1 kilometre from the drill rig;

- an area, about 3 km from the square tower, containing a pad; this area is connected to the tower area by a power or communication line;
- a secured housing area 15 km from the tower area, containing approximately ten buildings;
- a hard-surface airstrip approximately 1,600 metres long and 3 km from the housing area. In addition, the entire area is surrounded by an outer patrol road.[51]

Vance indicated that he had photographs proving that these facilities existed and proposed a technical visit to the site before the start of the World Conference for Action against Apartheid in Lagos, Nigeria, on 22 August and no later than 21 August.[52]

During this same period, the Western powers were mounting intense joint diplomatic efforts to induce South Africa not to conduct a nuclear test.[53] France in particular indicated that serious damage would be done to its relationship with Pretoria if the test were to be carried out. Although the South African government never acknowledged publicly the true objectives of its activities at Vastrap, the intense pressure exerted on South Africa following the initial Soviet démarche proved successful in modifying Pretoria's plans: Richardt Van der Walt, the individual responsible for test preparations at Vastrap, was notified by urgent telephone call on 17 August that he and his team were to hide all signs of test preparation and return to Pretoria immediately. The facility was then dismantled in a flurry of activity once it appeared that an inspection was imminent,[54] and by approximately 21 August – the date of Vance's proposed inspection – all evidence of the test preparations had been removed.[55]

Convinced for the time being that South Africa had been dissuaded from pursuing a nuclear-weapons programme, the

US briefed the Soviet Union on its findings. On 22 August, Warren Christopher delivered an oral statement to Soviet ambassador to the US Anatoly Dobrynin repeating South Africa's confirmation that it did not have a nuclear-explosive device or any plans to acquire one, saying 'we want your government to know about the results thus far of our discussions with the South African government'.[56] President Carter subsequently shared South Africa's assurances publicly in a 23 August press statement.[57] South Africa's Department of Foreign Affairs itself repeated this message in a 26 August cable to its embassies, noting that it had conveyed to France, the UK and the US, as well as the German foreign minister, that 'South Africa does not have or intend to develop a nuclear-explosive device for any purpose, peaceful or otherwise; the so-called Kalahari facility is not a testing facility for nuclear explosions; there will not be any nuclear explosive testing of any kind in South Africa'.[58]

As history has demonstrated, these assurances did not reflect South Africa's true intentions with regard to its nuclear-weapons programme. Even at the time, South Africa continued to hint at its nuclear ambitions while simultaneously denying its pursuit of a military arsenal. On 24 August, for example, Prime Minister Vorster delivered an address in which he highlighted the inequity of the nuclear club as codified by the NPT. In his speech, which reportedly elicited a powerful reaction from his audience, he asserted that:

> The USA, the Soviet Union and the United Kingdom are parties to the Treaty but they have fully protected their positions as nuclear weapon states with large nuclear arsenals … Such, ladies and gentlemen, are the double standards to which South Africa is subjected to in this world.[59]

Rather than acknowledge any wrongdoing, Vorster instead suggested that a South African nuclear deterrent was imminent. He concluded his remarks by stating that 'if these things continue and don't stop the time will arrive when South Africa will have no option, small as it is, to say to the world: so far and no further, do your damnedest if you so wish'.[60]

In spite of South Africa's external defiance, internal communications reveal Pretoria's concern over the fallout in the UN that would result from international opposition to its planned nuclear test. In a telegram to the secretary of foreign affairs, South African embassy officials in Washington anticipated that this outcome would

> be exploited to the full in the UN and elsewhere by our opponents who can be expected to make every possible use of the emotional factors involved in the alleged possession of the bomb by a government whose policies are the subject of worldwide condemnation. The prospect of a Chapter VII sanctions resolution is thus brought measurably nearer.[61]

They were also concerned that South Africa's capitulation to Western demands to halt the test preparations would incentivise Washington to continue its hardline approach toward Pretoria. The telegram continues:

> The response of the South African government to the representations from the Western powers and from the US in particular not to proceed with the testing of a nuclear device is once more being interpreted as further substantiation of the thesis of the Carter administration that pressure on South Africa is more productive of results than the [illegible] policy of

attempting to work with South Africa. This again is an incentive to step up the pressure.[62]

This fear was not misplaced: in November 1977, the US joined the USSR and the rest of the UN Security Council in a unanimous vote to adopt Resolution 418, which placed an arms embargo on South Africa.[63] It made compulsory 'the cancellation of corvettes and submarines; no more fighter aircraft made available; growth of SA arms industry (Armscor); [and] no USA fuel for Safari-1'.[64] This outcome manifested Washington's pivot away from apartheid South Africa under the Carter administration toward a position that was perceived as being more in line with evolving US foreign-policy objectives at the time.[65]

US and Soviet intelligence sharing and discovery of the test site

The availability of recently declassified information about the discovery of the Kalahari test site provides new insights into the significance of US and Soviet intelligence sharing in this case. These sources also counter a narrative proposed by several South African scholars and former members of the country's nuclear-weapons programme, who have suggested that the US knew about South Africa's plans for a nuclear-weapons test before being approached by the USSR in 1977. This theory has been perpetuated by Dieter Gerhardt himself, who has stated in interviews that Soviet representatives provided the US with intelligence regarding South Africa's weapons programme a year prior to the planned test. According to Gerhardt, the USSR even proposed a pre-emptive strike on South Africa's pilot enrichment plant, the Y-plant,[66] a suggestion that – if made – was clearly not taken up in Washington.[67]

Available open-source and declassified literature provides little support for this characterisation of events. It shows instead that the US examined – and dismissed – South Africa's nuclear ambitions prior to the summer of 1977. While the US Congress grew concerned that cooperation with South Africa on nuclear issues conveyed the appearance of condoning apartheid, the intelligence community remained unconcerned by South Africa's threshold nuclear programme.[68] These sources suggest that US officials would have remained unaware of South Africa's plans to conduct a nuclear test without Soviet assistance.

Numerous declassified documents from 1976 highlight the US intelligence community's persistent doubts over South Africa's intention and ability to develop nuclear weapons during the mid-1970s, in spite of evidence to the contrary.[69] Indeed, the CIA undertook a number of studies on this question before being approached by the USSR in 1977, including a secret report by the CIA's Office of Scientific Intelligence entitled 'South Africa Again Rumored to Be Working on Nuclear Weapons', which was released in September 1976. The analysis presented in the document references statements by a South African Atomic Energy Board official explicitly expressing the country's intention to develop a nuclear weapon. Nevertheless, it concludes that these 'may be intended specifically for US or other foreign audiences', as there is 'no convincing evidence that nuclear weapons are actually being developed at this time'.[70]

Some declassified documents suggest that the US intelligence community's failure to detect South Africa's nuclear ambitions could be attributed to a lack of resources devoted to the sub-Saharan region in the mid-1970s. A memorandum from the Director of Central Intelligence dated 6 May 1977 that reviews these resources describes a dwindling pool of analysts specialising in the region from the late 1960s to 1975, who subsequently found themselves overwhelmed by an increased demand for intelligence brought on by the civil war in Angola. The document notes the perspective of intelligence-community staff that the number of full-time or equivalent analysts dedicated to this area was 'near the minimum which can be devoted to sub-Saharan Africa and still provide the substantive intelligence required by policymakers, especially in light of the increased interest in sub-Saharan affairs displayed by the Carter administration. There is no "fat" in this total analytical effort.'[71]

Not only may this shortage of analysts have blinded the intelligence community to South Africa's nuclear ambitions, it also may have resulted in an incident that suggests the United States' obliviousness to Pretoria's plans prior to August 1977. According to media reports at the time, the CIA was prompted to investigate more closely its own photography of the area near Vastrap following Moscow's revelations regarding South Africa's nuclear-test site. In doing so, it found that one of its own satellites had, in fact, photographed the site already.[72] Indeed, reports suggest that the US satellite, likely the *Big Bird* 1977-56A (KH-11),[73] made between four and six passes over the Kalahari that summer[74] while pursuing a Soviet reconnaissance satellite that had shifted its orbit.[75] Although the US satellite was capable of digitally transmitting photographs to Washington for analysis in real time,[76] these images had been archived without being interpreted, leaving US officials unaware that a nuclear test was being planned.[77]

No declassified official documents confirm this incident and, as such, it is not possible to determine unequivocally whether the US intelligence community became aware of the Vastrap test site before or after being approached by the Soviet Union.[78] Nevertheless, media reports detailing the circumstances of this event were circulated throughout the CIA during this period. One such article published in the *New York Times* in December 1977 suggests that the failure to detect the test site in spite of photographic evidence of its existence became central to a debate over whether US intelligence efforts needed to be completely reoriented under the Carter administration.[79] It also prompted Kenneth Adelman, then former assistant to the secretary of defense, and Brigadier-General Albion Knight, writing in autumn 1979, to recommend continuous monitoring of Vastrap by US national technical means because 'if South Africa should reopen the Kalahari site, it would be better that the information be discovered first by the United States, rather than by the Soviet Union'.[80]

In spite of this incident, or perhaps as a result of the embarrassment it caused, some within the US intelligence community continued to doubt the authenticity of the test site even after its existence was confirmed. Their scepticism was rooted in peculiarities about the layout of the facility, as well as its lack of security.[81] The authors of a September 1977 report by the Lawrence Livermore National Laboratory Special Projects Division entitled 'South Africa: Motivations and Capabilities for Nuclear Proliferation', for example, concluded that South Africa could have constructed the test site with no intention of utilising it in order to blackmail Washington into restoring support for Pretoria.[82] This perspective was not shared by US allies, as was made clear in a letter from C.L.G. Mallaby of the UK Arms Control and Disarmament Department from September 1977. In it, Mallaby indicated his inclination 'to discount altogether the view which Mr. Nye [Joseph Nye] ascribed to "a few people in Washington" that the Kalahari facility was a dummy test site built by the South Africans in the belief that its discovery would frighten Western countries and deter them from putting too much pressure on South Africa over racial or other issues'.[83]

When taken in concert, the body of available open-source data does not reinforce the assertion that the US knew conclusively about South Africa's plans for a nuclear test before being informed by the Soviet Union. Instead, it demonstrates how fundamental Soviet intelligence sharing was to the US in learning about South Africa's nuclear ambitions, as it appears unlikely that officials in Washington would have uncovered or questioned them independently.

Motivations for cooperation

Whether or not the US was aware of – or took seriously – South Africa's nuclear-weapons programme before 1977, both the US and Soviet Union had clear motivations for cooperating to pressure South Africa to halt its nuclear programme once it came to light. From the Soviet perspective, a significant impetus was the fact that the USSR did not have diplomatic relations with Pretoria during summer 1977. As such, Moscow needed Washington to leverage the very relationship with Pretoria of which the Soviet media was so critical in order to persuade the country to halt its nuclear-weapons programme.[84] Additionally, both the USSR and the US recognised the need to coordinate their responses to South Africa's nuclear ambitions because of the impact they would have on the broader non-proliferation regime. As Moscow and Washington had cooperated closely in negotiating the NPT, ambassadors Roland Timerbaev and James Leonard agreed that the 'publicity over South Africa's nuclear intentions' could prove useful in strengthening support for it.[85]

Some members of South Africa's defence community have suggested that, in exposing the Vastrap test site, the USSR also hoped to force the US to change its foreign policy with regards to South Africa. This thesis is somewhat supported by publicly available information regarding the USSR's national interests in the region, as well as recently declassified cables from the lead-up to the World Conference for Action against

Apartheid in Lagos and the UN General Assembly meeting during autumn 1977.[86] One declassified National Intelligence Daily cable from 17 August 1977 does question Moscow's interest in exposing South Africa's nuclear ambitions. It highlights in particular a rash of publications in the Soviet media alleging that the US and NATO assisted South Africa in developing a nuclear weapon, noting that 'whatever the degree of genuine Soviet concern about South African nuclear developments, the timing of the Soviet campaign – one month before the UN General Assembly convenes – suggests that it is designed to gain political advantages for Moscow'.[87] Nevertheless, when confronted by his American counterpart about allegations of US–South Africa collusion propagated in the Soviet press, Soviet ambassador Victor Issraelyan countered that the Soviet Ministry of Foreign Affairs was 'not responsible for the precise language in these stories'.[88] His response suggests that, at least at the top levels of the Soviet government, any interest in using this case as an opportunity to discredit the US was matched by a desire to facilitate cooperation.

South African nuclear physicist Nic von Wielligh sees evidence of Moscow's interest in manipulating Washington's relationship with Pretoria elsewhere, suggesting that the Soviet Union obscured the fact that the planned nuclear test was 'cold' in order to further vilify South Africa and to force the US to agree to sanctions against it.[89] For support, he points to the fact that Soviet spy Dieter Gerhardt would presumably have been aware that the planned test in the Kalahari would not use fissile material, as South Africa's Y-plant had not produced enough to be used in a nuclear-explosive device by August 1977. If this were the case, von Wielligh speculates, Gerhardt would have shared this information with his Soviet handlers.

There is no mention of the cold nature of the planned test in any of the declassified documents that are available for analysis today. This suggests that – if Soviet officials knew that the test device would have no nuclear yield – they did not share this information with their American counterparts. Von Wielligh and others cite this omission as evidence that Moscow wished to use the incident in order to advance its own national interests rather than because it regarded South Africa's proliferation as a genuine threat to global security.[90] Without additional information, however, it is not possible to determine whether Moscow failed to share the specifics of South Africa's planned test for any reason other than genuine ignorance.

What is evident from the declassified literature is that the US agreed to press South Africa to halt its test preparations at least in part out of a desire to avoid being perceived as supporting Pretoria's nuclear ambitions. US concerns over its involvement in South Africa's nuclear programme were made explicit in a declassified 15 August 1977 cable between Secretary Vance and Galen Stone, US deputy representative to the IAEA, in Vienna. In this communiqué, Vance instructs Stone to

> make a highly discreet approach to appropriate IAEA official(s) on urgent but confidential basis with request for latest information available to agency on quantities, chemical forms, isotopics, locations and use currently being made of all special nuclear material, both HEU [highly enriched uranium] and PU [plutonium] obtained by South Africa from external sources.[91]

Worries among US officials over the potential diversion of American-supplied 'special nuclear material' to a South African military programme were not new. As early as 1971, the US National Security Council had drafted a memorandum for Secretary of State Henry Kissinger evaluating the merits of supplying South Africa with nuclear-fuel-enrichment services in the face of international and domestic concern over 'the possible military applications of the technology and materials involved'.[92] By publicly attributing South Africa's nuclear-weapons programme to US and NATO support (regardless of whether evidence of such support was substantiated),[93] the Soviet media played on long-standing doubts over the prudence of exporting nuclear material to Pretoria. These pushed Washington to confront South African officials over the Soviet allegations in order to preserve its international image as a supporter of the burgeoning non-proliferation and export-control regimes.[94] The perception this linkage created even appears to have influenced US nuclear foreign policy with regards to South Africa, which worsened dramatically in October 1977. A memorandum prepared at this time for the secretaries of state and defense by the National Security Council recommended terminating the export of military items to South Africa and an end to any 'further nuclear-fuel supplies until such a time as the South African government has agreed to adhere to adequate full-scope international safeguards' in response to the discovery of the nuclear-test preparations.[95]

Conclusion

While the US and the Soviet Union were each able to advance their own national interests by cooperating in this case, this process also entailed compromise on the part of both countries. In responding to Soviet pressure to assist in preventing the South African test, for example, Washington risked alienating the National Front for the Liberation of Angola (FNLA) and National Union for the Total Independence of Angola (UNITA) movements, which it was supporting alongside Pretoria in their fight against the Soviet-backed Popular Movement for the Liberation of Angola (MPLA) in Angola.[96] In sharing the satellite images of the test site it had acquired with Washington, conversely, Moscow risked exposing the human-intelligence source who had tipped them off to its existence.

No available open-source material indicates that the USSR acknowledged any information other than that acquired by national technical means to the US; nevertheless, it would have been difficult for the Americans to have concluded that the Soviet Union coincidentally was conducting satellite reconnaissance over the precise portion of the Kalahari Desert where two nuclear-test shafts had been dug. At the same time, because the Soviet Union did not have diplomatic relations with South Africa, officials in Moscow had to rely on the US to communicate their position and report back any progress. This arrangement required a substantial amount of trust on the part of the USSR, whose continuous satellite monitoring of the test site showed little change on the ground.[97] Positive cooperative experiences between Washington and Moscow in other non-proliferation fora, including the Strategic Arms Limitation Talks (SALT) I negotiations, the establishment of the Nuclear Suppliers Group, the IAEA and the NPT review process, may have contributed to their willingness to take these risks in order to work together on this specific case.

For both the Soviet Union and the US, one motivation to cooperate stemmed from their appreciation of the chance that South Africa's test preparations afforded them to improve their bilateral relations. The behaviour of both countries throughout autumn 1977 evidences their desire to seize upon this opportunity. Indeed, while Soviet Foreign Minister Andrei Gromyko could have made 'propaganda capital' out of US–South Africa nuclear cooperation at the UN General Assembly that year, he instead treated the issue in a way that US ambassador Leonard characterised as 'careful and moderate'[98] in his plenary statement. Gromyko's restraint was in line with a request issued by US permanent representative to the IAEA Gerard Smith in September 1977 not to hurt 'the chances of this delicate operation by stirring up strong international and public pressures'.[99] As Smith observed to his counterparts in the Soviet delegation to the London Club, doing so 'would only stiffen domestic South African resistance and make it more difficult for [the US] to provide the nuclear-fuel carrot that constituted our only leverage'.[100] Gromyko appears to have taken this request to heart.

A list of talking points drafted for a 21 September 1977 meeting between Secretary Vance and Gromyko on monitoring South Africa's nuclear activity is similarly restrained and concludes that 'the quiet cooperation in which we have engaged will be ... a significant development in its own right'.[101] Victor Issraelyan echoed this characterisation of events in a 23 September 1977 meeting with ambassador Leonard, where he stated that he 'would like to do better than just avoid confrontation with the US on non-proliferation, including the South African case – he would like to cooperate'.[102] Cognisant of the chance that this incident presented to work constructively with one another on an issue of importance to both – nuclear non-proliferation – in order to make the most of this unusual opportunity, the Soviet Union and the US compromised in ways they might not have otherwise.

The circumstances in which this cooperation occurred further underscore the commitment of both countries to working together to address the threat of a nuclear South Africa. These include the fact that, in the US, the Committee on the Present Danger had released a statement only eight months earlier characterising the 'Soviet drive for dominance based on an unparalleled military buildup' as the 'principle threat to our nation, to world peace and to the cause of human freedom'.[103] Additionally, both the US and the Soviet Union were involved in active proxy conflicts with one another around the world during this period.[104] Arms-reduction negotiations between the two countries had temporarily stalled and the Carter administration had begun to emphasise human-rights issues in its foreign-policy objectives. Each of these developments could have reduced support in Washington for working with the USSR on high-stakes non-proliferation issues.[105] Nevertheless, and in spite of these obstacles, this example of bilateral cooperation between the two countries was successful owing to the fact that it served the immediate interests of both governments while mitigating a shared threat to international peace and security in the long run. As a 24 August 1977 *Washington Post* editorial observed,

> a group of nations who otherwise compete on a wide range of matters, including nuclear ones, were able to get together and act forcefully and fast to indicate to a prospective new nuclear power what the consequences would be if it went ahead. Nothing like that, you will recall, occurred at the time of India's nuclear explosion in 1974.[106]

Although this type of productive US–Soviet cooperation on non-proliferation was by no means unprecedented, it highlights the prescience of both American and Soviet leaders in perceiving how working together served their mutual interests, in spite of challenging circumstances in their bilateral relationship. This case underscores the need for leaders in Moscow and Washington who can recognise when cooperation will advance their own objectives rather than rejecting such opportunities out of principle. Given the condition of today's bilateral relationship, this is a lesson that both countries would do well to review.

Peaceful nuclear explosions: from the Limited Test-Ban Treaty to the Non-Proliferation Treaty

Paul Warnke

Often overshadowed in Cold War history by other more prominent superpower arms-control negotiations, the issue of peaceful nuclear explosions (PNEs) provides an important window into US–Soviet cooperation in non-proliferation and arms control. In the face of geopolitical rivalries and strategic competition, both superpowers sought to regulate the application and proliferation of PNE technology, restricting their usage through test-ban treaties while halting their spread in the emerging nuclear order. They achieved – through probing diplomacy, an openness to compromise and mutual interests in non-proliferation – a framework on PNEs that evolved from minor, imprecise controls to a detailed treaty regime with verification measures.

On 19 September 1957, the United States detonated a 1.7-kiloton nuclear device inside a mesa at the Nevada Test Site, marking the first fully contained underground nuclear explosion. Amid mounting international opposition to atmospheric nuclear explosions, the *Operation Rainier* nuclear test, part of the *Operation Plumbbob* testing series, would not only alter the course of nuclear-weapons testing by demonstrating the feasibility of underground weapons development, but also validate the pursuit of a wholly different endeavour – the peaceful application of nuclear explosives. Designed to test the containment of radioactivity underground and the level of seismic activity produced by nuclear explosions, *Rainier* also gave credence to Project Plowshare, the US Atomic Energy Commission's (AEC's) incipient programme to explore non-military applications of nuclear explosions. The underground detonation confirmed the potential of using nuclear explosives for challenging industrial projects, such as the excavation of harbours and sea-level canals, the creation of void space for underground storage and the mining of deeply buried ore.[1] Born out of the technological enthusiasm and nuclear fervour of the 1950s, Plowshare initially embodied the ambitions of the US scientific community to harness the power of nuclear energy for peaceful ends. The scientific optimism and political support that propelled the US PNE programme through its first decade, however, gave way to declining industrial interest and growing concerns over radioactive fallout that ultimately led to Plowshare's downfall in 1977.

Following the Soviet's Union's inaugural nuclear-explosive test in 1949, its foreign minister, Andrei Vyshinsky, announced to the world the peaceful aims of the Soviet nuclear programme: 'We are razing mountains, we are irrigating deserts, we are cutting through the jungle, we are spreading life, happiness, prosperity and welfare in places where the human footstep has not been seen for thousands of years.'[2] Although few questioned the true intent of the Soviet Union's first nuclear test, Vyshinksky's words proved to be prescient. While Soviet interest in PNEs lagged behind Plowshare, by the 1970s the country had embarked on a far-reaching PNE programme of great industrial value to the Soviet economy. From an underground network of storage sites southwest of the Ural Mountains to a vast canal system joining the Pechora and Kama rivers, Soviet aspirations were ambitious.[3] Less constrained by public opinion and environmental standards, the Soviet programme ultimately surpassed the US Plowshare programme in both its scope and industrial use.[4]

Although their PNE programmes followed different chronological arcs and varied in scale, Soviet and US stances on PNEs often converged. As an issue significantly less contentious and geopolitically charged than the strategic arms-control negotiations, proxy conflicts and ideological schisms that came to shape the superpower relationship, PNEs offered a medium for US–Soviet cooperation through the highs and lows of the Cold War. Through informal bilateral talks and multilateral negotiations, the two superpowers pursued mutually beneficial arrangements that came to form the international framework for PNEs and determine their role in test-ban treaties. Yet the path of their relationship on PNEs was not straightforward, as bureaucratic disputes, unformed national policies and entrenched negotiating positions at times impeded progress. These obstacles, however, neither upended specific arms-control agreements nor threatened long-term engagement on the issue, which largely transcended the geopolitical struggles and strategic competition that came to define the US–Soviet relationship.

Reining in Plowshare with a test ban

Since the birth of the nuclear age, scientists and politicians alike recognised the potential of nuclear explosives to serve peaceful ends. In the technological fervour of the nuclear age's early days, they aspired to reshape the earth's landscape by harnessing the explosive energy of the atom. Initially, the paucity of nuclear materials, the low yields of nuclear explosives and the high radioactivity of early fission devices relegated PNEs to the realm of speculation. This quickly changed as a confluence of events in the 1950s generated political and industrial support for PNEs. The invention of 'cleaner' fusion devices with higher yields, the feasibility of underground testing and the establishment of Lawrence Livermore National Laboratory in California combined to justify a fully fledged PNE programme. In summer 1957, amid great excitement, Project Plowshare was officially established under the auspices of the AEC and Livermore.[5]

The US government quickly channelled this growing domestic optimism for PNEs abroad. At the Second United Nations International Conference on the Peaceful Uses of Atomic Energy, held in Geneva in 1958, US scientists unveiled to the international community the potential impact of PNEs on civil-engineering projects, such as harbour excavation and fracking.[6] While many welcomed the presentation of Plowshare with interest, the Soviet delegation harshly criticised the United States' nascent programme. Vasily Yemelyanov, the Soviet chairman of the conference, asserted that whatever their professed purpose, PNEs 'do not reach practical ends, but only political ends'.[7] He went on to publicly denounce Plowshare as a front for intensified nuclear-weapons testing.[8] The Soviet criticism of Plowshare as a political ploy and subterfuge for further weapons development would persist, turning PNEs into a point of contention in upcoming test-ban negotiations.

In July 1963, in the immediate wake of the Cuban Missile Crisis, and amid growing public outcry over atmospheric testing, the Soviet Union, the United Kingdom and the United States convened talks on a limited ban on nuclear-test explosions in outer space, under water and in the atmosphere. Shortly before the negotiations commenced, the AEC presented chief negotiator Averell Harriman and Undersecretary of State George Ball with a list of guidelines for PNEs, such as prohibiting device inspection and ensuring that Plowshare's cratering projects would be permissible under a Limited Test-Ban Treaty (LTBT).[9] Many of Plowshare's visionaries, including the AEC's then chairman, Glenn Seaborg, feared that legal constraints under a test ban would hobble the infant programme and severely limit the industrial applications for PNEs. Through either ambiguous language or an explicit exemption for PNEs, maintaining Plowshare's latitude was therefore essential.

The Kennedy administration, however, was far from unified in its support for Plowshare and a PNE exception under the proposed test ban. As Kennedy's top national-security officials formulated the US position on the eve of test-ban negotiations with the Soviet Union, Seaborg's proposal became especially contentious. In one June 1963 meeting, William Foster and Adrian Fisher, the Arms Control and Disarmament Agency's (ACDA's) then director and deputy director respectively, argued that a test-ban treaty and PNE exemption were mutually exclusive. Granting Plowshare experiments an exception, they believed, would diminish the practical and political value of a test ban to the point that a treaty would be meaningless. Others pointed out that including such a provision would demand a certain degree of device disclosure and an elaborate inspection regime to ensure against illicit weapons testing – an arrangement the Soviets would reject out of hand in the upcoming talks.[10] Although the AEC's proposal ultimately won out, the bureaucratic disagreement over Plowshare and its place in a test ban demonstrated the extent to which the priorities and biases of government agencies can colour decision-making as much as the broader national interest. For the most part, Seaborg was willing to dilute a significant arms-control agreement and complicate negotiations with the Soviets in order to safeguard the viability of Plowshare. ACDA and State Department officials, on the other hand, attached greater significance to building a robust test-ban treaty and easing tensions with the Soviets, even if it hamstrung the US PNE programme.

At the onset of the negotiations, the Soviet Union and the US tabled competing draft texts that closely resembled each other, apart from two major differences: PNEs and a withdrawal framework. Six days after the talks began, Harriman and US ambassador Foy Kohler met with Soviet Minister of Foreign Affairs Andrei Gromyko and his deputy Valerian Zorin to resolve the two sticking points. The US negotiators proposed a provision that would allow peaceful detonations in the prohibited environments pursuant to procedures specified in an annex.[11] While Harriman and his team attempted to engage their counterparts on PNEs, seeking to relax restrictions on Plowshare, the Soviets proved inflexible. Opposed to the lenient treatment of PNEs, Gromyko argued that granting such an exemption, on top of allowing underground tests, would dilute the treaty's political significance and diminish its 'worldwide appeal'.[12] Furthermore, he pointed out that the treaty still permitted parties to pursue underground PNE projects, thereby allowing the US to conduct a range of programmes. One member of the US negotiating team also attributed Soviet opposition to suspicions that an unchecked PNE programme could act as a thin disguise for advanced weapons tests.[13]

The US delegation ultimately viewed the PNE issue not only as a secondary item, but also as a useful bargaining chip to advance American interests in other areas. Following his conversations with Gromyko, Harriman proposed to President John F. Kennedy that the US concede the PNE provision in exchange for a withdrawal clause, granting states parties the right to pull out of the treaty. That Plowshare technology remained rudimentary and its industrial applicability still uncertain reinforced Harriman's belief that PNEs did not merit an exemption under the treaty. This trade-off proved even more appealing after the Soviets agreed to an amendment mechanism through which certain Plowshare projects could be sanctioned in the future.[14] Washington's response to Harriman, while acknowledging that the AEC would oppose the treaty's parameters, judged that a withdrawal clause took precedence and would facilitate Senate ratification of the treaty.[15] The conclusion of meaningful arms-control measures, undiluted by exemptions or loopholes, had prevailed over the future of Plowshare, the practical value of which was still marginal. More-over, the Kennedy administration's swift decision to abandon the PNE exemption in the face of Soviet opposition suggests that it never fully backed the AEC proposal. In many ways, its inclusion in the US negotiating position as an unfinished annex represented a balancing act – an attempt to synthesise competing bureaucratic interests into one uniform policy. Introducing the PNE exception to the proposals, however, ulti-mately proved fortuitous, as it gave US negotiators leverage to press the Soviet Union for concessions in other areas.

With the Soviets consenting to the exchange, the draft treaty was modified to include in Article I the phrase 'any other nuclear explosions' in the ban on nuclear tests in the prohibited environments. Imposing an additional proscription on PNEs, the new text prohibited underground nuclear explosions that caused 'radioactive debris to be present outside the territorial limits of the State under whose jurisdiction or control'[16] they were conducted. In exchange for these concessions, a with-drawal provision was added to the draft, along with a more flexible amendment process that required a simple majority rather than a two-thirds supermajority.[17] After the major barri-ers to agreement had been removed, the Soviet, UK and US delegations signed the LTBT in Moscow on 5 August 1963.

Although the LTBT's negotiations pitted the two super-powers against each other on PNEs and imposed considerable constraints on Plowshare, there were signs that both sides were amenable to future cooperation on the issue. On the sidelines of a US–Soviet track and field competition, a fitting backdrop to the closing days of the test-ban negotiations, Harriman and Khrushchev met privately to discuss the question of PNEs. The informal conversation shed light on the Soviet Union's long-term plans to employ the technology and uncovered a willingness to find common ground at a later date:

> [Khrushchev] told me of the various long range plans the Soviets had in mind such as building canals and diverting the Pechora River to flow south to Kazakhstan instead of north to the Arctic. This gave me opportunity to express surprise that he had thrown out our article on peaceful uses … He readily offered the view that we should have no difficulty in agreeing on such a matter when the subject has been more carefully explored … When tensions were relieved by a test ban and reduced by other understandings … peaceful uses would then meet popular approval.[18]

This high-level exchange unearthed a new-found Soviet interest in PNEs, which mirrored the aspirations of the Plowshare scientists, as well as indicated a readiness to establish a framework for PNEs once the technology and its applications were more feasible. Rallying Senate support for the LTBT, President Kennedy expressed in a letter to the Foreign Relations Committee his intent to 'vigorously pursue' Plowshare projects within the bounds of the treaty and 'seek international agreement' to exempt atmospheric PNEs once such uses became constructive.[19] Despite trading PNEs for a withdrawal provision, the US government was still determined to unfetter Plowshare from certain legal restraints, a course of action that required Soviet consent. For their part, the Soviets outwardly feared that an allowance for PNEs might weaken the political import of a limited test ban, but perhaps harboured deeper concerns that an unconstrained Plowshare would act as cover for advanced weapons development or significantly outpace a PNE programme of their own. In the end, the first international limitation on nuclear testing marked an important juncture in the US–Soviet relationship on PNEs; Moscow's mounting interest in the industrial applications of PNEs together with Plowshare's rapid development demanded deeper engagement and a more robust legal framework for their regulation.

Shortly after the LTBT's entry into force in October 1963, US–Soviet cooperation on PNEs intensified, bleeding into the international sphere as Plowshare looked to sell its services abroad. In stark contrast to 1958, at the 1964 Third International Conference on the Peaceful Uses of Atomic Energy the Soviet Union wholeheartedly supported the American presentation on Plowshare. Unveiling his country's plans to use PNEs in irrigation, excavation and gas-stimulation projects, the Soviet delegate even proposed the commencement of joint US–Soviet technical studies.[20] Beyond winning over the Soviet delegation, Plowshare's international campaign touting the industrial benefits of nuclear explosives piqued the interest of several developing nations, such as Brazil and India. According to Seaborg, deepening international cooperation on PNEs 'was the best chance of engendering enough enthusiasm for PNEs to make revision of the test ban treaty possible'.[21] While foreign interest in PNEs opened up potential markets for Plowshare's services, an economic boon for the AEC, the US and Soviet programmes likewise enticed other nations to pursue PNE programmes of their own, which many feared constituted a back door to a nuclear-weapons capability.

Sensing an opening in early 1965, Seaborg reported in a letter to Undersecretary Ball that the Soviet attitude towards nuclear excavation had 'materially improved since the period prior to the execution of the Limited Test Ban Treaty'.[22] A staunch proponent of Plowshare since its inception, Seaborg suggested that talks be initiated with the Soviets as a first step towards obtaining international involvement in Plowshare, since their stance 'would have an important bearing on the evolution of the program'.[23] Securing Soviet participation was therefore crucial to formulating an international arrangement on PNEs and to amending the LTBT to authorise large-scale excavation projects, both of which, in Seaborg's opinion, were vital to Plowshare's success.[24] Once an obstacle to US–Soviet cooperation in test-ban talks, the AEC's goal of relaxing the restraints on Plowshare could now be a source of deeper engagement between the two countries.

With the ink barely dry on the LTBT, US Secretary of State Dean Rusk, however, was reluctant to pursue an immediate amendment to the treaty, endorsing instead a cautious step-by-step approach to PNE talks with the Soviet Union. This course of action called for conducting Plowshare experiments strictly within the parameters of the LTBT while feeling out the Soviet position on PNEs, which seemed to be rapidly evolving. On 18 March 1966, Secretary Rusk held a lunch in Washington DC for Soviet ambassador Dobrynin. The two discussed US plans to excavate a sea-level canal at the Isthmus of Panama using nuclear explosives, a project that had come to vindicate the ambitions of Plowshare and provide a source of funding for its experiments. Although the US was still developing the nuclear-cratering and -excavation techniques required for a canal project, Secretary Rusk made it clear to the Soviet ambassador that the US was prepared to review the LTBT's limitations on PNE use, in particular the radioactive-debris provision that hampered large-scale excavation projects. He also sketched out what a basic verification system for PNEs would look like, noting that access to the nuclear device would be limited but observation of the operation made permissible to ensure its peaceful nature. Finally, 'not making any proposal but simply thinking out loud',[25] Rusk envisioned the creation of international machinery through which the US and Soviet Union could provide PNE services to interested countries. Dobrynin's response to Rusk's musings was terse and revealed little of the Soviet position. Nevertheless, the exchange was significant, as many of Rusk's suggestions contained the kernels of a framework for PNEs, which would constitute one section of a new, sprawling non-proliferation regime in which Soviet participation proved vital.[26]

Finding a place for PNEs in the emerging non-proliferation regime

While Plowshare's proponents in the US government sought an amendment to the LTBT, the international community had begun to confront the spread of nuclear weapons by commencing negotiation of a non-proliferation treaty (NPT). Through negotiations conducted in the Eighteen-Nation Disarmament Committee (ENDC) and the UN General Assembly from 1965 to 1968, members of the international community sought to check the proliferation of nuclear weapons by preventing the diversion of nuclear materials to explosive uses. United by their common interest in non-proliferation, the Soviet Union and the US were initially content with a treaty that codified the basic obligations of nuclear-weapons states (NWS) not to transfer, and non-nuclear-weapons states (NNWS) not to acquire or produce, nuclear weapons.[27] However, as the negotiations unfolded, the NNWS came to resist what they viewed as an inequitable pact that imposed on them the heavy burden of non-proliferation and demanded from the NWS little in return. Therefore, the fissures that emerged in the ENDC and UN General Assembly did not break along ideological or geopolitical lines, but formed around nuclear-weapons status. In these new, unfamiliar surroundings, the Soviet Union and the US found themselves in an unlikely political marriage.

The issue of PNEs did not divide the two superpowers during the NPT talks – as it had in the LTBT negotiations – but united them in a common approach. Both recognised that allowing NNWS to pursue their own PNE programmes would offer a back door to a nuclear-weapons capability and undermine the NPT. On the other hand, denying NNWS access to the peaceful benefits of nuclear explosives would widen the gap between nuclear 'haves' and nuclear 'have-nots', thereby reducing the treaty's appeal. To redress this imbalance, the US proposed the creation of an international PNE service under the NPT, in the mould of Seaborg and Rusk's original design. Although the Soviet Union neither identified itself as a potential supplier of PNEs nor developed the international machinery for PNEs, it endorsed and defended the US position in the ENDC negotiations. Both sides were also determined to preserve the freedom of their own PNE activities under the emerging non-proliferation regime and resisted the imposition of new legal constraints on their PNE programmes. During frequent bilateral discussions between high-level officials, the two sides slowly hashed out their positions on PNEs, agreeing on a course of action for the parallel multilateral deliberations. Cooperation on PNEs, however, did not follow a straight path, with bureaucratic disputes, political posturing and wavering positions at times hampering efforts to forge an agreement. Nevertheless, the two sides mostly collaborated in the ENDC and together wove PNEs into the intricate, layered fabric of the NPT.

In summer 1965, the Soviet Union and the US submitted to the ENDC competing draft treaties that neglected PNEs altogether, referring in Articles I and II only to 'nuclear weapons'.[28] More skeletal than a comprehensive text, the US original draft contained an additional provision for the definition of nuclear weapons, but it was left blank due to bureaucratic infighting over the PNE issue. According to Seaborg's account of the negotiations, ACDA sought to define nuclear weapons broadly to encompass all nuclear explosives, whatever their purpose, in the prohibitions stipulated in Articles I and II. Although willing to include 'other nuclear explosives' in Articles I and II, the AEC pushed for the addition of a separate provision that would permit NWS to conduct PNE services for other states under a new international framework.[29] In essence, the AEC proposed to transform Plowshare into an international service under the auspices of the NPT, in line with Seaborg's original concept. Many in the AEC, including Seaborg, viewed this internationalisation as central to Plowshare's health and longevity. Moreover, with the Soviet programme in its early stages, under the AEC's proposal the US would have enjoyed a monopoly in the international PNE market.[30]

This AEC position ultimately triumphed within the Johnson administration, paving the way for Seaborg's initiative. On 30 June 1966, almost three months after Secretary Rusk's discussion with ambassador Dobrynin on PNEs, an informal memorandum was sent to the Soviet ENDC delegation to ascertain its view of a potential PNE service under the auspices of the NPT. Again, the probe elicited little feedback from the Soviets, but, as Seaborg noted, 'sometimes in dealing with Soviets no reaction is a good reaction'.[31] As these periodic probes demonstrated, obtaining Soviet buy-in was pivotal for the AEC's initiative and, more generally, for Plowshare's future. Importantly, Soviet alignment with the US position would lend the international service greater legitimacy and help block attempts by NNWS to constrain the two superpowers' PNE programmes.

While the ENDC in summer 1966 had reached an impasse over nuclear-sharing arrangements in Europe, an issue that starkly divided the Soviet Union and the US at the beginning of the negotiations, momentum was building on a PNE consensus.[32] Some State Department officials viewed PNEs as a much-needed avenue for nuclear cooperation between the two superpowers at a time when more geopolitically fraught issues threatened to scuttle NPT talks. On 8 August 1966, Undersecretary Ball sent a lengthy memorandum to President Lyndon B. Johnson arguing the benefits of securing Soviet participation in an international PNE service. Under the proposed initiative, which built upon earlier concepts, the Soviet Union and the US would join together 'in a common undertaking to make available to all nations of the world – nuclear and non-nuclear alike – the benefits of Plowshare explosions for public works projects in their countries'.[33] This would entail the creation of an international entity in which the NNWS would enjoy fair representation, ensuring their participation in the control and utilisation of PNEs. At the same time, however, measures would be adopted to assure the confidentiality of the devices' technical make-up and verify that such services were not a guise for illicit-weapons testing.[34]

After sketching out its main features, Ball explained to President Johnson that the political benefits of developing an international framework for PNEs would most likely outstrip any economic or technological dividends. Less concerned with the welfare of Plowshare than the prospects of US–Soviet cooperation, Ball emphasised that 'by presenting the plan to the Soviets, we could begin a useful dialogue with them, based on our mutual interest in deterring proliferation and in sponsoring peaceful nuclear applications'.[35] Although a joint US–Soviet initiative in the context of the LTBT or NPT negotiations would mark a diplomatic breakthrough, 'the discussions themselves would be valuable, regardless of their outcome'.[36] Finally, as Ball acknowledged, should the economics and environmental hazards of Plowshare projects prove so intractable that PNE technology became infeasible, the very practice of instituting an international service would bear diplomatic fruit with the Soviets.[37]

For Ball, a high-ranking State Department official who was not involved in Plowshare, the perception of cooperation and the simple process of dialogue could carry the same weight as concrete action in US–Soviet relations. Progress in establishing an international PNE service was therefore not an end in itself, but a means to alleviate tensions and spur cooperation in other areas. Even more, deeper cooperation at the bilateral level would form the basis for renewed progress at the multilateral level, where deadlocked NPT talks threatened to damage the Soviet Union and United States' mutual interest in non-proliferation. In pushing for PNE discussions with the Soviets, Ball did not treat Plowshare as a discrete entity, the economic and technological success of which was paramount. Placed within the broader strategic context of US–Soviet relations, it was instead a vehicle for linkage: progress in one set of negotiations would lead to equivalent progress in another. The US programme had evolved from a bargaining chip to advance separate US interests in the LTBT negotiations into a lever for resolving more contentious, if not critical, non-proliferation issues.

Eager to introduce its PNE proposal to the international community, the US delegation injected the PNE issue into ENDC discussions on 9 August 1966, one day after Ball's memorandum to President Johnson. The chief US negotiator in the talks, ambassador Adrian Fisher, bluntly noted to the other delegations the 'inescapable technological fact' that 'the technology of making nuclear explosive devices for peaceful purposes is essentially indistinguishable from the technology of making nuclear weapons'.[38] Hence, any non-proliferation treaty that permitted NNWS to pursue indigenous PNE programmes would be ineffective in its stated purpose. After stressing the incompatibility between PNEs and non-proliferation objectives, Fisher drew attention to Plowshare, admitting that 'we still have problems to solve before we shall be able to demonstrate applications which are both technically sound and economically feasible'.[39] In addition to tempering expectations for Plowshare, he stressed that the economic and technological hurdles facing the US programme would be far greater for NNWS, as any nuclear-earthmoving project required highly sophisticated fusion devices. Therefore, any economic justification for the development of PNEs could appear to be disingenuous, an attempt to conceal a nuclear-weapons programme behind the facade of peaceful purposes. In effect, much of Fisher's opening statement on PNEs reflected ACDA's earlier recommendation to impose on NNWS a categorical prohibition of nuclear explosives, whatever their stated purpose, under the NPT.

To conclude his remarks, which were devoted entirely to PNEs, Fisher offered the NNWS the international service envisioned by Ball, Seaborg and others. The US proposed that, if and when PNEs proved technically and economically feasible, the NWS 'should make available to other states nuclear explosives for peaceful applications'.[40] Such a service would require international observation of PNE detonations and 'the nuclear device remaining in the custody and under the control of the state which performs the service'.[41] While its structure slowly came into focus, the international service, as the US initially proposed, did not impose on the NWS a legally binding, positive commitment to provide such a service. Instead, it would serve as an international vehicle for Plowshare's services as well as a bulwark against proliferation.

Although Fisher's opening salvo on PNEs effectively inserted the issue into the NPT talks as a bone of contention, the immediate reaction in the ENDC was 'sparse and mixed', revealing a lack of enthusiasm from the NNWS for the proposed PNE service.[42] The US delegation was forced to appeal to the conference two weeks later to confront the PNE issue and recognise 'the implications it has for our work'.[43] In keeping with its muted reactions to US propositions, the Soviet Union largely disregarded Fisher's remarks – perhaps reluctant to hand the US a diplomatic breakthrough when disagreements over nuclear sharing were ongoing.

Nevertheless, in private meetings with the US that ran parallel to the ENDC negotiations, the Soviets grew increasingly amenable to the international-service idea. On 20 October 1966, Gromyko and Dobrynin this time raised the PNE issue over dinner with Secretary Rusk and ACDA Director Foster. The Soviets expressed an interest in developing the PNE international arrangement that Rusk had introduced in private talks earlier in the year and were keen to hold formal discussions on the matter.[44] This new-found eagerness to construct an international PNE framework came three weeks after one of the first engineering accomplishments of the USSR's nascent programme. On 30 September, a PNE was used to extinguish a runaway gas fire at the Urta-Bulak gas field in Uzbekistan by sealing the well.[45] Although the Soviet Union did not yet identify itself as a supplier of PNE services on a par with Plowshare, its programme had progressed rapidly, employing nuclear explosives for industrial use before its US counterpart had. Therefore, a proposal that had once seemed purely conceptual now appeared more practical to the Soviet Union, as it would offer a means to loosen restrictions on its budding PNE programme.

Despite this newborn Soviet openness to PNE talks, US officials began to question the utility of hosting bilateral discussions, which some believed would undercut the parallel ENDC negotiations on the NPT. Shortly after Gromyko's dinner with Rusk, Fisher voiced his concern to the secretary of state that the timing of such US–Soviet talks, 'with their attendant publicity', would 'increase Indian reluctance to sign a non-proliferation treaty which denied the non-nuclear countries the option to develop peaceful nuclear explosives'.[46] Throughout the NPT's negotiations in the ENDC and UN General Assembly, India steadfastly resisted the obligation of waiving the right to manufacture, by its own means, nuclear explosives for peaceful ends. Along with Brazil, India opposed the creation of an international service, which it argued constituted an 'atomic commercial super-monopoly'.[47] Holding talks with the Soviets on PNE cooperation, Fisher worried, would heighten perceptions of the NPT's stratification and damage its appeal for influential states, such as India.

Fisher's recommendation marked a significant departure from Ball's earlier conceptualisation of PNE talks as a conduit for improved US–Soviet relations. Events at the multilateral level, such as India's hardened opposition to the NPT and the transformation of PNEs into a divisive issue, had overtaken the necessity to hold bilateral PNE talks. The optics of superpower collaboration on PNEs – a nuclear technology unavailable to much of the world – would undercut US attempts to frame the NPT as an equitable treaty and to dampen the interest of non-nuclear states in acquiring PNEs. As far as Fisher and ACDA were concerned, the PNE initiative was no longer a lever capable of unlocking progress in other areas, but a wrench to be thrown into NPT negotiations. Even if it led to a general improvement in US–Soviet relations and generated momentum for Plowshare projects, it would undermine efforts to construct a non-proliferation treaty with widespread adherence, then a priority for ACDA. This prioritisation of objectives and the contrast between Ball's and Fisher's views underscored not only the impact of bureaucratic disagreement on the policy-making process, but also the need for close coordination among bureaucratic stakeholders to implement effective policy.

Faced with the option to hold comprehensive PNE talks with the Soviets or postpone them until other non-prolifera-tion goals had been achieved, Secretary Rusk took the middle road. In a memo to President Johnson, he suggested that the administration narrow the scope of talks with the Soviets to cover only technical items, walled off from more sensitive non-proliferation and disarmament issues. A small delegation of technical experts, headed by AEC Commissioner Gerald Tape, would gauge Soviet interest and intentions regarding peace-ful uses of nuclear explosives. According to Rusk, this limited probe would lay the technical foundation for more complex and politically consequential endeavours, such as the creation of an international PNE service. Therefore, in early December, Llewellyn Thompson – the former US ambassador to the Soviet Union – met with Dobrynin in Washington DC to discuss the details and timing of the proposed technical talks.[48]

While US–Soviet diplomacy continued, the treatment of PNEs in the NPT negotiations grew increasingly urgent during the 1967 session of the ENDC. The introduction of the issue the year before had piqued the interest of several countries in pursu-ing PNEs to resolve long-standing development problems. US officials were particularly concerned that the growing appeal of PNEs would provide countries a back door to a nuclear-weapons capability, thereby diluting the impact of the NPT.

Brazil's and India's mounting resistance to the treaty, together with their clout among NNWS, only exacerbated the dilemma. Propelled by developments outside the US–Soviet bilateral context, non-proliferation and political questions had generated a momentum of their own and, as a result, had become inextricably linked with the technical side of PNE cooperation. Against this changing backdrop, Rusk met with Dobrynin on 18 January 1967, one month before talks resumed in the ENDC.

Originally intended to cover the technical side of PNE cooperation, the conversation quickly veered off course. Rusk opened up the meeting by highlighting the convergence of the PNE talks with the reopening of NPT negotiations, which broadened the scope of bilateral talks beyond what was previously agreed to. Unable to insulate the PNE issue from broader political considerations, Rusk bound technical cooperation with the question of a non-proliferation treaty. He insisted that a unified US–Soviet position on PNEs would be crucial in the face of mounting pressure from non-nuclear states. To discourage indigenous PNE programmes, both countries 'should be in a position to offer to conduct nuclear explosions for justified projects'.[49] Caught off guard by the secretary of state's digression, Dobrynin, however, was unprepared to marry PNE's technical and political aspects at that time.[50] Even though the political and technical sides of PNE cooperation had become interlocked with the resumption of NPT negotiations, the Soviet ambassador stressed that they should be pursued discretely, as one would involve an entirely different agenda and set of experts than the other.

Although Rusk and Dobrynin ended the discussion by both stressing the importance of separating the technical and political aspects of PNEs, the meeting was marked by misunderstanding and piecemeal agendas. In attempting to bridge two conflicting policies within the US government, Rusk had undermined the main features of both. The confinement of talks to technical matters effectively severed any linkage between PNE cooperation and more substantive political issues, while hosting bilateral talks parallel to the NPT negotiations risked heightening perceptions of superpower collusion on PNEs. Moreover, the bureaucratic process of synthesising conflicting positions had led to an incoherent policy. PNE cooperation and the goal of bolstering the NPT's appeal were not mutually exclusive, but engagement with the Soviets on both demanded a clearer course of action and the prioritisation of interests.

As the Soviet Union and the US tiptoed around the PNE issue in bilateral talks, multilateral deliberations on the NPT resumed in the ENDC on 21 February 1967. Ambassador Fisher opened with a message from President Johnson that underscored the need to cover all nuclear-explosive devices regardless of their purpose. So as not to impose any technological penalty on NNWS, however, the US was prepared to 'make available nuclear explosives services for peaceful purposes on a non-discriminatory basis under appropriate international safeguards'.[51] Unlike the 1966 session, which largely sidestepped the PNE issue, Johnson's statement touched off a contentious, detailed consideration of the problem at hand. Brazil and India were especially resolute in their opposition to a PNE ban, asserting that an indigenous programme did not constitute nuclear-weapons possession. Moreover, to bar access to nuclear explosions would impede the development of the peaceful uses of nuclear energy as well as codify a nuclear monopoly for the NWS.[52] Also opposed to the prescriptions set forth by the US, Sweden argued that a comprehensive nuclear-test-ban treaty, rather than the NPT, should regulate the usage of PNEs by NWS.[53] On the other hand, Mexico, which would play a leading role in the PNE debate, proposed as an immediate remedy the creation of an international body for the control of PNEs.[54]

On 14 March 1967, the Soviet delegation broke its long silence on the PNE issue in the ENDC. The statement, delivered by the Soviet representative to the ENDC, ambassador Nikolai Roshchin, characterised the use of PNEs as 'not a practical issue' at the 'present stage', curiously discounting altogether his country's growing PNE programme.[55] Roshchin maintained that the NPT must close all nuclear-proliferation loopholes, including the development of PNEs, but proposed that the issue of 'the procedure and conditions' governing PNEs be handled in an international instrument separate from the NPT. Roshchin's initial remarks on PNEs, however, conflated the new issue with the prevailing concern of the Soviet Union that West Germany was pursuing a nuclear-weapons capability. Even though it was not a member of the ENDC, much less a participant in the PNE debate, West Germany raised several public objections to the NPT during its negotiations. In particular, critics in Bonn worried that accession to the treaty would amount to a one-sided compromise with the Soviet Union and stunt the country's technical development.[56] Amid the fear of further nuclear-weapons programmes in Western Europe, Roshchin transformed the ENDC into a stage to reproach the West Germans for igniting the PNE issue, claiming they sought to erect 'new obstacles to the conclusion of a non-proliferation treaty'.[57]

Guided by a distrust of West German intentions and hardened geopolitical considerations, the Soviet Union appeared more concerned with stifling interest in PNEs and denying US allies pathways to a nuclear-weapons capability than forming an international PNE service. Despite showing openness to US proposals in bilateral consultations, it initially rebuffed them in a multilateral setting, instead transforming its first statement on PNEs at the ENDC into an indictment of West German activities. The dissonance of the Soviet position on PNEs, however, stemmed less from an opposition to US views than from the political posturing and pointed language characteristic of multilateral debate. International negotiations can resemble a rhetorical exercise where style matters more than substance and consistency more than change. The Soviet Union's opening PNE remarks in the ENDC largely followed this pattern, as Roshchin took the opportunity to charge West Germany with obstructing NPT negotiations rather than to address the new US proposals. The statement also reflected the tendency of Cold War relations to filter complex issues through a geopolitical prism, situating them within the familiar East–West context before addressing them as discrete items. Yet beneath these accusations and digressions lay the rough contours of a PNE framework that had begun to emerge in bilateral meetings between Soviet and US officials.

The vacillation and, at times, internal contradictions of the Soviet and US positions on PNEs during this period provide a window into the superpowers' multilayered relationship. At the multilateral level, political posturing and geopolitical concerns initially hindered efforts to form a united US–Soviet front on PNE issues. In NPT negotiations in Geneva, the Soviets appeared reluctant to back US proposals on PNEs, simply grouping them with others that, they contended, were aimed at undermining consensus on the NPT. Furthermore, India's growing interest in PNEs and its resistance to the NPT underscored the enmeshment of the multilateral and bilateral contexts when US officials appeared reluctant to pursue comprehensive PNE talks with the Soviet Union.

Nevertheless, unconstrained by the political rhetoric and publicity of multilateral negotiations, talks at the bilateral level were often more dynamic and constructive. Frequent, high-level discussions in Moscow and Washington DC had begun to generate a momentum of their own, as a mutual understanding on PNEs and a desire for deeper bilateral cooperation slowly emerged. After ambivalent responses to earlier US probes, the Soviet Union grew increasingly amenable to cooperation on the PNE front, revealing a greater willingness to engage with US proposals. Importantly, these meetings also provided a venue for both sides to feel out the intentions and priorities of the other – an iterative process that cultivated mutual trust between participants and laid the groundwork for future cooperation.

At the same time, the advances and retreats at these high-level meetings showed that diplomacy was a slow-acting, often disjointed process in which two steps forward were often followed by one step back. The inability of both the Soviet Union and the US to articulate a consistent policy on PNEs exposed not only internal disagreement, but unformed, irresolute philosophies. In a number of instances, bureaucratic division acted as a drag on the progress occurring at the bilateral level. The discordant views of ACDA and the AEC clashed on the issue of PNEs, producing a policy stitched together from competing visions. Determined to sustain Plowshare within the emerging non-proliferation regime, the AEC advocated for less stringent constraints on its PNE activities as well as an international service that would require Soviet backing. More concerned with building an effective, watertight NPT than preserving Plowshare, ACDA feared that PNEs had become too politically charged and that US–Soviet collaboration would only exacerbate the problem. Apart from this bureaucratic infighting, US officials pursued contradictory approaches to PNE cooperation, alternating between linking and compartmentalising issues. These differing views and strategies ultimately led to an incoherent approach to bilateral talks that wavered between the technical and political dimensions of PNEs, leaving the Soviet side at first confounded and tentative.

Although deciphering Soviet intentions can be challenging, the behaviour of its top emissaries with their US counterparts appears in the beginning to have been equally non-committal. Early probes from the US elicited little response from the Soviets, whose PNE programme was still in its infancy and shrouded in obscurity. Bilateral meetings were therefore largely one-sided during this earlier period of PNE cooperation. US officials drew the contours of potential PNE frameworks in discussions with Soviet envoys, who did not reject the schemes outright but provided little feedback in return. After it had successfully employed PNEs for industrial use and reached ostensible parity with Plowshare, however, the Soviet Union expressed greater interest in cooperation on this front. When the US changed tack in bilateral talks, prioritising the political side of PNEs due to the intensifying NPT debate, the Soviets nevertheless pushed back and insisted on a compartmentalised approach. They preferred to treat negotiations on the political and technical dimensions as separate processes, with progress in one immune to difficulties in the other. Ultimately, the technical talks that Secretary Rusk had proposed in late 1966 were not held until April 1969, but the seeds of cooperation between the Soviet Union and the US had finally begun to germinate in the multilateral venue of the ENDC.

As the PNE issue grew more charged in multilateral NPT talks, in March 1967 the US expanded on its concept of an international service. In addition to agreeing with the Soviet position that a separate international agreement should govern the PNE issue, ACDA Director Foster presented to the ENDC five principles for sharing the potential benefits of PNEs:[58]

1) The nuclear-weapons states would perform PNE services under appropriate international observation, with

nuclear devices remaining under the custody and control of the nuclear-weapons state.

2) Non-nuclear-weapons states would be able to request such services through an international body in which they would be represented.

3) Costs to non-nuclear-weapons states would be kept as low as possible and not include research and development costs.

4) If an amendment to the LTBT was needed to conduct major PNE projects, there would be full consultation between nuclear and non-nuclear parties to that treaty.

5) The conditions and procedures for international collaboration in PNE projects would be developed in full consultation with the non-nuclear-weapons states.

The Soviet delegation agreed with the substance of Foster's remarks and, in line with its earlier position, maintained that an independent agreement should govern PNEs.[59] These five precepts, which AEC officials primarily developed, ultimately shaped the ensuing debate on PNEs and formed the guideposts for Article V of the NPT.[60]

By summer 1967, the Soviet Union and the US had overcome the impasse surrounding nuclear-sharing arrangements in Europe.[61] The settlement of this once intractable issue opened up cooperation on other pressing questions, such as safeguards and PNEs, where strong mutual interests united rather than divided the two countries. As bilateral consultations intensified parallel to the multilateral NPT talks, the Soviet Union and the US submitted to the ENDC separate but identical draft treaties on 24 August 1967. The new draft codified, in Articles I and II, ACDA's view that a non-proliferation treaty must prohibit NWS from acquiring both nuclear weapons and 'other nuclear-explosive devices' – borrowing the language of the LTBT. Striking a balance between the two views on PNEs within the US government, the draft also reflected the AEC's five guiding principles for an international service in preamble. As Foster elaborated in the ensuing ENDC debate, the US expanded the legal reach of Articles I and II to preclude any interpretation, which the earlier draft text had left open, that the NPT permitted PNEs. To contain the political blowback from a more explicit PNE ban, the US delegation reiterated its pledge to share the benefits of such technology and even mentioned an upcoming Plowshare experiment for the stimulation of natural gas deep underground.[62] In a later session, the Soviet delegate reaffirmed the new draft's categorical rejection of PNEs in response to Brazil's insistence that states reserved the right to manufacture and conduct their own PNEs.[63]

While Brazil and India represented the minority view that PNEs be exempted under the NPT, other NNWS, including several non-aligned developing countries, supported banning the acquisition and use of PNEs by NNWS. Yet although they agreed with the proscriptions outlined in the NPT's opening articles, many found fault with the US–Soviet framework on PNEs. As a way to strengthen the positive obligation of NWS to provide PNEs to NNWS, Mexico proposed the addition of an operative paragraph, which would carry more legal weight than the preambular paragraph in the US–Soviet draft. According to Mexico, NNWS should be assured, 'categorically and unequivocally', that they could still enjoy the possible benefits of PNEs in exchange for renouncing the right to develop or explode their own. The Mexican delegation subsequently presented a draft text of a PNE article that mirrored the five principles articulated by the US and the preambular language of the recent draft treaty.[64] The Mexican proposal garnered widespread support in the ENDC, with Burma, Canada, Egypt,

Nigeria, Sweden and Switzerland all endorsing the insertion of an operative paragraph.

On 4 October 1967, ambassador Dobrynin invited ACDA Director Foster to the Soviet embassy to discuss the various suggestions tabled by the NNWS. The conversation centred primarily on the contentious issue of safeguards under the treaty, but the two also addressed the Mexican proposal. Although neither unequivocally endorsed the inclusion of a PNE article, both viewed the alteration to the draft text as 'possibly acceptable'.[65] A week after his meeting with Dobrynin, Fisher returned to Geneva and explained before the ENDC that the US would consider itself bound by the declaration of intention contained in the preamble. Furthermore, Fisher also expressed the willingness of the US to assess other legal constructions in which the commitment to share PNE benefits was more definite and binding.[66]

As the 1967 ENDC session came to a close, an overwhelming majority of ENDC members supported the PNE prohibition outlined in Articles I and II. The debates in Geneva had stressed the proliferation risks of PNEs, with many delegates subscribing to the view that there was no fundamental difference between nuclear explosives employed for peaceful purposes and those for military ends. Nevertheless, a growing chorus of countries called for the NWS to give firmer, more legally binding guarantees that they would provide PNE services on a non-discriminatory basis and at a low cost to NNWS.[67] In private consultations with US officials, several allies, including Italy, Japan and West Germany, voiced their concern that draft treaties would limit their access to the benefits of PNE technology. Even important Soviet allies, such as Czechoslovakia and Poland, expressed similar reservations about the current PNE architecture.[68]

Amid this pressure, ambassador Fisher and Soviet Deputy Foreign Minister Vasily Kuznetsov held a series of private discussions in New York at the end of 1967. Both were amenable to the Mexican proposal and agreed that the settlement of the PNE issue would facilitate the resolution of more pressing questions. Likewise, Foster and Dobrynin met again in Washington DC on 26 December, almost two weeks after the conclusion of the 1967 ENDC session. The discussion centred on the enunciation of Article III, which still remained a sticking point in the multilateral deliberations. In order to free up more time for the safeguards debate before the ENDC reconvened in January, Foster and Dobrynin welcomed the inclusion of an operative PNE article, which would not only assuage the concerns of the NNWS, but also bring the NPT closer to its completion.[69] As a result of these hasty meetings between different sets of Soviet and US officials, the two superpowers agreed to accede to NNWS demands for an operative paragraph on PNEs shortly before the NPT talks reconvened.

On 18 January 1968, at the opening ENDC session, the Soviet Union and the US tabled revised identical drafts that included a new operative paragraph on PNEs, which became Article V. Both delegations asserted that the reworked draft reflected the positions of a majority of ENDC members by ensuring, to a greater extent, access to the peaceful uses of nuclear energy for NNWS. Drawing largely from Mexico's earlier proposed language, Article V transformed the previous preambular statement of principle into a binding positive obligation. As Fisher explained to the ENDC, the new operative paragraph on PNEs 'should remove any concern by non-nuclear-weapon states that they might be dependent merely on the good will of the nuclear powers for the performance of nuclear explosive services for peaceful purposes'.[70] Although ambassador Roshchin did not identify the Soviet Union as a supplier of such services, he reaffirmed the right of NNWS to enjoy the benefits of PNEs on a non-discriminatory basis and according to favourable terms.[71] Amid a growing urgency to finalise a non-proliferation treaty, the Soviet Union and the US formed a united front on PNEs in the final ENDC session, decisively closing the PNE loophole while advancing the potential benefits of the international PNE service.

The promotion of the new draft and Article V continued in ensuing ENDC debates, as both the Soviet and the US delegations defended the merits of their strengthened obligations. Now that the provision of PNE services constituted a more binding commitment, ambassador Fisher unveiled, in great detail, Plowshare's technological progress in an attempt to market the potential benefits NNWS could obtain. Speaking before the ENDC, he announced the initial results of Project Gasbuggy, a test detonation to assess the feasibility of using nuclear explosives to stimulate and recover natural gas. As Fisher asserted, the public disclosure of technological advancements in the field along with deepened collaboration on civil-engineering projects underscored the seriousness with which the US would 'live up to the promise implied in Article V'.[72] In a following session, ambassador Roshchin did not speak to the recent successes of the nascent Soviet programme, which was still cloaked in secrecy, but strove to dissipate concerns of discrimination and limitations on the peaceful uses of nuclear energy. He also cogently highlighted the economic advantages contained in the new operative paragraph. NNWS would free themselves of the economic burden of producing nuclear explosives while reaping the benefits of their use.[73] The similarity of Soviet and US statements on PNEs in the 1968 session of the ENDC revealed a deep congruence of views and a willingness to defend the other's position. The collaboration, born out of the frequent, bilateral discussions between high-level officials, had finally started to shape a common front in the multilateral forum of the ENDC.

Despite the superpowers' attempts to rally support for Article V, several non-aligned members of the ENDC still disagreed with certain details of the new PNE framework. Sweden, which often called for tighter constraints on the NWS own PNE programmes, tabled an amendment that would eliminate any mention of bilateral arrangements.[74] At the behest of the AEC, the Soviet Union and the US inserted a provision for bilateral arrangements as the last sentence of Article V. The AEC argued that, in order to preserve the viability of Plowshare projects such as the new Panama Canal, it should not be weighed down by the requirement to seek multilateral approval.[75] However, a number of delegations in the ENDC feared that bilateral agreements might facilitate covert cooperation for nuclear-weapons programmes in the absence of international observation. PNE services that did not run through an international body could also fuel discrimination, as NWS would offer such services only to their allies. Lastly, opponents argued that bilateral arrangements would impede the establishment of international machinery for the provision of PNEs and the institutionalisation of generally accepted practices.[76] For many, a bilateral provision therefore represented a back door by which NWS could evade their commitments under Article V and undermine PNE multilateral mechanisms.

The Americans and Soviets refused to accept Sweden's proposals and strove to protect the inclusion of a bilateral provision. Samuel De Palma, a high-ranking ACDA official, gave assurances that the adequate representation of NNWS on the international body overseeing PNE services would safeguard against discrimination and guarantee their access to such benefits. Additionally, there would be no scarcity of devices for NNWS once the technology had been refined.[77] Speaking for the Soviet Union, ambassador Roshchin refuted the claim that bilateral arrangements would circumvent Article

I and II obligations, as such services would still be subject to international observation. He also emphasised that Article V set forth only the guiding principles for a PNE agreement and did not enumerate the technical details of such a framework, which would be settled at a later date.[78] Sweden ultimately relented after it was assured that, even when conducted under bilateral agreements, PNE projects would still be bound by international rules.[79] The two superpowers nevertheless hoped to preserve their prerogative and flexibility in the use of PNEs by establishing bilateral arrangements as a legal redoubt for their programmes.

On 14 March 1968, one day before the deadline imposed by the United Nations General Assembly (UNGA), the ENDC concluded its deliberations on the NPT. Only five members, primarily Soviet and US allies, endorsed the draft, whereas several non-aligned countries still voiced strong objections when the treaty was submitted to the UN. What ensued was two months of extensive and discordant debate in the UNGA, as differing positions slowly congealed into a final draft. Still contentious and far from settled, the PNE issue was not free from conflict and required further scrutiny. In consultation with Chile and Colombia, Mexico submitted revisions to Article V that would strengthen the commitment of NWS to provide PNE technology as well as ensure a high degree of international regulation. It also called for the immediate negotiation of the international organ responsible for overseeing PNE services, while insisting that assistance through such an international organ be prioritised over bilateral arrangements.[80] Reflecting the concerns of many NNWS, these proposals expanded on the blueprint for an international PNE architecture and sought to diminish the significance of the bilateral option.

As the NPT debate continued in the UNGA, Secretary Rusk invited Dobrynin and Deputy Foreign Minister Kuznetsov to

Washington DC on 17 May 1968. The meeting, which devoted more than an hour to the ongoing NPT talks, was a high point of cooperation between the two sides. As the marathon negotiations approached the finish line, Kuznetsov and Rusk expressed their appreciation for the close collaboration between the American and Soviet delegations and agreed that both would stand firm against sweeping changes to the draft text. Even so, the two concurred that minor revisions, designed to gain wider adherence to the treaty, should be considered. The discussion then turned to vote counting and the perspectives of different regional blocs. Kuznetsov, who had met privately with the Mexican delegate in New York, remarked that Mexico was prepared to endorse the draft text, but had tabled suggestions to Article V in order to sway the Latin American vote.[81] Initially, the Soviet Union and the US attempted to apply pressure against Mexico and convince it to drop its amendments.[82] However, because the proposals did not represent wholesale alterations to the text and might help bolster the receptiveness of NNWS to the NPT, the two superpowers ultimately accepted the Mexican changes to Article V. Through its amendments, the Mexican delegation significantly reinforced the positive obligations contained in Article V, which the Soviet Union and the US had unsuccessfully tried to dilute. It also helped mould the article to the satisfaction of many NNWS while not unduly aggravating the NWS, and in many ways served as a mediator between the two camps.

The Soviet Union and the US were quick to gather support for the final version of Article V in the waning days of the NPT talks. Highlighting its ongoing PNE research and development, the US vowed to extend Plowshare services, under the NPT's provisions, to NNWS without delay.[83] As multilateral negotiations neared an end and a vote on the NPT approached,

Kuznetsov also suggested before the UNGA that preparatory work on a PNE could commence before the NPT entered into force.[84] While a handful of delegations continued to oppose certain aspects of Article V, the PNE language had finally been settled. On 12 June 1968, with the debate on the NPT concluded, the UNGA voted 95 to four (with 21 abstentions) to 'commend' the NPT and promote the 'widest possible adherence to the treaty'.[85]

In prohibiting NNWS from acquiring their own PNEs, the NPT through Articles I and II imposed a significant constraint on the development and use of such technology. At the same time, however, it extended to the NNWS the industrial benefits of PNEs through an international service, a right embodied in Article V of the treaty. Aligned in their interests and resolute in their approach, the Soviet Union and the US cooperated in the formation of this balance. The two superpowers were determined to close the PNE loophole and reinforce the treaty's non-proliferation obligations, yet both recognised the advantages of providing PNEs to the world through an international mechanism. This service, along with a provision for bilateral arrangements, represented an economic lifeline for Plowshare, which had begun to face political opposition within the US. Although the Soviet Union had not publicly disclosed the scope and activities of its own programme and was more focused on domestic use than international projects, it nevertheless defended the merits and benefits of Article V. Both delegations also ensured for their programmes the freedom of manoeuvre under the NPT, resisting proposals from NNWS delegations to place additional legal constraints on PNE activities. In the end, the negotiation of the NPT offers an illustration of US–Soviet partnership, where frequent bilateral meetings and persistent, probing diplomacy uncovered common ground between the two superpowers.

Conclusion

Although the international PNE service envisioned in Article V of the NPT never materialised and PNEs have now become a relic of Cold War history, for more than two decades the Soviet Union and the US worked together both to regulate their PNE programmes and to ensure that other states did not pursue their own. From establishing PNE restrictions in test-ban treaties to curbing the spread of the technology in the emerging non-proliferation regime, the two superpowers overcame obstacles through compromise and determined diplomacy.

At the governmental level, bureaucratic dynamics drove US–Soviet cooperation as much as the broad national interest did. Relations with the Soviet Union were regularly filtered through the sieve of US bureaucratic interests and biases. Composed of functional and regional units, the US government tended to dissect its relations with the Soviet Union into discrete issues, often without reference to their impact on the broader bilateral context. Organisations instinctively pushed for policies that elevated their own priorities even if they appeared inconsistent with overall national policy. Hence, the AEC came to view the PNE restrictions of the LTBT as an impediment to Plowshare despite the treaty's contributions to the easing of tensions with the Soviet Union and wider arms-control and non-proliferation efforts. In the debate over PNE controls under a test ban, ACDA and the State Department provided a counterweight to the AEC, advocating deeper cooperation with the Soviet Union and a more watertight treaty. Far less concerned than the AEC was with the economic trajectory of Plowshare, these two agencies consistently viewed PNE cooperation with the Soviet Union in terms of its implications for the countries' political relationship and non-proliferation goals. In fact, given their functional roles and regional expertise within the US government, both ACDA and State often

acted as the bureaucratic standard-bearers for greater engagement with the Soviet Union.

It was important for US administrations, faced with competing bureaucratic priorities, to impose a hierarchy of interests as
a framework for decision-making and as a means to adminis-
ter coherent, sustainable policy. Pursuing nuclear cooperation
with the Soviet Union, which represented one of the most
consequential foreign policies for a Cold War administration,
demanded both broad-based agreement and close coordination within the bureaucracy for effective implementation.
For instance, the disagreement over PNE restrictions under
the LTBT, unresolved until the final stages of negotiations in
Moscow, came close to damaging a significant arms-control
and non-proliferation agreement. These internal divisions over
PNEs carried on into the Johnson administration and continued to complicate cooperation with the Soviet Union. Unable
to rank priorities and decide on one strategy of cooperation,
US officials were slow to articulate a consistent PNE policy – a
failure that initially hampered progress with the Soviet Union at
the bilateral level. When bureaucratic interests converged and
even complemented each other, though, the US government
set a firm course. The AEC's interest in promoting Plowshare
abroad and ACDA's objective of a strong non-proliferation
agreement intersected in Article V of the NPT. In the end, this
confluence along with a clarity of policy at the governmental
level helped form a common front between the Soviet Union
and the US, as the two worked together to develop a PNE
framework in the newborn non-proliferation regime.

The negotiation of the NPT in Geneva and parallel US–Soviet
consultations underscored the tightly knit relationship
between the multilateral and bilateral contexts. In meetings
at the Soviet embassy in Washington DC or discussions on
the sidelines of the UNGA, Soviet and US officials reached a

mutual understanding on how to weave PNEs into the fabric of the NPT. Pushback from NNWS and their proposals for wholesale changes to the NPT's PNE framework propelled the Soviet Union and the US into even closer coordination at the bilateral level, as ACDA officials and their Soviet counterparts together weighed amendments to the text. These bilateral consultations, often between the same sets of officials, translated into a harmony of views and a readiness to defend the other's position in the ENDC or UNGA. There were moments, however, when setbacks at one level stalled progress occurring in the other. India's interest in establishing an indigenous PNE programme and its rising antagonism in NPT deliberations initially precluded more comprehensive bilateral PNE cooperation. Events rarely occurred in a vacuum; progress or difficulties at one level produced second-order effects in another.

US–Soviet PNE cooperation did not end with the completion of Article V of the NPT. The two countries held a series of technical talks and scientific exchanges in 1969–75, and in 1976 signed the PNE Treaty (PNET), which established detailed restrictions on PNE usage and included a far-reaching verification system. However, the road of PNE cooperation, winding from the LTBT to the PNET, was neither direct nor free of obstacles. It resembled a disjointed, iterative process – defined as much by setbacks as by progress. Only through relentless engagement, meetings between high-level officials and an openness to compromise were the Soviet Union and the US able to surmount hurdles to cooperation. As the fabric of US–Russia cooperation on non-proliferation frays, it is even more important that officials in both countries revive the practice of dialogue and engagement.

Negotiating and sustaining the Non-Proliferation Treaty: challenges and lessons for US–Russia cooperation

Lewis A. Dunn

In the midst of the wider Cold War confrontation, nuclear non-proliferation stood out as an area of US–Soviet engagement and cooperation. Moscow and Washington took the lead in negotiating the Treaty on the Non-Proliferation of Nuclear Weapons (Non-Proliferation Treaty, or NPT) and later cooperated in 1985 to sustain that treaty.[1] With renewed confrontation between Russia and the US, an examination of the earlier history of non-proliferation cooperation, specifically the NPT, may help to identify possible lessons for rebuilding cooperative habits between the two countries.[2]

Negotiating the NPT

From the 1961 United Nations General Assembly (UNGA) resolution calling for negotiation of a non-proliferation treaty, to the opening for signature on 1 July 1968 of the NPT, the Soviet Union and the United States consulted each other and, as the negotiations advanced, cooperated closely to work through several difficult issues on which their initial positions differed significantly. The successful collaboration reflected a strong congruence of strategic interests.[3]

The negotiation of the NPT took place against the backdrop of the Cold War military confrontation in Europe. Soviet forces were deployed in East Germany and were seen by the US and its NATO allies as posing a continuing military threat. To reinforce deterrence and to reassure the West German government, Washington deployed large numbers of tactical nuclear weapons to NATO Europe and initiated so-called Programs of Cooperation, which entailed dual US and allies' control over nuclear weapons in the event of a European conflict. There was also ongoing consideration of the creation of a Multilateral Nuclear Force (MLF), which would have involved the deployment of US nuclear weapons on special-purpose NATO ships with dual US and NATO Europe crews. At the same time, the Soviet Union was 'fighting like hell against the multilateral nuclear force because they were afraid that the Germans might get access to a nuclear weapon'.[4]

Increasing concerns about nuclear proliferation also were an important part of the context for US–Soviet cooperation. US estimates at the time were that upwards of 20–30 countries could seek to acquire nuclear weapons in the decades ahead; the Soviets shared Washington's concern but also thought that effective international action could prevent such proliferation.[5] China's nuclear-weapon test in 1964, as well as ongoing debates in other countries about acquiring such weapons, reinforced these concerns. Projections at the time of the widespread use of nuclear energy for peaceful purposes were another factor, but the more specific concern, especially for Moscow, was that West Germany could acquire nuclear weapons, aided by its expanding reliance on nuclear energy.

For both Moscow and Washington, memories of the Cuban Missile Crisis also provided part of the background to their cooperation in negotiation of the NPT. The two countries' leaderships had approached the brink of a nuclear war and come away with a recognition of the importance of finding new ways to manage their own nuclear relationship, as well as of the dangers of nuclear proliferation. In the words of one of the key US NPT negotiators, George Bunn, 'there was … just a complete change in the attitudes and relationships between the two delegations, starting really with the Cuban Missile Crisis'.[6] Six months later, the quick and successful negotiation in June 1963 of the Limited Test-Ban Treaty signalled that recognition, and demonstrated the Soviet and US will, as well as ability, to cooperate.

Motivations and hurdles

The most important motivation for US–Soviet cooperation was a shared interest in nuclear non-proliferation. Both super-powers wanted to constrain any West German pursuit of nuclear weapons, and both wanted to prevent nuclear prolif-eration globally. Nonetheless, the relative importance of these two concerns to Moscow and Washington varied. US support for a possible MLF was the most significant obstacle to coop-eration, and not until Washington signalled its readiness to set aside the concept did negotiations begin on the possible features of a non-proliferation treaty. However, difficulties persisted in formulating the specific language of the Article I 'no transfer' provision, reflecting Soviet opposition to US nuclear-cooperation arrangements with its NATO allies, and Washington's unwillingness to renounce all such coopera-tion. Meanwhile, reaching agreement on the eventual Article III language on inspections and safeguards also proved diffi-cult. Soviet insistence that International Atomic Energy Agency (IAEA) inspections should take place in European Atomic Energy Community (EURATOM) states clashed with the latter's reluctance to accept such inspections. Washington's ongoing requirement to consult with its NATO allies, especially West

Germany, was an obstacle to US–Soviet efforts to find mutually acceptable compromises on these outstanding issues.

Once the US decided in 1966 to set aside the MLF concept, Soviet and US officials began a process of negotiations, consultations and informal engagement to resolve their differences on the most critical issues. In 1966, a working group comprising three Russians and three Americans developed mutually acceptable language for the 'no transfer' provision of Article I[7] and the 'not to receive the transfer' provision of Article II.[8] Two key players were George Bunn on the American side and Roland Timerbaev on the Soviet side.[9] The key compromise reflected Washington's readiness (with West German agreement) to abandon the MLF concept and a Soviet willingness to live in practice with limited US Programs of Cooperation with NATO allies, but stopping short of any allied peacetime control of nuclear weapons. The initial result was the tabling of identical draft treaties at the Eighteen-Nation Disarmament Committee (ENDC) in Geneva in August 1967. However, there were no safeguards-inspections provisions, because of continuing US–Soviet differences, or any Article VI nuclear-disarmament obligation, given the focus of both Moscow and Washington exclusively on non-proliferation.

A somewhat comparable process characterised efforts to resolve differences over safeguards issues and to arrive at language that would be mutually acceptable to both Moscow and Washington, as well as to the United States' European allies that were in EURATOM. Technical discussions between small teams of Soviet and US negotiators in Geneva were critical, with both Bunn and Timerbaev again playing key roles.[10] Building on professional and personal ties that had developed in the earlier negotiation process – and in an informal process that included discussing this issue while hiking around Geneva and sailing on Lac Leman – they articulated a solution and conveyed that back to Moscow and Washington. As reflected in Article III of the NPT, this solution provided that: 'Non-Nuclear-Weapon States Party to the Treaty shall conclude agreements with the International Atomic Energy Agency to meet the requirements of this Article either individually or together with other States'.[11] This compromise language was used in identical Soviet and US draft treaties tabled at the ENDC on 18 January 1968.[12]

The agreement of other articles in the 18 January 1968 ENDC draft treaties also involved US–Soviet cooperation, but these were less contentious and any differences less intractable. Agreement was reached between the superpowers on 'peaceful uses' (Article IV) and, in response to demands by Mexico, Sweden and other non-nuclear-weapons states (NNWS), on 'nuclear disarmament' (Article VI). By contrast, on security assurances to NNWS, Moscow and Washington, in effect, agreed to disagree. In 1966, Moscow had proposed including a clause prohibiting the use of nuclear weapons 'against non-nuclear states parties to the treaty, which have no nuclear weapons in their territory', but the US rejected such a clause, and the process went forward without it.[13]

Following the 18 January submission of the identical US–Soviet drafts, proposals were made by other participants in the ENDC to amend the NPT, including Article VI. These came prior to the joint US–Soviet submission to the UNGA on 11 March of a draft NPT. Further amendments were also proposed prior to the UNGA passage on 31 May of a resolution commending the NPT to UN members.[14] Moscow and Washington consulted closely and sought a 'common front' in determining how to respond to these proposed amendments, agreeing to accept some and dismiss others.[15] Close cooperation continued in the lobbying of countries to support the NPT, both before and after it was opened for signature on 1

July 1968. In the ensuing deliberations on the treaty (including over ratification), Soviet and US officials sought to keep each other informed and coordinate responses to requests for clarification or interpretation of the NPT's obligations.[16] The importance of guiding the NPT through the UN was greater than any possible concerns about a supposed superpower condominium.[17]

Sustaining the NPT's credibility at the 1985 Review Conference

The 1980 NPT Review Conference had been unable to reach agreement on a consensus final declaration because of differences on the issue of a Comprehensive Nuclear-Test-Ban Treaty (CTBT). Five years later, sustaining the credibility of the NPT depended on the avoidance of back-to-back failures to agree on a final declaration. Though less prominent and determinative than in the initial negotiation of the NPT, US–Soviet cooperation made an important contribution to shaping the structure and tone of the 1985 Review Conference and to the resolution of the most difficult issue, that of the CTBT.[18]

The context in the immediate run-up to and at the third NPT Review Conference (27 August–21 September 1985) was one of prospective positive change. Only six months earlier – and a year and a half after the Soviet delegation had withdrawn in November 1983 from the negotiations respectively on intermediate-range nuclear forces and in December 1983 on strategic nuclear forces – on 12 March 1985, the Soviet Union and the US began new arms-control negotiations on defence and space systems, strategic nuclear forces and intermediate-range nuclear forces. This resumption of negotiations took place one day after Mikhail Gorbachev had become the general secretary of the Communist Party of the Soviet Union. In turn, Moscow and Washington agreed to a summit meeting between

President Ronald Reagan and Gorbachev, to take place in Geneva on 19–21 November 1985.

On the non-proliferation front, Moscow and Washington agreed to establish biannual formal, high-level bilateral non-proliferation consultations. The initiation of this process had been proposed by Soviet officials some months after Moscow's withdrawal from arms-control talks in November and December 1983, in an apparent signal of a desire to sustain this aspect of the arms-control relationship. Building on earlier, less formal exchanges, the first meeting took place in Moscow in December 1984. The US team was led by ambassador-at-large for non-proliferation Richard T. Kennedy and included Lewis Dunn, who also was then heading US preparations for the NPT Review Conference. The Soviet team was led by A.M. Petrosyants, chairman of the Soviet State Committee for Atomic Energy, and included both Vladimir Petrovsky, head of the Soviet Ministry of Foreign Affairs' Department of International Organisations, and ambassador Timerbaev. Very quickly, the delegation leaders and their teams developed a strong working relationship. In both countries, the initiation and then success of these initial non-proliferation consultations were seen as signalling a broader readiness to improve US–Soviet relations.

Nonetheless, this resumption of bilateral arms-control negotiations, the upcoming Reagan–Gorbachev summit (and other senior-level contacts) and the resumed non-proliferation dialogue all took place against a backdrop of continuing confrontation and suspicion. The 1984 and 1985 US report on 'Soviet Compliance with Arms Control Agreements' alleged multiple violations of existing arms-control agreements. In addition, the US was providing covert military support to the mujahideen fighting Soviet forces in Afghanistan, the military confrontation persisted in Europe, Soviet concerns were growing about President Reagan's Strategic Defense Initiative and each country's strategic nuclear forces remained on high alert.

Globally, the nuclear non-proliferation situation was troubling. Pakistan was moving towards the acquisition of nuclear weapons, putting pressure on an India that had tested a nuclear-explosive device a decade earlier, in 1974. Israel's 1981 attack on Saddam Hussein's Osirak research reactor had set back Iraq's nuclear-weapon ambitions but had also created new fissures in the IAEA. In 1982, the IAEA General Conference decided not to accept Israel's credentials, barring Israeli partnership in the IAEA and leading to a temporary US suspension of American participation in the organisation. Elsewhere, in the Middle East and beyond, other states figured prominently at least in US assessments of proliferation problem countries.[19] In terms of the NPT, there were concerns that a lack of progress on peaceful uses and nuclear disarmament could disrupt the 1985 Review Conference and undermine the NPT's credibility.[20]

Their shared interest in sustaining the NPT, as well as in preventing nuclear proliferation, provided the underlying incentive for US–Soviet cooperation in the 1985 Review Conference process. A desire to avoid successive review-conference failures also played a role. Moreover, the prospect of the Reagan–Gorbachev November 1985 summit gave both Moscow and Washington a strong incentive to cooperate. Both countries' officials recognised that cooperation at the Review Conference would create a better atmosphere for the summit, while contentious debate between the two countries about who bore the most responsibility for the lack of progress in implementing Article VI's disarmament obligations would send a very different message.

By contrast, continuing political and military confrontation remained an obstacle to cooperation. The desire within the Reagan administration to hold the Soviets to account on arms-control non-compliance – joined by a Soviet desire to respond by making counter-charges – was another obstacle to working together at the Review Conference. This combination could have led to acrimonious polemics across the many Review Conference fora. There were also mutual suspicions about how the other would act at the Review Conference, either pursuing shared interests or making it a medium for charge and counter-charge.

During the preparatory-committee phase of the 1985 Review Conference process, US and Soviet officials consulted closely and frequently on how to ensure that the conference was a success. These consultations took place partly within the now-formalised process of bilateral consultations, which provided a valuable venue for US officials to engage formally and informally with key Soviet officials, including Timerbaev, and to build ties with them. Timerbaev would now be a key player in helping shape Moscow's policy on the 1985 Review Conference. At one point in this process, Timerbaev informally told the author that he would do his best to ensure Soviet cooperation with the United States at the Review Conference. Still other US–Soviet consultations took place in the near-monthly trips to Geneva in 1984–85 taken by the author.

In addition to ensuring that each superpower understood how the other was approaching the Review Conference, these consultations focused on gaining Soviet support for a US proposal to revise the Review Conference's committee structure.[21] At the first and second conferences, in 1975 and 1980, work had been carried out in two so-called main committees, one dealing with non-proliferation, safeguards and peaceful uses of nuclear energy, and one with nuclear disarmament. The US proposal, made at the second preparatory-committee meeting in October 1984, was to create a new main committee so that there would be three such committees, dealing respectively with non-proliferation and safeguards, peaceful uses of nuclear energy and nuclear disarmament. US officials argued – and other participants in the review process agreed – that this new breakdown more accurately reflected what came to be known as the 'three pillars' of the NPT, and would allow for more thorough discussion of non-proliferation matters. (In turn, the creation of an additional main committee also enabled each of the three main NPT groupings – the Western Group, the Eastern Group and the Non-Aligned Group – to chair a main committee.) With support from the Soviets and all three of these groupings, this change of structure was recommended by the preparatory committee and agreed to at the start of the conference.[22]

Meanwhile, US representatives – including at very senior levels – emphasised to their Soviet counterparts that Moscow and Washington had an interest in taking a positive approach to the Review Conference, avoiding polemics that would turn it into a spectacle of charge and counter-charge, which could only could hurt the NPT. One month before the 1985 Review Conference, as they discussed the overall state of US–Soviet relations and the upcoming Reagan–Gorbachev summit, US Secretary of State George P. Shultz told his counterpart, Soviet Minister of Foreign Affairs Eduard Shevardnadze, that at 'the Review Conference itself we should stay away from polemics and the US will conduct itself this way'.[23] There were indications that Moscow thought that this positive approach made sense for both countries but questioned its implementation.

Moscow's agreement to a 'no polemics' approach became clear only at the start of the Review Conference. Following the positive US plenary statement by Arms Control and Disarmament Agency (ACDA) Director Kenneth Adelman, head of the US delegation, ambassador Victor Issraelyan, head of the Soviet delegation, spoke, focusing only on Soviet accomplishments in implementing the NPT. Like Adelman, he eschewed polemics. However, two speeches had apparently been prepared for Issraelyan – one that took the positive approach and one to be used if Adelman used the US plenary statement to blame the Soviet Union for arms-control non-compliance and lack of progress in implementing Article VI. The decision to take a 'no polemics' approach was said to have been made high up in the Soviet system.[24]

During the Review Conference, the most difficult substantive issue concerned the language to be used on a CTBT in the final declaration. In the middle of the final week, the conference faced possible deadlock over US unwillingness to agree to language regretting failure to conclude a ban on nuclear testing and calling for its urgent negotiation. One further session, involving a small group of countries from across the NPT's membership, was called to try to formulate a compromise, including Mexico as the leading voice on the issue, as well as the US and the Soviet Union, which had made clear its support for resumed CTBT negotiations. With a deadlock still looming, the US delegation proposed one final compromise approach, in which the final declaration would state that: 'The Conference, except for certain States whose views are reflected in the following subparagraph, deeply regretted that a [CTBT] had not been concluded … and, therefore, called on all the nuclear-weapon States Party to the Treaty to resume trilateral negotiations in 1985.'[25] Except for one delegation, all parties participating in the small group negotiation were prepared to support this compromise approach. The exception was the East German delegate, who pressed the US to make clear which countries other than the United Kingdom and the US had opposed a CTBT during the Review Conference. Very quickly, Soviet ambassador Issraelyan looked over to the East German representative and told him to leave the matter alone and in effect to be quiet. That Soviet intervention sealed agreement on the CTBT compromise. Though several other issues still had to be resolved, this outcome on a CTBT was essential for US agreement to the eventual consensus final document – and to avoiding damaging back-to-back failures of the review conferences.

Shared, if not identical, Soviet and US interests in preventing the spread of nuclear weapons constituted an underlying and continuing reason for successful cooperation in negotiating the NPT. By the early 1960s, growing concern about the proliferation threat had led both countries' leaderships to similar conclusions, even if initially the Soviet focus may have been on preventing West Germany's acquisition of nuclear weapons[26] and the US focus was on a perceived problem of possible widespread proliferation. As this process advanced, both Moscow and Washington kept their attention focused on their fundamental goal of a non-proliferation treaty, whether in accommodating demands from non-nuclear states to include a disarmament article or in agreeing to disagree on the issue of negative security assurances. 'This common understanding and mutual trust ... helped to overcome innumerable problems' during the negotiations.[27]

This shared interest in preventing nuclear proliferation – amid the growing risk of nuclear conflict – was reinforced by the events of the Cuban Missile Crisis. Both countries agreed on assigning the 'highest importance' to the NPT because of the danger of nuclear war.[28] However, the growing resistance among US NATO allies, other than West Germany, to the concept of the MLF was in part responsible for this cooperation. The resistance of its allies to the MLF made it easier for Washington to change its position on nuclear cooperation within NATO, thereby opening the way for the Soviet Union and the US to work together in negotiating the NPT.

Regarding cooperation to sustain the NPT in 1985, a historic shared interest in the NPT insulated the early preparatory process[29] from the wider breakdown of US–Soviet bilateral arms-control negotiations, particularly during the difficult period following the withdrawal of the Soviet Union from arms-control talks in late 1983. Both parties felt a sense of responsibility for a treaty that they had jointly played leading roles in creating. In turn, the mid-1984 Soviet proposal for more formal, high-level bilateral non-proliferation consultations – and US acceptance of that offer – signalled recognition of the importance of continuing one area of arms-control cooperation. At the same time, for both countries, the risks of nuclear proliferation and the challenges facing the wider non-proliferation regime (including the NPT and the IAEA) provided a logic for consultations. This dimension of shared interest continued to be a motive for cooperation into the 1985 Review Conference. Neither Moscow nor Washington wanted or would have benefited from successive failures to reach agreement on a final declaration, as well as the all-but-inevitable perceptions that would have followed of the 'NPT on the rocks'.

Gorbachev's coming to power in the Soviet Union reinforced that motivation. The arms-control process resumed and accelerated, and there was a new emphasis in both countries on pursuing a more cooperative US–Soviet relationship. Moreover, at the 1985 Review Conference itself, the prospect of the November Reagan–Gorbachev summit was almost certainly a powerful reason for both countries to adopt a no-polemics approach and to cooperate to make the conference a success.

Institutions and people also help explain successful cooperation during the NPT negotiations and the sustaining of the NPT at the 1985 Review Conference. The creation of the US Arms Control and Disarmament Agency in 1961 established a strong advocate for the NPT, as well as a bureaucratic opponent to the MLF, which was advocated by the State Department. The close working and personal relationships among key figures in negotiating teams also proved critical to resolving difficult issues. Key negotiators such as Bunn and Timerbaev had a shared commitment to 'the vital need to stop the proliferation of nuclear weapons'.[30] In addition, habits of consultation, coordination and cooperation developed, which continued once the NPT was opened for signature and ratification.

ACDA was similarly able to dedicate significant staff and senior-level resources to preparations for the 1985 NPT Review Conference. Indeed, sustaining the NPT was one of the top ACDA priorities. One result of this was repeated consultations between US diplomats and their Soviet counterparts in Geneva (and within the wider bilateral non-proliferation process) over the two years before the conference on the issues likely to arise, the benefits to both countries of taking a positive approach and the importance of cooperation to serve both countries' interests in a successful conference. At the same time, though ambassador Kennedy was not directly involved in implementing US NPT diplomacy, his credibility with his Soviet counterparts, as well as their strong working relationships developed in the wider non-proliferation bilateral process, reinforced the arguments for cooperation. On the Soviet side, Timerbaev was heavily involved in all aspects of Soviet preparations for the 1985 Review Conference. He was committed to the NPT and to ensuring a conference outcome that strengthened the treaty, which he had played a critical role in helping to create. Timerbaev also made clear his intention to work in Moscow towards Soviet–US cooperation that protected the NPT. Institutionally, US–Soviet consultations for the 1985 NPT Review Conference also reflected a recognition of the leading roles that the countries had played in the creation of the NPT. This was so although there also were continuing consultations with the UK, as one of the three NPT Depositaries, and the then-three nuclear-weapons-states parties (China and France were not yet parties). Overall, the institutional structure of the NPT, with key roles played by the Soviet Union and the US at this point, may have contributed to sustaining the treaty's credibility at the 1985 Review Conference.[31]

Conclusion

Shared interests in non-proliferation and the NPT have repeatedly provided the underlying foundation for US–Soviet cooperation. A primary lesson for future US–Russia cooperation is the need to go 'back to basics' – for a full and frank official dialogue on both countries' NPT-related interests. Though both powers share opposition to the newly negotiated Treaty on the Prohibition of Nuclear Weapons (TPNW), as well as common rhetoric that such negotiation will undermine the NPT, what is their shared stake in an effective and legitimate NPT? How might such legitimacy and effectiveness erode in the years ahead, perhaps accelerated by the long-avoided back-to-back failure of review conferences, if the 2020 conference repeats the pattern of the 2015 one? Most importantly, what are the two countries – together and with others – prepared to do to protect shared interests in the NPT as the keystone of the global non-proliferation structure, and what are the most important obstacles to such cooperation?

During the Cold War, NPT cooperation between Moscow and Washington took place within a broader process of bilateral non-proliferation engagement. This was especially evident immediately before and after the 1985 NPT Review Conference, and suggests that there is a strong argument to re-establish a high-level, sustained process of bilateral non-proliferation consultations, including on the NPT.[32] Substantively, those consultations would provide a venue within which to go 'back to basics'. Restored high-level consultations also could help create bureaucratic and institutional centres of gravity committed to rebuilding habits of cooperation in each country. Re-establishing bilateral non-proliferation consultations would signal both countries' readiness to rebuild habits of cooperation, including eventually on the wider set of strategic issues now dividing them. Renewed high-level US–Russia bilateral consultations would need to be harmonised with the P5 consultations, as well as other bilateral US consultations on non-proliferation matters. From the professional and personal relationships of the US–Soviet NPT-related negotiations, a further lesson is that strong working ties repeatedly contributed to the success of Moscow and Washington in resolving the NPT-related issues dividing them and in carrying forward their shared objectives.

Over time, a rebuilt process of formal high-level bilateral consultations could well help to re-establish such relationships; however, other approaches should also be explored. Joint analyses of pressing NPT-related issues could be undertaken by officials and experts, including revisiting the lessons from earlier US–Russia technical analysis of nuclear-warhead verification; reducing the risk of use of nuclear weapons in a proliferation-related crisis; and actions that Russia and the US could take to reduce to an absolute minimum any risk of accidental or unintentional detonation of a nuclear weapon. Meanwhile, joint US–Russia NPT 'gaming' by officials and experts from both countries could be undertaken, for example on the evolution and consequences of North Korea's continuing deployment of nuclear weapons or on scenarios involving significant erosion of the NPT and how to prevent them.

Motivated by frustration at the nuclear-disarmament stalemate and concerns about the risk of use of nuclear weapons, more than 100 NNWS – supported and encouraged by advocacy non-governmental organisations – have successfully negotiated and opened for signature the TPNW. More than 50 countries have so far adhered, and the treaty will likely acquire prior to the 2020 NPT Review Conference the 50 ratifications needed for its entry into force. The successful negotiation of the TPNW has changed the global nuclear-disarmament debate and the overall global nuclear landscape, even though it will not eliminate a single nuclear weapon because all of the countries that possess nuclear weapons have made clear that they will not adhere to the treaty. More important, the legitimacy and effectiveness of the NPT could erode significantly if there is increasingly divisive debate over the treaty at the 2020 NPT Review Conference.

In response to this changed landscape, it is becoming ever more important for Russia and the US – along with the other NPT nuclear-weapons states – to identify and pursue, cooperatively, new approaches to regain the nuclear-disarmament initiative and to address the concerns that led to the TPNW. One priority area would be cooperation to reduce to an absolute minimum the risk of use of a nuclear weapon. This step would respond directly to concerns among many NNWS that nuclear risk is significant and increasing. In so doing, it would help to lessen the divisions among NPT parties that endanger the NPT's legitimacy and support. Such cooperation also would reflect the historic and continuing interest of Moscow and Washington in the treaty that they worked so hard to create nearly five decades ago.[33]

Looking back at successful NPT cooperation between Moscow and Washington, starting with the NPT's negotiation, offers important lessons about the incentives, obstacles and reasons for successful cooperation. Looking ahead, there also are valuable lessons and important implications to be drawn from that past experience. In that regard, just as in the mid-

1980s, the revitalisation of high-level bilateral consultations and related direct engagement on NPT issues may again be the first step toward a process of re-engagement on the fuller set of strategic issues now dividing the two countries. That outcome would serve both countries' continuing interests, not only in the NPT but also in a more cooperative and stable US–Russia strategic relationship.

CHAPTER FIVE

The establishment of the London Club and nuclear-export controls[1]

Sarah Bidgood

During the first decades of the nuclear age, the Soviet Union and the United States used the export of nuclear technology as a mechanism to advance their Cold War foreign-policy objectives. Moscow sold nuclear power plants to developing nations as a way to cultivate and strengthen new alliance relationships, while Washington exported research and light-water reactors that relied on US-produced nuclear fuel in an attempt to constrain proliferation, boost its market dominance and counter Soviet influence.[2] In 1974, however, India's 'peaceful nuclear explosion' demonstrated unequivocally the harmful consequences of these practices. It was against this backdrop that Washington approached Moscow with a view to forming a conference of major nuclear suppliers to coordinate their export policies. Their initial bilateral discussions, as well as their interactions in what came to be known as the London Club, constitute important examples of cooperation for non-proliferation between the two countries.

Motivations for multilateral export controls

As noted in Chapter One, following the passage of the 1954 Atomic Energy Act, the US abandoned its policy of secrecy and denial and quickly emerged as the leading global exporter of nuclear knowledge, materials and equipment. Under pressure to deliver on the promises made in President Dwight Eisenhower's 1953 'Atoms for Peace' speech, the US government encouraged commercial nuclear-industry representatives to export nuclear research and reactors overseas, in part as a way to counter the appeal of communism in developing nations. Despite the fact that efficient, large-scale nuclear-energy production had yet to be realised, even within the US, Eisenhower perceived that there were significant 'psychological benefits' to be derived from these activities that trumped economic and security concerns.[3] Reflecting these priorities, US nuclear exports during this period were conditioned on the receipt of political, rather than technical, assurances of their long-term peaceful applications.[4]

The US was matched in its enthusiasm for the peaceful atom – as well as its disregard for its proliferation potential – by the Soviet Union.[5] By the mid-1950s, Moscow had positioned itself as the main source of nuclear assistance and exports to countries within the communist bloc.[6] Throughout the next decade, the Soviet Union and the US sought to outdo one another in their promotion and supply of nuclear energy as part of an effort to increase their influence abroad. Their competition in this arena resulted in the global dissemination of sensitive dual-use technologies and material, including to some countries that would eventually develop nuclear weapons, with inadequate regard to the consequences of these practices.[7]

The Cuban Missile Crisis, coupled with rising concern in Washington over the threat of 'Nth country' proliferation during John F. Kennedy's presidency, prompted the Soviet Union and the US to explore mechanisms to limit the spread of nuclear weapons in the early 1960s. By 1967, the two countries were engaged in close cooperation on the negotiation of the Treaty on the Non-Proliferation of Nuclear Weapons (Non-Proliferation Treaty, or NPT), which opened for signature in 1968.[8] This watershed agreement codified the inalienable right of its parties to peaceful nuclear energy in exchange for the commitment of the non-nuclear-weapons states (NNWS) not to proliferate. It obligated them to conclude safeguards agreements with the International Atomic Energy Agency (IAEA) and prohibited any state parties from providing 'source or special fissionable material … or equipment or material especially designed or prepared for the processing, use or production of special fissionable material' to NNWS, without safeguards. The negotiation of this provision, codified in Article III.2 of the treaty, itself required close US–Soviet cooperation (see Chapter Six). Its conclusion prompted the first informal multilateral efforts to coordinate export policies among major nuclear suppliers.

Under the chairmanship of Professor Claude Zangger of Switzerland, a group of NPT and non-NPT states began negotiations in 1971 on a list of nuclear-related equipment that would trigger the application of IAEA safeguards.[9] While their efforts were of significant importance to the implementation of the NPT, they did not impact the export of items outside those identified in the treaty. This limitation of the trigger list's scope became apparent when India conducted its peaceful nuclear explosion in May 1974. India's nuclear device had been created using plutonium from a Canada-supplied research reactor, a diversion of dual-use technology that underscored the need for expanded, coordinated multilateral controls, guidelines and safeguards provisions across nuclear suppliers to curtail the spread of nuclear weapons to states outside the burgeoning non-proliferation regime. The need to close this loophole was especially evident to legislators and policymakers in Washington because the US had supplied the heavy-water moderator used in India's CANDU (Canadian Deuterium Uranium) reactor.

Despite the muted official response to India's peaceful nuclear explosion in the US, coordinating the conditions of supply and expanding the items that warranted the application of safeguards with other major nuclear suppliers quickly became a priority for Washington. An update to US National Security Study Memorandum 156 from May 1974 explored the implications for US policy of India's peaceful nuclear explosion and acknowledged the need for a response to this 'setback to our nonproliferation efforts'.[10] Its authors advised taking action both to prevent the spread of nuclear weapons and to fight the misperception that 'the US no longer took the proliferation issue seriously'.[11] Such efforts became a high priority in light of the IAEA director general's complaints over the 'lack of a vigorous US (and USSR) response' to this event.[12]

At the same time, however, nuclear exports were proving to be a commercially lucrative business for both the Soviet Union and the US, and the two countries increasingly found themselves competing with one another for market dominance.[13] The 1973–74 oil crisis led analysts at the time to project that demand for nuclear energy would only continue to rise. Fearing that the global supply of uranium would run out, they speculated that these conditions would necessitate the reprocessing of plutonium for use in nuclear-power reactors, a practice with significant negative implications for non-proliferation.[14] At the same time, non-NPT states such as France and West Germany were exporting sensitive nuclear material and equipment to aspiring proliferators with minimal assurances of its peaceful applications.[15] This competitive economic environment forced each supplier to consider carefully how adopting more stringent export controls, which were prudent from a non-proliferation standpoint, would impact on their commercial interests.

With these considerations in mind, the US National Security Council recommended in a May 1974 report that President Richard Nixon approve consultations to encourage 'other countries [to] adopt export controls, comparable to those of the US, governing international activities of their citizens in the fields of unclassified nuclear technology transfer and assistance related to the production of special fissionable material', among other outcomes.[16] By way of National Security Decision Memorandum 255, issued in June 1974, Nixon charged the US Department of State with coordinating initial consultations aimed at 'reaching some common principles regarding the supply of sensitive enrichment technology or equipment'.[17] By July of that year, Secretary of State Henry Kissinger and his analytical staff were busy examining how to implement these directives.[18]

At Kissinger's insistence, consulting with the USSR and securing their support for these efforts was identified as a top priority, particularly in light of an upcoming trip to India where he would seek New Delhi's agreement to safeguard any future nuclear exports.[19] In his words, there was 'absolutely no sense in taking on India, and driving them to the Soviet Union on that issue' without 'an understanding with the Soviet Union of cooperative action' on coordinating their conditions of nuclear supply. In light of the urgency of this issue, he gave the Arms Control and Disarmament Agency (ACDA) and the State Department's Policy Planning division ten days to identify a concrete strategy. He asked them to lay out an approach to get 'what we want from the suppliers and what we want from the recipients'.[20]

By 2 August 1974, ACDA Director Fred Ikle and Director of the Policy Planning Staff Winston Lord had crafted a 'Strategic Action Plan' for Kissinger's review. They proposed that the US convene a conference with other nuclear exporters to 'tighten up further these export controls' and secure assurances that they would not attempt to undercut one another.[21] Kissinger was averse to any approach that would position the US as 'everybody's maiden aunt around the world, clucking to each country with ... a shopping list of various things we might do'. His advisers reassured him, however, that the USSR was likely to 'be prepared to go quite a long way with us' in pushing for more stringent multilateral export controls.[22]

This perspective reflects two primary assumptions in Washington about Soviet priorities and interests during the early 1970s. Chief among these was the belief that the USSR's experience with China had impressed upon its leaders how nuclear assistance could be diverted for military purposes without appropriate safeguards.[23] In fact, State Department official Herman Pollack reported to Kissinger in July 1974 that Soviet representatives in Vienna had chided the US for 'not doing enough about India'.[24] As a result, there was good reason to assume that Moscow would be eager to prevent future diversions of nuclear exports without compromising its own economic interests, particularly if the US led these efforts.

More broadly, US policymakers expected that their Soviet counterparts would support strengthening export controls as a way to advance their shared interest in non-proliferation. As the National Security Council Undersecretaries Committee observed in a June 1974 report, the acquisition by other states of nuclear arsenals would complicate the 'maintenance of a stable US–Soviet nuclear relationship'.[25] This outcome would have disrupted progress on the implementation of the Anti-Ballistic Missile Treaty, preparations for the first NPT Review Conference and negotiations on the control of peaceful nuclear explosions, a chemical-weapons convention and a comprehensive test ban, all of which were in process at this time.[26] In light of the importance to the detente process that both Soviet premier Leonid Brezhnev and Nixon – and, later, President Gerald Ford – placed on concluding these agreements, any interruption to these concurrent efforts would have been especially damaging.[27]

With this premise, Ikle and Lord presented Kissinger with an action memorandum on 26 August 1974 that reflected the need for a joint approach to export policy and the likelihood that the USSR would be a receptive partner in this endeavour. Specifically, they proposed a conference of 'key nuclear industrial states' aimed at 'realising a coordinated approach in placing effective controls, including safeguards and security measures, over transfers of commercial nuclear equipment and materials'.[28] While recommending eventual multilateral negotiations with Canada, France, Japan, the United Kingdom and West Germany, the two policymakers advocated speaking first with the 'French and the Soviets to ensure their support' before initiating discussions with other states.[29] This approach accommodated Kissinger's reluctance to put the US 'out in front' on the issue of strengthening nuclear-export controls and nonproliferation more broadly.

Ikle and Lord's proposal reflected the view that US–Soviet leadership on export controls was necessary to engender multilateral support for it.[30] As Pollack observed to Kissinger, moving forward side by side with the Soviet Union in efforts to coordinate their export policies would entice Canada and the UK to follow suit. Their participation could then incentivise suppliers outside the NPT – namely France – to strengthen their export policies correspondingly.[31] It is noteworthy that Kissinger and his advisers regarded US–Soviet leadership as the key to engaging other major suppliers – including their own allies – in adopting more stringent export practices. The importance they placed on Moscow's involvement in these efforts underscores the legitimacy that superpower cooperation lent to major non-proliferation initiatives during the early 1970s. Nevertheless, the secretary of state and his advisers were also aware of the ways in which this approach could backfire. They were wary of creating the impression of superpower collusion, particularly in any activities that could be perceived as restricting the access to the peaceful use of nuclear energy promised under the NPT.[32]

This concern was not shared by Soviet Minister of Foreign Affairs Andrei Gromyko. When Kissinger observed that his Russian counterpart 'wouldn't want some of his allies to get the impression of condominium' from any joint efforts to coordinate nuclear-export policies with the US, Gromyko was dismissive: 'If you mean our real allies,' the Soviet official replied, reportedly with a smile, 'it is no problem.'[33] Kissinger could not be so certain that he would receive similar support from the Western states, but he had pressing reasons to try. As he lamented to Gromyko, 'France has sold four reactors to Iran, and we don't know what safeguards there were'.[34] Recognising the potential proliferation consequences of this deal and the difficulties he was likely to face in convincing Paris to take steps to minimise them, he concluded that 'if we two can agree on safeguards, then we could go to the Europeans'.[35] Against this backdrop, the two sides initiated a series of bilateral US–Soviet consultations on export controls in October 1974 in Moscow.

US–Soviet bilateral consultations on export controls

Soviet and US policymakers had good reason to expect that their deliberations on export-control issues would be productive, based on their prior cooperative experiences. As US Deputy Secretary of State Robert Ingersoll reminded the US delegation in his initial instructions to them, 'we have frequent consultations with the Soviets on IAEA matters through our respective missions to the IAEA, with an excellent record of cooperation and mutual support in this field'.[36] He went on to note that 'there are no export areas in which the Soviets have a less restrictive policy than we do, and the main purposes to be pursued in discussion with them would be to discuss our interest in further coordination of supplier policies'.[37] These sentiments were echoed by Igor Morokhov, First Deputy Chairman of the Soviet State Committee for the Utilisation of Atomic Energy and head of the Soviet delegation to these meetings, who confirmed that 'much of what [the US] said meets with Soviet understanding' of export-control issues.[38]

In fact, Moscow and Washington were already working on a bilateral basis to coordinate their responses to specific export-related challenges before they commenced their bilateral consultations on export controls in October 1974. For example, when Argentina attempted to exclude duration and termination concepts from a safeguards agreement with Canada for the supply of a nuclear reactor in August of that year, the US mission to the IAEA placed a special emphasis on engaging the Soviet mission to ensure that the USSR was part of 'a common suppliers' front' in their response to this issue.[39] This effort reflected the close cooperation in which the Soviet Union and the US had engaged in refining the Zangger Committee's trigger list, even when the Soviet delegation was not invited to take part in these negotiations in a formal capacity.[40] At the first plenary session of their bilateral consultations in October, US delegation head Walter Stoessel recalled the constructive role played by the USSR in these negotiations as 'an important step in achieving common nuclear export policies'.[41]

Prior cooperative experiences also provided the participants with an understanding of how to engage on this issue smoothly and productively. For example, in light of the vital importance with which Ikle and Lord regarded Soviet participation in coordinating export controls, they were prepared to represent

Moscow's views in a multilateral setting if the Soviet Union found it politically difficult to participate.[42] This approach was one the two sides had used successfully in the context of the Zangger Committee negotiations. For his part, Morokhov suggested early on that he and Stoessel share responsibility for leading their bilateral consultations, with each assuming the role of chairman at every other session. This model served them well during the Threshold Test-Ban Treaty (TTBT) and the Peaceful Nuclear Explosions Treaty (PNET) negotiations, which were being conducted at approximately the same time.[43] Both sides likewise agreed to hold their consultations at the Ministry of Medium Machine Building in Moscow, the site of their negotiations on the TTBT and PNET. These procedural decisions illustrate how interaction on one non-proliferation issue could influence the outcome of another, even if the two were not linked at a broader strategic level.

Despite the apparent closeness of their existing export policies and their successful history of cooperation on export-control issues, however, the Soviet and US representatives had very different views about the scope of their discussions in Moscow. At their initial meeting on 22 October 1974, Morokhov presented the US delegation with an issue paper that identified 12 topics for negotiation. These went far beyond discussions about the application of safeguards against the diversion of nuclear technology and materials to a host of other non-proliferation issues, such as the 'creation of a more favorable regime for NPT parties with regard to receiving assistance in the peaceful uses of nuclear energy'.[44] The US, meanwhile, had produced a short, five-point aide-memoire, which contained a series of proposed guidelines for international nuclear exports. As this initial exchange demonstrated, Moscow viewed negotiations on nuclear-export policy as one part of a 'whole complex of measures to consolidate [the] NPT regime',[45] while Washington perceived it as a subject that could be addressed in isolation. While the broad Soviet interest in advancing non-proliferation made Moscow a willing partner in strengthening export controls, its incongruity with the United States' focused approach to this issue instead quickly threatened to derail discussions.

Both sides left their first meeting with promises to study one another's proposals, but this closer read only revealed greater differences between the initial Soviet and US positions.[46] In particular, ACDA and State Department representatives were alarmed by the fact that the Soviet delegation had not referenced in the 12-point issue paper the need to 'obtain explicit assurances from non-nuclear-weapons states that would preclude use of nuclear material in any … nuclear-explosive device, whether for peaceful purposes or for weapons'. Similarly, there was no mention of the need for 'developing stringent conditions on the supply of sensitive nuclear material to countries in regions of instability or conflict'.[47] US policymakers considered these elements to be critical components of any multilateral approach to strengthening safeguards and coordinating export policies. They instructed the US delegation to confirm in subsequent meetings that their Soviet counterparts felt the same.[48]

In attempting to resolve their differences, the US delegation sought to 'strike a balance between being reasonably responsive and not pre-negotiating bilaterally with the Soviets the conference results'.[49] Although ACDA and State Department officials advised the US representatives to focus on obtaining 'agreement both on the outline of a multilateral safeguards approach and on the desirability of a conference of key suppliers' at their bilateral sessions,[50] bridging the gaps in the two countries' positions continued to prove difficult. The Soviet delegation persisted in pressing for engagement on a wide range of non-proliferation challenges, noting that 'if you are really worried about non-proliferation of nuclear weapons then we need a whole range of measures to put things in order'.[51] Meanwhile, the US delegation maintained that the bilateral sessions should 'be devoted to specific problems, in particular, multilateral agreements to strengthen safeguards and control over exports and develop a common policy among the key suppliers'.[52]

Throughout these consultations, representatives on the US side sought to convince their Soviet counterparts that 'a multilateral approach is indispensable to the success of a safeguards strategy'.[53] They saw how a 'purely bilateral approach in this field could be easily circumvented by other key suppliers and would ultimately be self-defeating'.[54] On this basis, the Department of State advised the US delegation to avoid getting into 'detailed bilateral consultations' at their meetings and to save these discussions for a key-suppliers conference.[55] By the conclusion of the fourth and final meeting in November 1974, however, there seemed to be little hope that this event would transpire at all.

Soviet opposition to the conference stemmed in part from doubts that a meeting of nuclear suppliers could amount to anything more than 'competing exporting countries … seeking to ensure their markets'.[56] Further, they observed that some of the countries that participated in the Zangger Committee negotiations had not even adopted its trigger list,[57] and they wanted assurance that any subsequent attempts to coordinate export controls would be more effective. The Soviet Union was also concerned more broadly about the IAEA's capacity to implement any guidelines that the nuclear suppliers agreed upon. In Morokhov's view:

> Even if the exporters' conference should come up with a decision on controls, the verification problem will be up to the IAEA which, so far, is the only recognized international organ and control apparatus to deal

with nuclear materials and equipment for nuclear and non-nuclear states. Thus, the burden will fall on the shoulders of IAEA which, as you know, is in a very unsatisfactory shape.[58]

Morokhov did not believe that the IAEA could take on this role, in part because its safeguards department was significantly understaffed, with only 65 out of 101 vacancies having been filled. Out of these 65, individuals from non-NPT countries occupied nearly half, a situation that, from the Soviet perspective, suggested that the agency did not support the development of a successful verification regime for the NPT.[59]

In spite of these reservations, Soviet ambassador Roland Timerbaev hinted to one of the US delegates following their final bilateral meeting that the Soviet Union might be receptive to attending the nuclear-exporters conference that the US side proposed. This apparent softening in the Soviet position came with the proviso that it 'would be very useful if we could establish [a] procedure for regular periodic consultations on a non-proliferation policy'.[60] When Timerbaev spoke with Stoessel by phone on 29 November to inform him that the USSR agreed 'in principle' to participating in a nuclear-exporters conference, he reiterated Moscow's desire to hold a general discussion on 'enlargement of participation in the NPT, the review conference, the IAEA panel on PNEs' and other non-proliferation issues with Washington.[61] Perhaps seeing a quid pro quo for Soviet participation in multilateral negotiations on export controls, Kissinger instructed Stoessel to 'accept [the] Soviet proposal for continued bilaterals on non-proliferation topics'.[62] By late December 1974, the Soviet side had informed a number of other delegations of their intention to participate, and in early January 1975, they were pressing the US for information about when this conference would occur.[63]

A Nuclear Suppliers Conference in London

Ensuring Soviet participation in the first gathering of what would come to be known as the London Club of nuclear exporters had been a priority for the US throughout autumn 1974, but by the end of the year, determining which other delegations would attend was proving no less challenging. US representatives had begun approaching key nuclear exporters about the possibility of convening a small coordinating meeting at the same time that they were engaged in bilateral discussions on nuclear exports in Moscow. They sought feedback on their proposed guidelines for nuclear export from these parties and reported back to their Soviet counterparts on their progress.[64] For their part, Soviet officials were initially opposed to discussing strengthening export controls with any non-NPT parties, a position rooted in their concerns that these states would not be subject to international safeguards as stipulated by the treaty. Further, as Kissinger had anticipated, Soviet officials wished to see greater representation of the 'Socialist Bloc' among the conference participants.

Timerbaev proposed that East Germany (the German Democratic Republic, or GDR) be invited as the eighth participant in the inaugural suppliers' conference to address the political challenges that West Germany's participation would pose for his delegation.[65] While agreeing to report this request to his superiors in Washington, Stoessel observed that including the GDR would make it difficult to prevent other interested parties, including Italy and the Netherlands, from participating. On this basis, the US continued to place a priority on participation by Canada, France, Japan, the UK, the USSR and West Germany at the first meeting of the group of nuclear suppliers,[66] while acknowledging to Moscow that it would be 'possible to consider alternative forms of consultations and coordination with such smaller suppliers outside of [the] proposed conference'.[67] This decision illustrates both the extent and the limits to which Washington was willing to go to accommodate Moscow's preferences.

While the Soviet request for the GDR's participation eventually proved to be perfunctory (Kissinger correctly read it as a 'predictable but low-key approach upon which [the] Soviets are unlikely to insist'[68]), securing France's support for the US draft export guidelines and for multilateral negotiations on them became a very real barrier to convening a nuclear-suppliers conference. France's reluctance to join the group was tied to its opposition to making full-scope safeguards a condition of supply for enrichment and reprocessing facilities and technology. Its position was not unanticipated: when the Zangger Committee decided on a list of items that would trigger full-scope IAEA safeguards in 1973, for example, France declined to commit to abide by these guidelines, although it had pledged to act as though it were an NPT member in other respects. Nevertheless, the imperative to include France in the exporters group increased as Paris considered whether to supply Argentina, Brazil, Pakistan, the Republic of Korea and other 'states which have given evidence of nuclear-weapons aspirations' with enrichment and reprocessing facilities.[69] Furthermore, it was thought unlikely that Japan and West Germany would join the group without French participation.[70]

To avoid this outcome, US policymakers tried a number of approaches to convince France to take part in the first meeting of the nuclear exporters. Some of the concessions they were willing to make required breaking rank with the USSR, whose support Kissinger had considered so critical to securing French buy-in initially. During a bilateral meeting between President Ford and French President Valéry Giscard d'Estaing in December 1974, for example, Kissinger assured Giscard that France would not be required to accede to the NPT in order to participate, even though this departed from the Soviet focus on strengthening the newly concluded treaty. He promised that while 'the Soviet Union has persistently sought to engage us in joint pressures on the NPT we refused to pressure you or the PRC'.[71] Nevertheless, Kissinger found himself both unable to convince France to attend the conference and unable to proceed without its participation. Out of other options, he threatened to hold the first meeting without the French delegation, calculating that their desire not to be isolated would impel them to attend.[72] His approach worked, and by April 1975 France agreed to attend an 'exploratory meeting' to be hosted by the UK that spring.[73]

Securing French participation in the London Club, while necessary, meant that the US increasingly found itself mediating between Paris's positions on nuclear exports and those of the other delegations, particularly the USSR. France consistently objected to proposals that full-scope safeguards be made a condition of supply throughout 1975, forcing the US – which had planned to support Soviet insistence on stringent safeguards requirements – to change tack.[74] The French delegation clearly recognised that the US would not push it to make concessions for fear that it would leave the negotiations. Even prior to the exploratory meeting, which was held on 23 April 1975, Kissinger had assured French Minister of Foreign Affairs Jean Sauvagnargues that 'there could be appropriate provisions for exceptions to or release from commitments made by the nuclear suppliers', particularly taking into account 'the limits of possibilities for the commitments France would be willing to make in an eventual conference'.[75] These accommodations did not escape Soviet attention. In July 1975, Morokhov observed to Stoessel that the 'US seemed to have a "flexible" position' on the adoption of strong export controls favoured by Canada, the UK and the USSR, but opposed by France and Germany.[76] As

he had observed previously, six of the seven suppliers participating in the negotiations supported full-scope safeguards.
Morokhov indicated that the Soviet delegation would attempt
to bring the French in line with the majority in bilateral consultations of its own.[77]

By autumn 1975, the US began to suspect that its hands were
tied on the issue of safeguards. Nevertheless, in a September
1975 memorandum to Kissinger, members of the National
Security Council's Verification Panel Working Group explored
ways to bring the French position in line with that of the other
nuclear suppliers. They observed that capitulating to France
would negatively impact the United States' public image, as
the international community had become aware of what were
now known as the London Club meetings. Its members would
expect the nuclear suppliers to prohibit the export of enrichment
and reprocessing technology of the sort that France was planning to export without full-scope safeguards. Nevertheless, the
working group recognised that 'an attempt to take the "high
road" at this time would suffer from a lack of leverage, would
be inconsistent with previous assurances, and could result in a
collapse of the suppliers' talks'.[78]

Hoping to encourage France to embrace more stringent
export-control guidelines without going back on the promises
the US had made to secure their participation in the conference, the working group investigated whether modifying US
domestic policies on nuclear exports could bridge the gap
between Paris and the hardline supporters of full-scope safeguards in Moscow. To this end, in a set of instructions for the
third London Club meeting, they recommended insisting on
stronger multilateral controls at the London Club meetings in
exchange for the 'liberalisation of US COCOM [Coordinating
Committee for Multilateral Export Controls] policy on nuclear
reactor exports; relaxation of US licensing requirements on

French licenses of US firms; and relaxation of [US] policy of requiring the return of uranium tails when the Soviets provide toll enrichment services'.[79]

The working group had good reason to expect that this quid pro quo for France's constructive participation in the meetings might work. Rumours at the time suggested that France was concluding a deal to export between six and 12 Westinghouse-designed and Framatome-licenced light-water reactors to the USSR.[80] However, in accordance with National Security Decision Memorandum 261 (22 July 1974), US policy required the application of either US or IAEA safeguards on nuclear exports by COCOM member states to communist countries.[81] Because the USSR, as a nuclear-weapons state under the NPT, had refused to accept voluntary safeguards agreements,[82] France's proposed light-water-reactor sale would have required Washington to grant an exception. Representatives from the French embassy in Washington suggested that, under these circumstances, the desired level of export control could come from 'commitments France might agree to in the context of multilateral nuclear supplier understandings' instead.[83]

While hopeful that these 'few additional compromises' might enable the suppliers to reach an agreement on a list of export guidelines, the working group recognised that its proposal was risky and anticipated that it would be difficult to get buy-in from the US Congress.[84] To hedge against these outcomes, the US insisted in a bilateral conversation with the French the week prior to the September 1975 London Club meeting that the USSR must provide assurances that the reactors would be used for peaceful purposes and agree to supply the uranium ore to fuel them if the US was to approve the deal.[85] This bargain left the US representatives to the London Club in a curious position. While the US was relaxing its own safeguards requirements to secure France's support for more stringent safeguards requirements,[86] the Soviet Union, which insisted upon full-scope safeguards as a condition of supply, was itself refusing to accept safeguards on the reactors it was purchasing from France.

In the end, the leverage the US attempted to exact to change France's position on safeguards was ineffective. The French delegation to the London Club remained staunchly opposed to making full-scope safeguards a condition of supply. A memorandum summarising US views on the outcome of the 16–17 September 1975 London Club meeting concluded that 'remaining differences on the extent of safeguards coverage to be required as a condition of nuclear exports precluded the adoption of a complete set of common guidelines at this meeting'.[87] Its author 'urged the Canadians, British, and Soviets to be realistic, and plan to stay in close touch with all delegations over the next few weeks as the key countries conduct internal reviews and bilateral discussions aimed at achieving an informal compromise'.[88]

The Soviet delegation to the deliberations clearly recognised the position in which the US found itself in the final months of 1975. In a follow-up to a bilateral discussion with US representatives the week after the September London Club meeting, Timerbaev himself remarked on the 'importance of avoiding excessive pressure on [the] French'.[89] Nevertheless, he said that his delegation saw France's interest in reaching a consensus agreement on guidelines as an indication that, 'if approached at [a] high political level prior to [the] next meeting of the group', Paris might acquiesce to supporting full-scope safeguards as a condition of supply.[90] Morokhov accordingly pushed for a delay of a few months before the next meeting in which to conduct these overtures.

At the same time, Morokhov remarked upon the fact that US–Soviet cooperation on the peaceful uses of atomic energy 'had remained good even in periods of strained relations between the two countries'.[91] It was his recommendation that their successful cooperation in this arena 'should be continued'.[92] Perhaps in the interest of preserving these positive interactions, at the November 1975 London Club meeting, the Soviet delegation joined the other supplier countries in agreeing to an initial set of guidelines for nuclear transfers that did not require comprehensive safeguards.[93] In January 1976, the seven participants exchanged notes to confirm their commitment to abide by these guidelines.[94]

As these deliberations illustrate, during negotiations in the emerging Nuclear Suppliers Group, the US frequently acted as a broker between delegations with opposing, and even contradictory, viewpoints. This role required flexibility and a willingness to make sacrifices in the interest of achieving consensus, even though this approach meant that the seven suppliers often operated on a lowest-common-denominator basis. It also required close working relationships with the Soviet representatives to the London Club as the US delegation sought to 'make choices as to what balance is to be struck between diplomatic imperatives and public perceptions of a vigorous, coherent, nuclear policy'.[95] The foundation of trust that the two sides established through their bilateral negotiations both before and during the London Club negotiations became especially important in 1976 as the suppliers faced proliferation challenges that tested their commitment to the initial guidelines they had adopted.

The suppliers' efforts to apply the guidelines to a West German proposal to export a full nuclear-fuel cycle to Brazil in February 1976 constitute a vivid example of this dynamic. The preceding year, Brazil had concluded a deal with Germany for the supply of two new enrichment plants but refused to accept full-scope safeguards on its nuclear-fuel cycle.[96] Throughout the course of the London Club negotiations, US officials had grown increasingly concerned about the proliferation consequences of this arrangement and had gone so far as to issue a démarche to Bonn.[97] Their concerns were shared by the Soviet Union, as Soviet representative Marat Antiasov conveyed in a July 1975 bilateral consultation with representatives from the US mission to the IAEA. He told his US counterparts that the Soviet government was 'very unhappy' with the West Germany–Brazil nuclear agreement and cited critical articles in *Pravda* and *Izvestia* as evidence of the stir it had created in Moscow.[98]

In an attempt to mitigate the proliferation risks this deal posed and uphold the newly agreed London Club guidelines, the US advocated for the conclusion of a tripartite safeguards agreement between Brazil, Germany and the IAEA. The three parties negotiated an agreed text during several rounds of consultations that, in Bonn's view, went beyond the London Club guidelines and ensured US support for it.[99] In anticipation of a vote on the tripartite safeguards agreement at the IAEA Board of Governors meeting in February 1976, the US held consultations with various delegations to ascertain their support for – or concerns with – the proposed agreement text. These activities once again cast the US as the mediator, this time between the Soviet Union and West Germany, whose strained relations threatened to preclude an agreement.

Despite supporting the objectives of the London Club negotiations, the German foreign ministry perceived in early 1975 that any guidelines adopted by the London Club could limit its ability to fulfil Brazil's order, which Bonn saw as critical to its future as an industrial nation.[100] Its concerns proved to be prescient. In February 1976, the Soviet delegation to the IAEA signalled to its US counterparts that it would seek to postpone consideration of the tripartite agreement until June 1976. This was at least in part because, under the agreement, the start date for the application of safeguards was linked to the 'first transfer of relevant technological information rather than [the] date of completion of construction of [the] first facility using such information', as stipulated in the London Club guidelines.[101] The Soviet side attributed great significance to implementing the agreement the right way, given that it was the first to be negotiated 'after the signature of the nuclear suppliers agreement'.[102] Bonn, conversely, read Moscow's objections as an attempt to set the 'precedent that [West German] exports were subject to USSR veto'.[103]

The German delegation looked to the US to serve as an intermediary with Moscow in resolving this matter. In a personal appeal to Secretary Ingersoll two weeks before the vote at the IAEA Board of Governors meeting, ambassador Berndt von Staden, the West German representative to the negotiations, requested that the US take bilateral steps to convince several of the board members 'not to agree to a possible postponement'.[104] In a 19 February 1976 discussion with Walter Stoessel, Soviet Ministry of Foreign Affairs counsellor Anatoly Byelov seemed to hold a similar view, observing that 'close consultation between the US and Soviet delegations would go far toward dealing with such problems'.[105] While maintaining close contact between the two sides, the US encouraged West Germany to hold its own discussions with the USSR. Washington advised its German counterparts to 'identify all problems other [delegations] had and to find ways, perhaps by explanatory statement at [the IAEA] board meeting, to provide answers'.[106] At the same time, at the urging of US ambassador to the IAEA Gerald Tape, the Soviet ambassador to the IAEA Vladimir Erofeev approached one of the West German representatives the week before the vote. He indicated that his delegation 'did not intend to be obstructionist, and if concerns could be met,

[the] agreement could be approved'.[107] They agreed to consult further the morning before the vote, leading the US to express mild optimism that a solution was forthcoming. In a cable back to the capital, the US delegation noted that it would continue its efforts to mediate between the sides, which 'appears to be helpful in working out such solutions'.[108]

The night before the vote at the IAEA on the tripartite safeguards agreement, the Canadian ambassador proposed a meeting of the London Club delegations the following morning to discuss each representative's stance on the proposed text before moving into formal plenary. Five of the delegations agreed to attend under the condition that the US and the Soviet Union participate, but it was eventually 'agreed that [the] US would host [the] meeting and inform [the] USSR'.[109] Following these small group deliberations, a formal debate was held at the IAEA Board of Governors meeting. Although in its statement the USSR highlighted the difficulties to which the safeguards agreement had given rise, the delegation indicated that 'explanations by [West Germany] and Brazil had eliminated them'.[110] As a result of the understanding facilitated by the US between the USSR and West Germany, the board was able to reach the consensus that the '[IAEA] Director General be authorised to conclude and implement the agreement'.[111]

Conclusion

In the pursuit of a consensus list of export-control guidelines, the US frequently found itself caught between Soviet support for strengthened export controls, which it likewise supported, and the need to keep 'France from being "isolated" on key issues such as full-scope safeguards'.[112] Similarly, when faced with the first major test of the London Club guidelines, the US was both sympathetic to Soviet concerns about the Brazil–West Germany deal and unwilling to let consensus fall apart over them. For its part, the Soviet Union appeared to view the US as a genuine ally on export-control issues, and one that attempted to address its concerns seriously. On this basis, the Soviet delegations to the London Club and the IAEA demonstrated a willingness to show flexibility and embrace the compromises the US sought to orchestrate, even when they fell short of Moscow's preferences.

The positive dynamic of US–Soviet interactions on export controls persisted beyond 1976 and continued as the London Club – and subsequently as the rebranded Nuclear Suppliers Group (NSG) – attempted to strengthen further the members' export guidelines the following year. In at least one instance, this pattern of cooperation between the two sides contributed to preventing the NSG from collapsing completely. In September 1977, the Soviet delegation informed its US counterparts that it was considering withdrawing from participation because of France's unwillingness to support a joint UK–USSR effort to make full-scope safeguards a condition of supply. While the US supported this initiative, they sensed that France was feeling 'squeezed in the London Suppliers Forum to agree to apply full-scope safeguards' and might leave the group itself.[113] In a series of hasty bilateral consultations with its Soviet counterpart, the US delegation 'stressed the importance of continuing cooperative non-proliferation efforts in a multilateral context', highlighting how the 'breakup of [the] London Suppliers Group would be perceived as a failure of Soviet–US non-proliferation efforts'.[114] It successfully appealed to the Soviet delegation to 'go along with compromise'[115] in the interest of maintaining the integrity of the group and both countries' international image. While the outcome – an agreement to review safeguards requirements in the future – fell short of what either side hoped to achieve, it constituted 'a significant strengthening of the existing provisions on these subjects' and, from Washington's point of view, 'demonstrated the continued ability of the group to make some tangible progress'.[116]

These interactions illustrate why ACDA and the Department of State were correct in their initial belief that Moscow would prove to be a reliable partner on export-control issues. By taking a hard line on issues like full-scope safeguards, the Soviet delegation addressed Kissinger's 'reluctance to have the United States go charging around the world like Don Quixote' while still enabling him to fulfil the non-proliferation policy objectives that the Ford administration had prioritised.[117] Meanwhile, in acting as an intermediary between Soviet positions on key issues and those of other participants, the US helped to ensure that Moscow had an equal voice on export-control issues, which it was not afforded in the Zangger Committee negotiations.[118]

The ways in which the two sides helped one another advance their national objectives in the London Club context reveals some of Moscow's and Washington's primary motivations for cooperating and the approaches they used to overcome barriers in the process. Firstly, through their interactions in the London Club, the Soviet Union and the US were able to develop export guidelines that better served both their commercial interests and their non-proliferation commitments. Both superpowers would have faced significant commercial losses had they attempted to strengthen their export controls unilaterally. In this respect, economic interests served as a major driver for the two nuclear suppliers to work together on a consensus set of conditions for nuclear exports. At the same time, as noted in a 1976 US Department of State action memorandum on the Ford administration's nuclear-policy review, 'domestic pressures have substantially increased for fuller public expressions of what we have pursued privately' in the non-proliferation space.[119] As a result, policymakers in Washington saw the London Club – and cooperation with Moscow in this context

– as an opportunity to demonstrate their commitment to non-proliferation at home and abroad.

Secondly, India's peaceful nuclear explosion increased pressure on both the Soviet Union and the US to ensure that more states did not proliferate. Amid concerns that Pakistan would follow India's example, and wary that countries close to ratifying the NPT – West Germany, Japan and Italy – could have second thoughts, policymakers in both capitals recognised the imperative of preventing prospective proliferators from acquiring the necessary materials and technologies to act. This threat perception was a significant motivator for both sides to work expediently and in earnest on this issue. It also compelled the two sides to ensure that they coordinated their positions on export controls, particularly in light of the positive influence that they perceived their joint efforts could have on other nuclear exporters.

Thirdly, previous and concurrent successful examples of US–Soviet non-proliferation cooperation helped create trust and confidence between the two delegations that enabled them to interact productively in the London Club context. That the US had reliably represented Soviet interests in the context of negotiating the Zangger Committee guidelines, for example, reassured Moscow that Washington could be trusted to represent Soviet interests in multilateral negotiations in London. This conclusion certainly contributed to the United States' ability to mediate between the USSR, a forceful proponent of full-scope safeguards, and their staunchest opponents, most significantly France. It also likely induced the Soviet delegation to be more receptive to compromise in the London Club context, recognising that the US would make genuine efforts to support Moscow's positions whenever feasible.

In spite of the close cooperation between the Soviet Union and the US on nuclear-export policies, however, disagreements among NSG members over whether full-scope safeguards should be a condition of supply ultimately proved to be insurmountable. This central tension precluded efforts to further strengthen multilateral export controls for more than a decade, bringing meetings of the NSG to a halt between 1978 and 1990. Nevertheless, the process of establishing the London Club, and navigating the major issues that arose in its deliberations, yields valuable insights into the conditions and circumstances that allowed these efforts to succeed, particularly as they pertain to US–Soviet relations.

IAEA safeguards: patterns of interaction and their applicability beyond the Cold War

Nikolai Sokov

Cooperation between the Soviet Union and the United States with respect to nuclear non-proliferation or the International Atomic Energy Agency (IAEA) was rooted in a shared interest in preventing the spread of nuclear weapons, occasional disagreements notwithstanding. It was also characterised by an appreciation of the motives and concerns behind one another's approaches, and a willingness to compromise in pursuit of objectives that were seen as serving both countries' national-security interests. One of these objectives was to strengthen the IAEA safeguards system.

The system of safeguards, which is intended to prevent the diversion of 'source or special fissionable material' for use in nuclear weapons or other nuclear-explosive devices, is a vital element of the nuclear non-proliferation regime. Principal safeguards obligations by states parties to the 1968 Treaty on the Non-Proliferation of Nuclear Weapons (Non-Proliferation Treaty, or NPT) are contained in Article III of the treaty, which also designates the IAEA as the body responsible for the implementation of that system. The requirement to accept safeguards applies only to non-nuclear-weapons states (NNWS) parties to the NPT. However, all of the NPT-recognised nuclear-weapons states (NWS) – China, France, the Soviet Union (now Russia), the United Kingdom and the United States – eventually agreed as a confidence-building measure to accept voluntary safeguards with respect to elements of their non-military nuclear complexes.

Two specific elements of the safeguards regime are pertinent to insights into the mechanics of US–Soviet cooperation, and provide a better understanding of the conditions that enabled such cooperation. These are paragraphs one and four of Article III, which define the obligations of NNWS with regard to safeguards in all peaceful nuclear activities within the territory of the state, under its jurisdiction or carried out under its control anywhere, and paragraph two, which bans the provision of 'source or special fissionable material' or 'equipment or material especially designed or prepared for the processing, use or production of special fissionable material' to a NNWS, unless the source or special fissionable material is placed under safeguards.[1]

Although the two countries shared a strong interest in a nuclear non-proliferation regime and, more specifically, in a reliable safeguards system, cooperation on that matter was hardly preordained. In fact, more than once in the course of negotiations and subsequently, their positions differed in a significant way. Yet each time they succeeded in finding a mutually acceptable resolution to those differences. In fact, cooperation on Article III was close enough to be classified by some NNWS critics as a case of 'superpower condominium'. That track record stands in contrast to the interactions between Russia and the US in recent years – although the two countries continue to share an interest in the maintenance of the nuclear non-proliferation regime, the degree of cooperation appears to be far lower. This comparison suggests that shared interest is a necessary but hardly sufficient condition for such cooperation: other determinants that made a high degree of US–Soviet cooperation possible have apparently factored in that relationship.

The negotiations relating to the safeguards system provide particularly useful information for examining the role of these suspected external determinants to US–Soviet cooperation. Each party had to manage other international and domestic issues, such as alliance relationships, to make sure that they did not derail non-proliferation initiatives. These challenges were particularly serious for the US, and as such, it was not unusual for Washington to promote positions that had been diluted in terms of the priority attached to its non-proliferation objectives, leaving Moscow to decide whether to reject the US approach out of hand or seek to negotiate a compromise.

Safeguards-related issues on the US–Soviet agenda

The beginning of US–Soviet cooperation on Article III can be dated with considerable precision. In 1965, Moscow agreed to the principle of on-site inspections as part of IAEA safeguards. Previously, the Soviet Union had categorically rejected all on-site inspections, anywhere and under any international regime – an attitude inherited from the 1950s.[2] This change in Moscow's position opened a direct path toward US–Soviet collaboration on Article III.

The Soviet acceptance of such inspections in the context of IAEA safeguards was, however, limited and conditional. For example, Moscow would not agree to inspections on its own territory (which meant, in practice, on the territory of any NWS). Still, it did accept inspections for all NNWS, including its own allies. Furthermore, US–Soviet deliberations on Article III were kept separate from work on other elements of the future treaty.

The Soviet Union and the US shared the fundamental principle that, as a condition for membership of the NPT, each non-nuclear country was obligated to sign an agreement with the IAEA on the application of safeguards to its nuclear programme. They also regarded such an agreement as a prerequisite for the receipt of technical assistance from the IAEA in the development of peaceful nuclear programmes.

This common view of the key elements of the future safeguards regime did not result in an early agreement between the Soviet Union and the US on the text of Article III, however. In fact, disagreements on safeguards persisted longer than those on other elements of the treaty. The draft NPT text, which the Soviet Union and the US tabled in their capacity as co-chairs of the United Nations Eighteen-Nation Disarmament Committee (ENDC), contained only a placeholder for Article III. The US aide-memoire that accompanied the draft noted that 'discussions between the co-chairmen are continuing in an effort to reach agreement on an article on safeguards (Article III) for subsequent submission to the ENDC'.[3] Delays in reaching an agreement on Article III reflected the United States' need for additional time to coordinate its position with its allies and then to coordinate that common position with Moscow. It is significant that Moscow demonstrated understanding of the challenges Washington faced by agreeing to leave a placeholder in the draft NPT text for Article III and by not raising it at the ENDC or other venues in a confrontational manner.

At the centre of the conundrum the US faced was the issue of how safeguards would be applied to members of the European Atomic Energy Community (EURATOM), who were also US allies. EURATOM members rejected the principle of bilateral IAEA safeguards – namely, that each country would conclude a safeguards agreement with the IAEA in an individual capacity. Instead, they insisted that safeguards be applied by EURATOM itself, which would, in turn, conclude an agreement with the IAEA. By way of rationale, they claimed that EURATOM's regional safeguards were more reliable and stricter than the bilateral ones administered by the IAEA – a characterisation that may have been accurate under pre-NPT 1950s safeguards but would not necessarily apply in the post-NPT period. The issue was not framed in terms of the reliability of safeguards, however. Rather, it centred on the concern that other regional groups might emerge in the future that would refuse the direct application of IAEA safeguards and claim the right to self-inspection, thereby potentially weakening the regime and setting a precedent that would be deleterious to the ability of the IAEA to implement its mission. That challenge could prove particularly serious if such groups refused to accept for internal purposes more stringent safeguards that could be developed at a later date. This concern was the central motive behind the Soviet Union's insistence that all safeguards agreements be bilateral. Soviet decision-makers worried that special treatment given to US allies could deny the IAEA – and Moscow – sufficiently reliable information about national or joint nuclear programmes, most importantly those involving West Germany.

The US was deeply divided on the advisability of accepting regional EURATOM safeguards within the NPT. As early as the 1950s, the US Atomic Energy Commission had fought the self-inspection principle during negotiations on the US–EURATOM Cooperation Agreement, which was concluded in 1958, but was overruled by the Eisenhower administration. In the end, the US acquiesced, and agreed with EURATOM that 'if or when the IAEA had established an international safeguards and control system, the US and EURATOM would "consult" regarding the assumption by that Agency [the IAEA] of the safeguards and control over fissionable material'.[4]

The language of the 1958 agreement did not preordain that the US would accept the EURATOM-proposed safeguards formula for the NPT; the obligation to consult did not equal acceptance. Indeed, in the early 1960s, the US government was deeply concerned about Franco-German cooperation on civil nuclear affairs, particularly with respect to West German involvement in the creation of a uranium-enrichment capacity in France. Recently declassified documents demonstrate that the Kennedy administration was acutely aware of the possible implications of that programme for suspected West German nuclear-weapons aspirations and clearly did not regard EURATOM safeguards as a sufficient defence against such developments.[5] Although concerns about Franco-German cooperation had largely abated by 1964, Washington nevertheless remained watchful.

These concerns paved the way to full agreement with the Soviet Union. Yet at the other end of the scale for the US were broader issues of transatlantic cooperation. Refusal to consider EURATOM arrangements for safeguarding allies' nuclear programmes entailed certain risks for alliance solidarity, to which some US governmental agencies – first and foremost the Department of State – were highly sensitive. Dominating these concerns was the prospect that a tougher non-proliferation approach by the US could lead West Germany to entertain a nuclear-weapons programme of its own, a development that proposals for a NATO Multilateral Nuclear Force (MLF) – an idea that had been abandoned only a few years earlier – was intended to forestall. As explained by President John F. Kennedy to Soviet Minister of Foreign Affairs Andrei Gromyko in 1963, one of the reasons for an MLF was 'to make it less possible for the Germans to press for nuclear weapons of their own, weapons which could be used without US consent'.[6] Similarly, the refusal to accept EURATOM safeguards as part of the future NPT, it was argued, could undermine the still very tenuous agreement by West Germany to join that regime.

These internal conflicts in the formulation of US policy need to be put in a proper perspective. At no time did Washington deviate from the broad principle of the need for reliable safeguards. The Department of State's own Office for International Technological and Scientific Affairs insisted that:

> A nonproliferation treaty should include a strong provision providing for international safeguards … The Joint Committee on Atomic Energy has expressed itself strongly on this issue on several occasions. There appears to be significant Congressional support for an effective safeguards clause in any nonproliferation treaty.[7]

That attitude was shared by the US Joint Chiefs of Staff. In a memorandum addressed to the State Department, the Joint Chiefs noted that they supported the latest draft of the NPT, except that 'there is no provision for clearly defined adequate safeguards on peaceful nuclear facilities and other peaceful programs to prevent non-nuclear states from developing nuclear weapons under the guise of peaceful research'. The Joint Chiefs insisted on 'clearly defined adequate safeguards' as a condition for the NPT.[8] Even the Department of State remained uncertain about the wisdom of making a concession to EURATOM. As US Secretary of State Dean Rusk put it, that exception created the possibility of a 'little family group which would inspect itself and deny outside inspection'.[9]

Commitment to strong safeguards notwithstanding, the US needed to avoid the risk of antagonising its allies, especially West Germany, which was suspected of secretly harbouring intentions to acquire nuclear weapons. In the end, Washington chose to accommodate EURATOM's preferences, fully cognisant of the potential risks that decision entailed. The US draft of the NPT tabled in August 1965 foresaw the establishment of 'International Atomic Energy Agency or equivalent international safeguards'.[10] The underlying justification for its acceptance of EURATOM safeguards in place of IAEA safeguards was their assessed reliability and the belief that a special arrangement made for Europe would not undermine the effectiveness of the safeguards regime. The 1966 National Intelligence Estimate agreed with the claims of the United States' European allies that IAEA and EURATOM safeguards were equally efficient.[11] The US Arms Control and Disarmament Agency (ACDA), similarly, claimed that 'EURATOM safeguards [were] in our opinion dependable'.[12]

Now Washington needed to convince Moscow that a departure from the strictest possible treatment of the future safeguards regime would still be acceptable. The risk of making an exception for EURATOM was well understood in the US, including in the State Department, which was its key proponent. That task was by no means simple. ACDA admitted in a December 1966 report to the president that Soviet objections to the self-inspection principle were serious, since acceptance of EURATOM safeguards 'would be, in effect, inspection by our allies of our allies'. The US, this report said, should seek 'a formulation which would achieve [the objective of enlisting Soviet support] and at the same time protect the interests of our allies'. [13]

Negotiations with the Soviet Union on the US-preferred language granting a safeguards exception to EURATOM, and potentially other regional groups, were not straightforward. The Soviet Union could have continued to resist, and might have invoked the same right for Moscow's allies; this probably would have been unacceptable to the US, and perhaps even EURATOM. Strong opposition to the 'EURATOM exception' would have been predictable and understandable, given perennial Soviet concerns about the possibility that West Germany might decide to acquire nuclear weapons. Instead, apparently motivated primarily by securing the early conclusion of the NPT (which meant accepting satisfactory rather than optimal terms), Moscow agreed to accommodate the US.

A considerable part in the successful resolution of the controversy belonged to Soviet and US diplomats permanently posted in Geneva. They succeeded in developing personal trust, which was key to successful negotiations. Furthermore, these negotiators were given considerable leeway by their respective capitals in reaching agreement *ad referendum*. This arrangement enabled diplomats to probe in depth the motivations behind the other party's position, correctly identify the limits of its flexibility and explore options for compromise. It is conceivable that the more traditional pattern of negotiation, in which every decision is made in capitals and must pass through the inter-agency process before submission to the other side, might have yielded the same outcome. However, it almost certainly would have taken considerably longer.

One innovative method Soviet and US negotiators devised to secure final approval for nuclear-safeguards-related language on which they had themselves informally agreed was to submit the proposed joint draft text to their respective capitals in a fashion that presented the proposal as an initiative of the other side. In other words, in Washington it was known as the 'Roshchin draft', while in Moscow it was referred to as the 'Foster draft' (the names of the chief negotiators). This approach ensured that agencies in the capitals involved in the negotiations were presented with a 'yes–no' choice about whether or not to approve the draft, rather than having the opportunity to craft instructions for their representatives on how to proceed.[14]

Here, the highly concentrated decision-making system in the Soviet Union referred to above played a role. Furthermore, since the foreign ministry could initiate political decisions (in the form of an action proposal, or *zapiska*) and proposals could be channelled from the ministry directly to the highest level, Soviet negotiators had considerable weight. Although with respect to the issue of EURATOM safeguards there is no explicit evidence in Soviet declassified documents to support this conclusion, it would be surprising if the issue had not been resolved in that manner.[15]

The compromise language arrived at by the two sides allowed EURATOM as a whole to conclude an agreement with the IAEA. Paragraph 4 of Article III of the NPT stated that an agreement with the IAEA should be concluded 'individually or together with other States'.[16] The nature of that compromise is significant. In effect, the Soviet Union accepted an outcome on the more narrow issue of stringent safeguards that did not achieve its ideal position in order to secure the larger goal of establishing an international nuclear non-proliferation regime.

There is also every reason to believe that Moscow clearly understood the motivation behind the US position – namely, Washington's problems in its relations with allies. Given the Soviet Union's long-standing concerns about a possible West German nuclear programme, compromise on the safeguards issue could have proven untenable. However, in this case, an overriding interest in the NPT and, apparently, the belief that the US shared that interest and would do everything in its power to preserve the integrity of the future non-proliferation regime, persuaded Moscow to accept this less than ideal outcome. Accommodating the US position in this respect involved a degree of trust that would have been unthinkable in the previous decade. The compromise also reflected the overall improvement in US–Soviet relations, which began in 1963 during the Kennedy administration. The positive change in that relationship and the expectation of further improvement likely affected Soviet estimates of future US–Soviet cooperation on non-proliferation and the perception of the US as a reliable partner in these efforts.

Beyond the question of EURATOM, the Soviet Union and the US also successfully engaged on other issues pertaining to safeguards within the framework of the NPT. These examples of cooperation shed light on the factors that enabled such constructive joint work to take place.

The first issue involved the question of whether NWS would be obligated under the NPT to place their civil nuclear facilities under IAEA safeguards. This requirement was advocated by a large number of NNWS, including some US allies in Europe, who saw it as a means to ensure that NPT safeguards would not be too intrusive and/or as a way to make the regime more equitable. The US eventually accepted this concept in 1968[17] and, after some wavering, was joined by the United Kingdom. However, the Soviet Union, supported by France, strongly objected, insisting that the nuclear sectors in NWS remained exempt from safeguards. In no small measure, this position was rooted in the nature of the Soviet nuclear industry, in which defence and civil components were intermixed. Soviet opposition was reinforced by its general aversion to intrusive, on-site inspections. In the end, and in the interests of concluding negotiations, the US acquiesced to the French and Soviet view, agreeing that the placement of nuclear facilities under safeguards measures in the NWS should be a voluntary option. Indeed, the Soviet Union initially did not place any of its nuclear facilities under safeguards and concluded a relevant agreement with the IAEA only in 1985.

The second issue, which took considerable time to resolve, concerned the adequacy of safeguards that existed at the time for the implementation of Article III of the NPT. This issue was neither high profile nor especially controversial. Rather, it was one on which the two countries genuinely sought the best outcome, at least from their shared perspective. Moscow and Washington eventually reached a common view that revision of the existing procedures was unnecessary and that safeguards adopted before the NPT's entry into force (known as item-specific safeguards) generally were sufficiently flexible and modifiable to be used for the purposes of the NPT. Nevertheless, the agreement of the two sides on this issue did not preclude cooperation to create the next generation of safeguards. Moscow was also prepared to insist on more extensive and novel approaches to bilateral safeguards in specific instances (e.g. with respect to the heavy water that it provided to India).

The third issue concerned the resources necessary for the implementation of such safeguards. In 1967, the Soviet Union proposed the creation of a Safeguards Department within the IAEA. The US, in contrast, sought to postpone the decision, bowing to resistance from some of its allies.[18] Eventually, after the signing of the NPT, the two countries cooperated in the decision by the General Conference of the IAEA to create such a department in 1970.

While not inconsequential in terms of their potential impact on the effectiveness of the new non-proliferation regime, a common feature of these three issues was their essentially technical nature. As such, the issues lent themselves to an approach in which each party sought to maximise the chance of achieving its goals, rather than selecting the first choice that was 'good enough'. This was probably one reason why the negotiations took a relatively long time to resolve – they simply did not attract enough attention to be raised to higher-level authorities, who were primarily focused on more politically relevant elements of the NPT.

Informal cooperation: the Soviet Union, the Zangger Committee and the London Club

The issue of safeguards also arose within nuclear export-control regimes, specifically the Zangger Committee and the London Club. The US and USSR engaged in close cooperation in these bodies, including on whether the export of sensitive nuclear materials and equipment should require mandatory IAEA safeguards on the part of the importer.

The Zangger Committee represents a particularly interesting case because the Soviet Union had not been invited to join it during the initial negotiations on its 'trigger list'. This decision by the Western group of countries was apparently driven by political and procedural, rather than substantive, reasons, but the USSR clearly shared the goals and also the rules adopted by that body. Indeed, as noted in background material prepared by ACDA in advance of consultations in Moscow in 1974, 'the Soviets did not join in the deliberations of the (Zangger) Committee, but were kept advised of its progress'.[19] Furthermore, the document continued, 'in September 1974, the Soviets formally notified the Director General of the IAEA that their export policies were in accord with the Zangger Committee guidelines'.[20] Cooperation between the two parties stretched so far that the US informally represented the Soviet Union in the Zangger Committee and consulted Moscow with regard to the issues on the committee's agenda, to make sure that Moscow remained on board with and supportive of its decisions.

Beyond adopting the Zangger Committee guidelines itself, Moscow also brought the export-control policies of its allies in line with the committee's provisions, a move that was facilitated by the aforementioned nature of Soviet alliance relations, in which Moscow exercised extensive control over its allies' nuclear-energy programmes and trade.[21]

Summarising a detailed overview of Soviet policy on the issue, ACDA noted that 'there are no export control areas in which the Soviets have a less restrictive policy than we do' and assessed the pattern of US–Soviet cooperation on these matters as 'excellent'.[22]

Cable traffic between Washington and relevant US embassies and missions in the early 1970s also shows that the USSR adhered in practice to stringent export-control policies. For example, requests for clarification of the Soviet position on nuclear exports to various countries as diverse as India, Libya and Spain typically were met with confirmation from Soviet representatives that the export of nuclear-related goods and services (such as the enrichment of uranium) would be in compliance with Soviet NPT obligations, subject to IAEA safeguards and in line with common export-control guidelines as specified by the Zangger Committee. This degree of cooperation and the shared approach to nuclear exports was cited by US officials as part of the rationale for securing the 'buy-in' of their counterparts in Moscow before the first multilateral London Club meetings in 1975.

Despite this close coincidence of policies, ally relationships again impacted on US–Soviet cooperation on the application of safeguards, even in such informal settings. A 1974 memorandum prepared by the State Department noted, for example, that the

> Canadians supported by the UK and Soviets pushed for a requirement that recipients put all their nuclear facilities under safeguards (the 'full fuel cycle safeguards' approach). The French, with support from the FRG [West Germany] and Japan, were only willing to agree to requiring safeguards on supplier-transferred items (the 'project specific safeguards' approach).[23]

A cable sent from the US Department of State to the US Embassy in India similarly points to that rift, and further shows that the US position had been to 'fully support common supplier policy of this kind if acceptable to all other participants'.[24] In other words, the US was already considering the more limited, 'project specific safeguards' concept in the name of achieving consensus within the Western group of states, even though its own preference coincided with the Soviet approach. The Soviet Union, in contrast, continued to push for the stricter application of safeguards, and, in September 1976, Soviet representative to the IAEA Board of Governors Ivan Morokhov insisted, according to his US interlocutors, that 'full fuel cycle safeguards should be required as a condition of export'.[25] It is not unlikely that the strong Soviet position helped Washington in opposing the softer approach preferred by some US allies.

The issue of 'superpower condominium'

US–Soviet cooperation during the NPT negotiations (including the joint drafts of Article III submitted to the ENDC in 1967), their interaction with regard to the Zangger Committee and preparations for Soviet membership of the London Club brought to the fore the highly sensitive issue of 'superpower condominium'. From Moscow's standpoint, it was desirable for the two countries to continue this pattern – namely, to discuss all outstanding matters dealing with non-proliferation on a bilateral basis and then present a common position to the rest of the international community, closely coordinating any changes in that common position. This desire to approach nuclear issues on a bilateral basis with the US first, before undertaking multilateral negotiations, also reflected the broader interest of the Soviet leadership in positioning itself as a superpower equal to the US. In this respect, the special relationship between the two countries could serve multiple but reinforcing objectives.

In Washington, however, the experience of 1967 was perceived differently. Close coordination and joint actions by the Soviet Union and the US made some countries, including US allies, resentful and suspicious of the emerging superpower condominium. Afterwards, Washington carefully sought to avoid creating a similar impression, even if it meant forgoing opportunities to find common language with Moscow and press on with the shared non-proliferation agenda. Specifically, the US insisted that consultations with allies should precede interactions with the Soviet Union, and that the positions of allies would be taken into account as much as possible.

The previously referenced ACDA background material prepared for consultations in Moscow on export controls clearly indicated Washington's desire to avoid the impression of 'strict bilateralism' on NPT issues. Its authors identified, as the second objective, the intention

> to lead the Soviets beyond the bilateral dimension toward the concept of involving all key suppliers in export controls. We must attempt to persuade the Soviets that only multilateral action in this field can be effective and that, while we value bilateral consultations, a strictly bilateral approach could be easily restricted or circumvented by other key suppliers ... Obviously, we want to avoid any signs of US–Soviet condominium in light of relations with our allies and the Chinese.[26]

The image of the Soviet position represented in this ACDA document may be misleading, as there is every indication that Moscow appreciated the need for multilateralism in export controls, as well as in other elements of the nuclear non-proliferation regime. Rather, Moscow appeared to insist that the Soviet Union and the US reach an agreement before presenting the common position to the rest of the world, after which negotiations could take place in a multilateral but coordinated fashion. Morokhov explained this approach in 1976. According to his US interlocutors, Morokhov reprimanded the US for an action in Vienna that had not been cleared with Moscow in advance: 'He viewed US Mission action of giving [a] paper to the IAEA Secretariat, without first obtaining [the] views of [the] USSR, as amounting to [a] breach of faith' because 'a number of points made in the paper ... were unacceptable to [the] USSR'.[27] The parties also disagreed on the location of consultations – while the US declared that these should be conducted in Vienna in the context of the IAEA, Morokhov demanded that the consultations be held in Moscow on a bilateral basis.[28]

Washington, however, drew the line here. No matter how much it valued consistently strong cooperation with Moscow on nuclear non-proliferation, it was reluctant to sacrifice its relations with allies and other partners to a condominium. Instead, it sought to carefully balance these elements of its policy.

Nevertheless, and in spite of these disagreements in approach, the period of the late 1960s and early 1970s was one in which the two superpowers were able to engage in a productive and constructive non-proliferation relationship. This cooperation was apparent in their ability to arrive at joint positions both on broad political issues and on practical technical and legal matters. The foundation for cooperation that developed during that period endured throughout most of the remainder of the Cold War.[29]

Conclusion

Analysis of US–Soviet interactions on IAEA safeguards during the 1960s and early 1970s demonstrates that close cooperation between the two countries was not based solely on a shared interest in the nuclear non-proliferation regime. Several other variables external to the non-proliferation issue area facilitated cooperation and increased the probability of successful outcomes. Three such variables stand out.

Impact of external factors

The first is the nature of alliance relationships. The US needed to contend with the interests and the positions of its allies, sometimes to the detriment of its own preferences. The Soviet Union, in contrast, could act almost as a unitary player, whose policies were only minimally affected by the interests and positions of its allies or any other states. This arrangement enabled Moscow to make compromises when necessary more readily than Washington, as the issue of EURATOM exception demonstrates. At the same time, the experience of very close collaboration between the two countries displayed in 1967, during negotiations on the draft text of Article III of the NPT, made US allies suspicious that in the future Washington might disregard their interests in favour of cooperation with Moscow. The US responded to these concerns by emphasising consultations with allies and demonstratively placing a higher priority on these than on bilateral interactions with the Soviet Union. The pattern that emerged during the NPT negotiations could be detected in other areas, such as intra-NATO consultations in the context of bilateral strategic arms-control negotiations (including both the Strategic Arms Limitation Talks (SALT) and the Strategic Arms Reduction Treaty (START) stages in the 1970s and 1980s).

The second external variable involved the differences in the decision-making procedures in the two capitals. In Washington, the process emphasised inter-agency consensus and, consequently, US positions tended to reflect a compromise among key bureaucratic actors. Moreover, the president rarely sought to overrule the governmental bureaucracy. US policymaking also was distinguished by the need to consult with the US Congress on controversial points. These conditions severely constrained US negotiators with respect to the compromises they could fashion. As a result, considerations that might have appeared to be of secondary importance on occasion forced the US to modify its position, sometimes to the detriment of a more stringent non-proliferation policy.

In contrast, the far more centralised Soviet system of policymaking afforded its negotiators greater flexibility, including an opportunity to make concessions on important issues for the sake of a greater goal – as long as these concessions were sanctioned by a higher echelon. On the other hand, Soviet negotiators could also find their hands tied if 'reasonable' policy options were either ignored by senior policymakers or regarded by the Politburo as off limits.

The third variable was the impact of the overall state of US–Soviet relations, which improved significantly while the NPT was being negotiated. During this period, the two countries were approaching or had already entered detente, and a high level of cooperation and an even higher level of expectations for future cooperation on a broad range of international and bilateral issues defined relations. There existed an atmosphere of emerging trust and the propensity to accept the rationales for policy presented by the other side. Against this backdrop, it became easier for both sides to make concessions, when these were necessary, to reach an accord. Later, when trust dissipated and the two countries entered a period in the 1980s sometimes defined as the 'second Cold War', the non-proliferation regime was already sufficiently mature to help insulate it from conflicts that permeated the overall bilateral relationship.

While the two countries continued to share a strong interest in the maintenance and the strengthening of the nuclear non-proliferation regime, some of the factors that facilitated cooperation in the past are no longer present or exist in a very different fashion. Although non-proliferation cooperation in general and safeguards cooperation in particular remained strong in the 1990s, in many respects this period appears to be an outlier.

Post-Cold War relations

During the immediate post-Soviet period, Russia's policymaking was in turmoil. Indeed, the 'chaos of the 1990s weakened the positions of Russian negotiators, [and] forced them into the position of a "student" trying to justify mistakes to the "teacher"'.[30] By the end of the 1990s, the Russian attitude on a broad range of international issues, including non-proliferation, had begun to change. Subtle at first, this shift became clear in the second decade of the twenty-first century. In 2011, vocal Russian opposition to the state-level approach to the implementation of safeguards by the IAEA, whereby 'all available and relevant information about a state's nuclear program is used to guide the Agency's safeguards activities in that state, instead of focusing on specific facilities',[31] brought these changes into focus. Although, on the surface, conflict over this issue was related to the actions of the IAEA secretariat, it represented a far more serious confrontation with the US and other Western states over fundamental issues regarding safeguards policies. The scale and the depth of the confrontation stood in stark contrast to the pattern of close US–Soviet cooperation during the Cold War.

Arguably, conflict of this kind – in terms of both its substance and its public nature – would have been unlikely during the Cold War, given the shared interest of the two countries in the maintenance of a strong non-proliferation regime, including with respect to IAEA safeguards. Indeed, prior to 2011, the two countries' perspectives on IAEA safeguards were remarkably similar. One possible explanation for the conflict relates to broader changes in Russian foreign-policy objectives and priorities, and the increasing politicisation of the IAEA, as well as the perceived use of the nuclear non-proliferation regime to justify and promote largely unrelated policies, such as the war with Iraq in 2003. It is noteworthy that the state-level approach to safeguards did not directly affect Russia's own interests in a tangible way, but rather was seen in Moscow as an unfair and politically motivated application of safeguards that disadvantaged the interests and disregarded the concerns of other states. The underlying motive for this change in Russian policy appears to have had little to do with the safeguards themselves and more with concerns about US and Western efforts to shape IAEA policy in a direction that Moscow regarded as discriminating against some of its potential allies in the multipolar international system. In essence, non-proliferation and, more narrowly, safeguards policy, no longer enjoyed the same degree of priority over other elements of foreign policy as they had in the Soviet Union.

A second major factor in Moscow's changing approach to non-proliferation is the steady worsening of overall relations between Russia and the US over the last two decades. Some commentators have suggested that the Russian 'revolt' against the IAEA secretariat was caused in no small measure by this broader trend. According to one observer, 'Most people will tell you that Russia's problem with the [state-level approach] isn't fundamentally about safeguards … it's really about Russia's relationship with the US and the West'.[32] Furthermore, many Russians believe that the IAEA has lost its independence and become an instrument of US policy.[33]

Meanwhile, the Russian decision-making system underwent significant change. Although it remained highly concentrated, with the president exercising nearly complete control over all important decisions, governmental agencies acquired greater latitude in determining and defending their organisational interests. This change was most visible in the greater influence exerted in the post-Soviet period by the nuclear industry. Today, the Russian nuclear industry (RosAtom) is actively engaged in commercial activities abroad and weighs in on all decisions that could affect its ability to market its products abroad. Although RosAtom has the status of a 'state corporation' (that is, owned by the state), in many respects it operates like a private company. From RosAtom's standpoint, the perceived 'politicisation' of safeguards under the state-level approach represented unfair commercial practices that prevented it from doing business with countries such as Iran. Although it took time for RosAtom's concerns to affect the Russian government's policy on safeguards, the IAEA's report on the 'possible military dimension' of the Iranian nuclear programme, published in November 2011, provided a major impetus. The report enabled Russia to come quickly to the defence of Iran and other states disenchanted with the IAEA's stance, who are also potential investment targets for Russia's nuclear industry.

One of the central factors defining US–Soviet interaction in the 1960s and 1970s – the shared interest in a strong nuclear-safeguards regime – remained in place throughout the post-Soviet period. However, this was not sufficient to ensure the same degree of cooperative relations. US–Russia interaction on nuclear safeguards is not yet in crisis, but is certainly strained and could deteriorate further, as the Chemical Weapons Convention example demonstrates. In just two years, Russia and the US went in 2015 from close cooperation on the removal of chemical weapons from Syria to a highly visible confrontation in 2017 over the question of who had used chemical weapons in that country. Russian support for the Organisation for the Prohibition of Chemical Weapons now appears tenuous, and Moscow and Washington routinely clash at the UN Security Council over the issue of chemical-weapons use. These events serve as a stark reminder of how quickly cooperation on the non-proliferation of weapons of mass destruction can collapse.

CHAPTER SEVEN

Negotiating the draft Radiological Weapons Convention

Lesley Kucharski, Sarah Bidgood and Paul Warnke

A shared interest in preventing the proliferation of radiological weapons paved the way for cooperation between the Soviet Union and the United States on a draft Radiological Weapons Convention (RWC) between 1979 and 1992. Frequent bilateral discussions between the two sides took place between 1977 and 1979 on the sidelines of the UN Conference of the Committee on Disarmament (CCD), which had succeeded the Eighteen-Nation Disarmament Committee (ENDC) in 1969. This dialogue took place in parallel with negotiations for the control of chemical weapons, trilateral negotiations with the United Kingdom on a Comprehensive Nuclear-Test-Ban Treaty (CTBT) and the second round of Strategic Arms Limitation Talks (SALT II). This context contributed to the ability of the Soviet and US negotiators to work together productively, even in the face of revelations about US plans to develop enhanced radiation weapons (ERWs). Linkages between the success of the RWC and other, more ambitious arms-control efforts also motivated Moscow and Washington to resolve their opposing positions on the scope of the convention itself.

In 1979, US President Jimmy Carter and Soviet General Secretary Leonid Brezhnev declared in the concluding communiqué of the Vienna Summit on SALT II that the US and USSR had reached an agreement on major elements of a treaty banning the development, production, stockpiling and use of radiological weapons (RW).[1] The two countries then submitted their working draft to the UN Conference on Disarmament (CD), which succeeded the CCD that same year. The following year, the CD established an ad hoc working group to consider the draft, with the aim of negotiating a new multilateral treaty. For the next 12 years, the US and USSR (and later, Russia) advocated for their joint proposal and criticised many suggested modifications proposed by other states. By 1992, however, negotiations for the Chemical Weapons Convention (CWC) and the CTBT had directed priorities away from the activities of this working group. The CD decided to remove RWC negotiations from its agenda the following year, without agreeing on a final document.

The negotiating history of the draft treaty can be roughly divided into three phases: origins (1969–76); US–Soviet bilateral negotiations (1977–79); and multilateral negotiations at the CD (1980–92). Bilateral cooperation on this issue took time to materialise, with the Soviet Union and the US initially unable to agree on the scope of a potential RW ban. The USSR sought to negotiate a convention that would prohibit new types of weapons of mass destruction (WMD) in general, while the US maintained that new instruments should focus on prohibiting specific WMD individually. When the US began advocating for the negotiation of an RW agreement in 1976, the USSR continued to push for a blanket prohibition of new WMD capabilities while engaging Washington in efforts to ban radiological weapons. Both sides sought to prevent these differences from impeding progress in concurrent arms-control negotiations. However, despite their efforts it became increasingly difficult in mid-1977 to delink the different negotiations when allocations for the development and deployment of ERWs in the US defence budget became the focus of international attention.

While the two sides ultimately were able to overcome obstacles to a bilateral accord, the draft RWC now collects dust in the archives of the CD. Nevertheless, Moscow and Washington's joint efforts to ban RW constitute a significant – if often overlooked – arms-control accomplishment.[2] Using documents from the CD, declassified US diplomatic cables, and interviews with former Soviet, Russian and US diplomats involved in the negotiations, it is possible to understand the factors that both facilitated and impeded US–Soviet cooperation on this topic, and explain why the CD ultimately failed to adopt the draft RWC.

Origins of a convention to prohibit radiological weapons (1969–75)

It can be argued that the goal of controlling radiological weapons has been on the international agenda since the founding of the United Nations. In its first resolution, the General Assembly established the Commission to Deal with the Problems Raised by the Discovery of Atomic Energy. The mandate of the commission included submitting proposals 'for the elimination from national armaments of atomic weapons and of all other major weapons adaptable to mass destruction'.[3] In the wake of the bombing of Hiroshima and Nagasaki, nuclear weapons were largely the focus of this commission. The term 'other major weapons adaptable to mass destruction' was left undefined until 1948, when the Security Council Commission on Conventional Armaments defined WMD to include 'atomic explosive weapons, radioactive material weapons, lethal chemical and biological weapons, and any weapons developed in the future which have characteristics comparable in destructive effect to those of the atomic bomb or other weapons mentioned above'.[4] As far back as 1948, the UN had identified the elimination of RW as one of its goals. For more than 20 years, however, the issue of controlling RW remained on the shelves of the international disarmament agenda.

In December 1969, one year after the international community negotiated the Treaty on the Non-Proliferation of Nuclear Weapons (Non-Proliferation Treaty, or NPT), the Maltese delegation introduced a draft resolution at the United Nations General Assembly (UNGA) First Committee, which deals with disarmament and international security matters, calling on the ENDC to consider ways to restrict radiological warfare and an RW arms race.[5] Although Malta acknowledged that RW were not 'particularly important militarily', it stressed that the rate of technological progress in this field made the production and use of RW more feasible and therefore an emerging threat that needed to be contained. The Maltese resolution was incorporated into UNGA Resolution (UNGAR) 2602 (XXIV) as part C, which was adopted by a vote of 79 to 0, with 37 abstentions. The US and USSR were among the 37 abstaining states.

The large number of abstentions on this resolution reflected a popular view that radiological warfare was not plausible in the foreseeable future and therefore should not be prioritised over other more pressing disarmament matters. For example, the UK delegation, led by Lord Chalfont, explained its abstention in the following way:

> I think that in the Conference of the Committee on Disarmament at Geneva we already have a very large number of important and urgent issues to which we ought to address ourselves and deal with before we come to expend time, money and resources on these

interesting and slightly esoteric concepts of future weapon systems.[6]

The US, among others, aligned itself with this statement.[7] Whereas the US delegation found fault primarily with the resolution's substantive elements, the Soviet Union did so with its procedural ones. Speaking before the UN, Soviet ambassador Nikolai Roshchin emphasised that the proposal's recommendations had not been properly debated, since Malta submitted the resolution toward the end of the UN First Committee.[8] He went on to note that 'the competent organs of the various states' needed time to consider this new question of RW arms control before debating the issue at the UN. Roshchin ended his statement with the premonition that the rate of technological and scientific development would lead to 'some unforeseen developments in this field' that would demand greater attention in the future.[9]

In accordance with UNGAR 2602 (XXIV), the CCD considered the Maltese proposal the following year. The proposal was swiftly rejected. Building on the argument made by Lord Chalfont, the Netherlands submitted a working paper, which concluded that 'it is difficult to see the practical usefulness of discussing arms control measures related to radiological warfare'.[10] The working paper received such overwhelming support, including from the US, that its conclusion was incorporated into the CCD's annual report to the UNGA. After that, RW arms control receded to the periphery of the international disarmament agenda.[11] Importantly, though, the subtle differences that first emerged between the Soviet and US positions would enlarge into divergent approaches to RW arms control as the issue became more urgent.

The topic of RW was reintroduced at the UNGA five years later, in September 1975, albeit indirectly, by a draft resolution submitted by the USSR on the 'Prohibition of the Development and Manufacture of New Types of Weapons of Mass Destruction and of New Systems of Such Weapons'.[12] This proposal originated from Brezhnev's June 1975 election speech, in which he called for a multilateral agreement on the prohibition of the development of new WMD.[13] Purportedly initiated by the premier himself, this proposal reflected the view that emerging technology could enable the creation of new weapons 'more terrifying' than nuclear weapons.[14] The resolution that accompanied the Soviet draft agreement in the UNGA likewise noted that 'modern science and technology have reached a level where a serious danger arises of the development of new, still more destructive types of weapons of mass destruction and of new systems of such weapons'.[15]

The draft resolution submitted by the Soviet Union stressed the necessity of 'concluding an appropriate international treaty or agreement, for the prohibition of the development and manufacture of new types of weapons of mass destruction and new systems of such weapons'.[16] In introducing the proposal, Soviet Foreign Minister Andrei Gromyko cited past experience to argue that pre-emptively banning new types of WMD before they were developed and deployed, rather than eliminating weapons already in national arsenals, was the best approach to halting the arms race, both qualitatively and quantitatively.[17] The Soviet Union, however, omitted from its draft resolution any definition of the types of weapons states parties would commit to forgo, noting instead that these would be 'specified through negotiations on the subject'.[18] These ambiguities elicited a tepid response from US policymakers, who were reluctant to engage in even initial discussions without a more concrete understanding of the proposal's scope.[19]

Subsequent bilateral efforts to clarify how 'new types' of weapons would be defined following the introduction of the

Soviet draft proposal to the UNGA underscored the dissonance between Soviet and US thinking on RW.[20] At a late September 1975 meeting with USSR Embassy Ministry counselor Vladelin Vasev, for example, US Arms Control and Disarmament (ACDA) Assistant Director Thomas Davies reported that the US government faced difficulties in formulating a response to the proposal 'in concrete terms'.[21] While offering to respond to any requests for clarification, Vasev himself acknowledged that the Soviet initiative was not 'a substantial measure of hardware dismantlement'.[22] Two months later, at a November 1975 meeting with his Soviet counterparts, US representative Joseph Martin highlighted another drawback of the proposal. He observed that the ambiguous scope of the Soviet disarmament initiative could cause confusion and interfere with existing treaties and negotiations, such as the Biological Weapons Convention (BWC) and the ongoing SALT II and chemical-weapons negotiations. He cited in particular 'corridor gossip' suggesting that the Soviet proposal would include binary chemical weapons, the B-1 bomb and *Trident* ballistic-missile system, and explained that the US could not support a resolution which 'prejudges the issue [of new WMD]'.[23] In response to these concerns, Soviet ambassador Victor Issraelyan was quick to assure his counterparts in Washington that the proposal was not meant to interfere with other ongoing arms-control efforts. He noted instead that the draft agreement and resolution were entirely procedural in nature, and that the USSR was open-minded about how best to move forward.[24]

The unilateral introduction of the Soviet proposal to the UNGA without prior consultation with the US was a departure from the typical approach to non-proliferation cooperation adopted by both Moscow and Washington in the mid-1970s. As illustrated in other chapters, the two countries often preferred to consult on a bilateral basis to secure one another's support before engaging in multilateral negotiations on important WMD-related initiatives. This idiosyncrasy of the Soviet WMD proposal was not lost on Washington. At the same November 1975 meeting referenced above, US ambassador Albert Sherer asked Issraelyan outright why the USSR had not approached the US with the proposal before introducing it at the UNGA. Issraelyan responded that his government was not opposed to bilateral discussions but observed that the views of other militarily developed countries on this issue needed to be taken into account.[25]

This atypical approach may be attributable in part to the Soviet Union's underlying motivation for introducing its initiative to prohibit new WMD. Starting sometime in the early 1970s, Soviet Foreign Minister Gromyko began to present a seemingly important and urgent proposal on disarmament to the UNGA each year. The content of the proposal was dictated by the Soviet General Committee and derived from military and political analysis of reports on US military research and development, including the annual US Defense Posture Statement to Congress. Former Soviet diplomats have described the WMD proposal as an annual propaganda stunt aimed at bolstering the USSR's disarmament credentials in the eyes of the Non-Aligned Movement (NAM), while simultaneously portraying the US as a warmonger. An additional, though more difficult to accomplish, objective in tabling this proposal was to gain intelligence on US progress in weapons development.[26] This characterisation is reinforced by Soviet ambassador Roland Timerbaev's acknowledgement in December 1975 to his US counterparts that even Soviet-led efforts to solicit concrete examples of the types of weapons that could be covered by the agreement from experts in the USSR yielded virtually no results.[27] With these motivations, rather than genuine progress on non-proliferation, little stood to be gained from US support, making bilateral discussions on the proposal in advance unnecessary.

Even if political posturing rather than genuine threat perception was behind Soviet interest in prohibiting WMD, the US government did not reject the proposal outright. As noted in a November 1975 cable from the Department of State to the US Mission in New York, despite disagreement over the proposal's intended scope, the US government shared 'concern over dangers posed by possible development of new mass destruction weapons and would be prepared to consider any practical steps toward preventing such dangers'.[28] The State Department 'could go along with [the] UNGA recommendation calling for examination of [the] subject provided support for [the] recommendation did not constitute commitment to adopt restraints'.[29] On this basis, the USSR proposed establishing a group of qualified governmental experts to consider the scope of the treaty. This idea was incorporated into the revised Soviet resolution on its proposal, which was submitted to the UNGA on 2 December 1975. While UNGAR 3479 (XXX) was adopted by 112 votes to 1, with 15 abstentions,[30] the US and many of its Western allies were among the states that abstained on the vote.[31] Washington's position was tied to the USSR's unwillingness to 'modify the resolution to make it acceptable to the US, for example, by dropping the assertion of the "necessity" of concluding such a convention'.[32]

Perhaps reflecting Soviet recognition that US support would be necessary for this initiative to succeed, a *Pravda* article from 16 December 1975 written by Issraelyan under the pseudonym 'V. Levonov' did not criticise the US or its allies for abstaining on the resolution vote. Instead, as US ambassador to the Soviet Union Walter Stoessel reports in a cable to the US Department of State, Issraelyan 'recounts the number of delegations which voted for each of the resolutions, but singles out the PRC which is one [sic] the receiving end of a full paragraph of abuse as having voted against them'.[33] As Timerbaev intimated to his American counterparts, the US abstention was regarded as a 'sympathetic veto' [sic] in Moscow rather than an indication that Washington would be unwilling to cooperate on a draft WMD convention.[34] Despite the United States' initial lack of interest in bilateral exchanges with the USSR on their WMD proposal, Timerbaev's assessment proved to be prescient. In April 1976, the USSR initiated a series of three informal meetings attended by experts and diplomats, including US representatives, to more concretely define the scope of the proposed agreement to ban new WMD and systems.[35]

Talking points for the first of these meetings show that the US was not ready to make a substantive intervention on WMD issues without additional clarification on the scope of Moscow's initiative.[36] While Soviet representative Roshchin emphasised that the task of defining WMD was the responsibility of all delegations,[37] he privately inquired if US representative Martin felt that the committee should hold more informal meetings on the question of defining new types of WMD. Martin indicated that he did not envision the US sending experts to future discussions because he did not see how they could make a substantive contribution unless the USSR was ready to identify specific weapons and weapons systems.[38] Nevertheless, if the 'Soviets were prepared to designate specific areas or topics as the subject for consideration', the US would be able to determine whether to send experts to participate in a subsequent round of meetings.[39]

A little more than a month later, Anatoly Dobrynin, Soviet ambassador to the US, suggested an exchange of Soviet and US views on their proposed ban on new types of WMD in the lead-up to the summer session of the CCD. State Department officials speculated that the offer for bilateral consultations was likely an effort to avoid 'embarrassment in the event of US non-participation' in further discussions at the CCD.[40] Despite initial misgivings, the US agreed to hold a series of bilateral meetings on the Soviet initiative on 6–12 August 1976.[41] These discussions focused primarily on a working paper submitted by the USSR to the CCD, which proposed that specific weapons be included in the ban based on 'qualitatively new principles of action' that were comparable to or exceeded traditional WMD.[42] This overture from Soviet officials, to consult with their US counterparts on multilateral nuclear initiatives, contrasted sharply with the year before, when Moscow had introduced to the UNGA its WMD-ban proposal without notifying Washington. Nevertheless, deeper diplomatic engagement at the bilateral level was not enough to overcome enduring disagreements over the substance of the Soviet proposal, which continued to impede headway in multilateral talks.

Definitions and the scope of prohibitions in the Soviet proposal constituted the major obstacles to progress. In the Soviet working paper to the CCD, a weapon was classified as a new type of WMD if it met at least one of three criteria relating to 'the means, target or nature of its effect'.[43] Washington responded negatively to the broad definition, which it contended would 'support characterizing virtually anything (including the jaw-bone of an ass) a weapon of mass destruction'.[44] Furthermore, US representatives suspected that the USSR was using this definition to look for intelligence on US weapons systems.[45] Finally, they objected to the inclusion of biological and chemical weapons in the list of WMD banned under the Soviet proposal, asserting that such a prohibition would encroach on the BWC, as well as undercut ongoing negotiations on a chemical-weapons convention.

In their interventions in the CCD and during bilateral meetings, US officials advocated, as an alternative to the Soviet definition of WMD, adoption of the language used in the UN Security Council's Commission for Conventional Armaments in 1948.[46] They argued that many of the weapons described in the Soviet paper fell 'outside the scope of our perception of reasonable meaning', for they stretched the conceptual boundaries established by the UN for classifying WMD. By the end of the bilateral sessions, two Soviet experts, Yuri Fokin and Colonel Surikov, agreed to acknowledge the definition of WMD arrived at in 1948, yet were unwilling to use it as the template for the Soviet proposal.[47] Even though Soviet officials refused to budge on the scope question, their recognition of divergent definitions for WMD marked a success for the US. During the autumn 1976 round of expert discussions, the main objective of the US delegation had been 'to impose on discussions the comparability standard set forth in 1948 as [the] basis for identifying any new candidate weapon type as a weapon of mass destruction'.[48]

Moving beyond an impasse: the US proposal to ban radiological weapons

Against the backdrop of diminishing international interest in the Soviet proposal to ban new WMD, the US launched a diplomatic initiative in late 1976 that initially competed with the Soviet WMD proposal, but which would ultimately pave the way for US–Soviet cooperation on radiological weapons.[49] On 16 November 1976, Fred Ikle, director of ACDA, notified Soviet Chargé d'Affaires Yuli Vorontsov of Washington's intention to introduce a measure prohibiting RW. According to Ikle, the need to fill 'a gap in the 1925 Geneva Convention', which does not cover radiological agents, and to regulate growing 'reactor waste and radiological material' motivated the US to put forward an RW ban.[50] The meeting amounted to more of an overture than a detailed discussion on the proposal's substance, with Ikle suggesting that Moscow and Washington speak at greater length about the proposal's implementation in the future. Vorontsov reportedly responded favourably and viewed the initiative as a 'nice move in the right direction'.[51]

Ikle publicly introduced the initiative at the autumn 1976 session of the UN First Committee, asserting that control over RW was the appropriate response to the rapid accumulation of radioactive materials throughout the world.[52] Declassified cables suggest that this proposal was an offshoot of a US nuclear-energy policy announced the previous month by President Gerald Ford. This cited 'the terrible increase of violence and terrorism throughout the world' as one urgent factor necessitating this new approach.[53] Therefore, at least publicly, threat perceptions and national-security concerns drove the US diplomatic push to outlaw RW. Privately, however, US officials saw RW arms control as a 'secondary' concern and did not 'attribute exaggerated importance' to the issue, much like other countries had done in the past.[54] More than strategic concerns or issues of radioactive waste, the potential for political gains guided US policy on RW arms control. Declassified documents from early 1977 show that Washington saw its RW proposal as an alternative to the Soviet WMD ban, which enjoyed fading international support.[55] The introduction of a competing disarmament measure would not only detract from the Soviet measure, but also enhance the United States' international standing and disarmament credentials in the CCD.

The Soviet Union viewed the US initiative in a wholly different light. Soviet ambassador Victor Issraelyan interpreted it as evidence of 'considerable change' in Washington's attitude toward Moscow's proposal to ban new WMD,[56] despite a lack of evidence for this assessment. Soviet Deputy Minister of Foreign Affairs Vasily Kuznetsov concluded 'that it seemed the US also kept its eye on MDW [WMD]' after all.[57] In a meeting with Ikle in November 1976, Kuznetsov argued that addressing specific types of WMD and seeking a comprehensive prohibition on all new WMD were not mutually exclusive approaches and could be pursued in tandem. His openness to both approaches, however, foreshadowed the difficulties the two sides would confront in reconciling their two overlapping and, at times, competing initiatives.

Even though the Soviet Union revealed a readiness to consider the RW initiative, the US continued to rebuff the Soviet WMD effort at the CCD. In February 1977, the State Department instructed its delegation to the CCD to reject any consideration of specific provisions under the Soviet agreement. At the same time, though, US officials saw 'some political advantages in refraining from boycotting [the] MDW [WMD] experts meeting' scheduled for March 1977. While the US delegation assured its allies that its 'decision to send experts to MDW talks ... in no way changes our attitude toward the MDW proposal', the US would still be willing to engage in 'consultations with [the] Soviets at CCD ... but not exclusively on MDW'.[58] As the US had withheld its experts from previous meetings, the decision marked a diplomatic opening of sorts and a slight change in tack. The new approach towards the WMD initiative was two-pronged, as the US scaled back its diplomatic offensive against the Soviet proposal, while at the same time launching an initiative of its own that it viewed as more appealing and practical.

This small yet pivotal change in US policy towards the Soviet WMD initiative stemmed partly from a change in administrations. Jimmy Carter entered the White House in January 1977 with the goal of improving relations with the Soviet Union and swiftly concluding a SALT II agreement.[59] The desire to avoid overt confrontation and make strides in the area of arms control most likely influenced the way that US representatives publicly treated Moscow's WMD proposal, even if their internal assessment of its utility and feasibility remained highly critical. This attitude was visible in the flexible US explanation for why RW was not already covered by the Soviet WMD proposal.[60] During the fourth round of expert negotiations on the Soviet initiative in Geneva in March 1977, the US representative acknowledged that RW did indeed fall under the 1948 UN definition of WMD. He conceded that, in this light, it 'might be appropriate for CCD to look at radiological weapons as MDW [WMD] in the future consistent with its work program priorities'.[61]

That same month, at the first high-level meeting between Carter administration officials and their Soviet counterparts in Moscow, Secretary of State Cyrus Vance advanced the new strategy of advocating for the RW proposal while tempering US hostility to the Soviet initiative. Although the primary purpose of Vance's trip was to lay the conceptual groundwork for a SALT II agreement, the US secretary of state and Soviet Foreign Minister Gromyko also discussed the potential for RW arms control. When Gromyko expressed a desire for joint efforts on the Soviet WMD ban, Vance agreed to 'continue bilateral talks on this, in any case and specifically with respect to radiological weapons', in spite of ongoing divisions over the scope of Moscow's proposal.[62] This conversation resulted in an agreement to create a number of working groups to discuss outstanding issues, including RW. The decision represented a positive result to an otherwise contentious visit, where substantial disagreements arose over SALT II and the attention the Carter administration gave to Soviet dissidents.[63]

US–Soviet bilateral efforts (1977–79)

Following Vance's trip to Moscow, Soviet and US officials met in five rounds of a bilateral working group on the sidelines of the CCD between May 1977 and July 1979 that ran parallel to multilateral discussions on the WMD proposal. The two sides agreed to discuss both RW and new WMD in the same setting, although the Soviet delegation referred to the bilateral forum as a working group addressing new types and systems of WMD and RW, while Washington reversed these priorities in its formulation.[64] At the first of these meetings, in May 1977, the US delegation trod lightly with its RW initiative, drawing only the rough contours of an RW agreement, while remaining open to international mechanisms that limited new WMD. When presenting the US view, for example, ambassador Robert Buchheim noted that 'the US government has not yet come to any firm conclusions on the specific content of such a possible agreement'.[65]

At the onset of these bilateral working groups, US officials for the most part tiptoed around the substantive aspects of RW arms control, intent only on establishing a general framework for the talks. On the eve of the first round of US–Soviet consultations in Geneva, Washington instructed its delegates that 'organizational and technical' matters would have to be explored before initiating discussions of the text of any agreement.[66] This deliberate effort to dodge substantive talks on an RW or WMD treaty appears to reflect in part US concerns over the perception of superpower collusion and the recognition of the need to engage allies.[67] It may also point to the belief of the new US administration that the initiation of talks, however general and vague they might be, would carry symbolic weight and create a more favourable environment for SALT II negotiations.[68] In the eyes of US officials, the very existence of the bilateral discussions outweighed any tangible outcome. It would appear, therefore, that since its genesis, the RW initiative was less an effort to conclude a new, discrete arms-control measure than a political ploy to both undercut the Soviet WMD proposal and deepen US–Soviet cooperation on arms-control issues generally.

While US officials were non-committal at first, their Soviet counterparts expressed a growing openness to consider a specific RW instrument, despite their preference for a wider-reaching WMD agreement.[69] At the first working group, Viktor Likhatchev, the Soviet representative to the CCD, continually referred to the bilateral discussions as 'negotiations', underscoring the importance Moscow attached to talks that Washington approached with initial indifference. In fact, the Soviets appeared intent on transforming the meetings into a forum where the two sides would hammer out a treaty and submit it to the CCD. Although approaches still differed, by the conclusion of the first session of the working group, the Soviet side had agreed to pursue a separate agreement on banning RW. This shift represented an important starting point for serious cooperative efforts between the two super-powers.[70]

The logic of political expediency that drove US thinking on RW arms control had begun to change when the two sides held another round of bilateral meetings in August 1977. In a cable to ACDA Director Paul Warnke detailing the outcome of the talks, the head of the US delegation, Adrian Fisher, highlighted the 'symbolic value' a joint initiative on RW would hold for US–Soviet relations. Although Fisher had reiterated to his Soviet counterparts the US delegation's reluctance to discuss substantive details of an RW agreement, he mentioned to Warnke that agreeing to a rough framework with the Soviet Union would represent 'the first tangible result' of the working groups, and contribute to the future work of the CCD. At the end of his cable, Fisher stressed that the window of opportunity for launching such an initiative might quickly be closing and therefore required prompt action on the part of the US.[71] As the bilateral working groups progressed, and Soviet interest in deeper cooperation mounted, US officials in Geneva had begun to feel a growing urgency to show concrete progress in the area of RW arms control.

Fisher's premonition that the window of opportunity was quickly closing proved prescient. The bilateral working groups hit a significant and unanticipated snag when US plans to produce ERWs (a type of hydrogen bomb that releases radiation in the form of neutrons without radioactive contamination; in other words, a neutron bomb) were revealed in a summer 1977 *Washington Post* article. ERWs allow the user to inflict casualties from a blast wave and radiation exposure while minimising damage to the surrounding infrastructure. US and NATO military officials came to view the ERW as a tactical, war-fighting asset that would offset the numerical asymmetry between NATO and Warsaw Pact tank forces, given the weapon's ability to penetrate heavily armoured tanks with radiation.[72]

ERWs were first discussed in the US in the 1960s, as nuclear-deterrence policy evolved from a strategy of massive retaliation to one of 'flexible response'.[73] President Ford secretly authorised the production and stockpiling of ERWs for missiles and artillery guns in 1976.[74] These plans remained secret until 6 June 1977, when journalist Walter Pincus uncovered them.[75] In addition to sparking a public debate on the ERWs, Pincus's article created a significant obstacle for arms-control negotiations with the Soviet Union, which launched a massive propaganda campaign against the 'inhumane' weapon and threatened to discontinue SALT II negotiations if the US moved forward with ERW production and deployment.[76]

The deployment of ERWs to Europe represented a strategic threat to the Soviet Union, one that struck at the heart of its Central Europe military strategy – the massed-tank attack.[77] Moscow therefore moved quickly to incorporate ERWs into the RW/WMD negotiations. In August 1977, it submitted to the CCD an updated proposal on the scope of the WMD treaty, replacing its previous criteria of weapons with four specific categories, the second of which described ERWs. The four categories included:

1) radiological means of the non-explosive type acting with the aid of radioactive materials;
2) technical means of inflicting radiation injury based on the use of charged or neutral particles to affect biological targets;
3) infrasonic means using acoustic radiation to affect biological targets; and
4) means using electromagnetic radiation to affect biological targets.[78]

The US delegation, led by Fisher, rejected the Soviet proposal out of hand. Fisher claimed that 'the so-called neutron bomb is clearly a nuclear explosive device' and noted that the US had been 'proceeding on the basis that [the] RW convention would not include nuclear explosive devices'.[79]

The public disclosure of the ERW plans and the subsequent effort by Moscow to incorporate the capability into the RW/WMD framework ultimately led to the suspension of informal US–Soviet bilateral negotiations in the latter half of 1977. By tying up RW talks with the ERW issue, Soviet officials in Geneva had employed a strategy of negative linkage: difficulties in one compartment of negotiations would freeze progress in another. The US, however, was adamantly opposed to this coupling of issues and asserted that the condition for resuming negotiations was their delinking. This impasse over ERWs continued into 1978 and threatened to bury the RW joint initiative.

With negotiations mired in a deadlock, a number of external events began to influence the course of US–Soviet cooperation on RW. Amid a deteriorating security environment, along with Soviet propaganda efforts to widen cleavages in NATO, it grew increasingly imperative to shore up the transatlantic alliance and revamp its defence posture. Officials from both sides of the Atlantic feared that the Soviet development of the RSD-10 *Pioner* (SS-20 *Saber*), a new road-mobile intermediate-range ballistic missile, would drastically alter the balance of power in Europe. The Soviet Union was also on the political offensive in Europe. Sensing growing strain between the US and its European allies, it had ramped up its propaganda campaign and 'peace diplomacy' to rouse public opposition against NATO's defence policy and nuclear-weapons deployments in Europe. After its revelation in the *Washington Post*, the neutron bomb inserted itself into this delicate situation, not only as a possible remedy to the military imbalance in Europe, but as a lightning rod for Soviet propaganda. While the weapon's deployment in Europe could contribute to NATO's defence capabilities, namely by deterring a conventional attack by Warsaw Pact forces, its future had also become inextricably linked to questions surrounding the Alliance's unity.

Despite the neutron bomb's growing strategic and political importance for NATO, its production and deployment faced several hurdles. Western media portrayals of ERWs as a weapon that 'kills people but spares property' began to stir up public outrage, putting Western leaders in a precarious political position.[80] To exploit growing dissension within NATO, the Soviet Union launched a publicity campaign against the neutron bomb, helping incite demonstrations against the weapon in Europe.[81] In West Germany, the swell of opposition was particularly strong, where political opponents portrayed ERWs as unethical and a catalyst for renewed East–West confrontation.[82]

On top of its propaganda efforts, the Soviet Union put heavy pressure on NATO countries through direct diplomatic channels. As the neutron-bomb controversy escalated in late 1977, Brezhnev sent personal letters to several European leaders in which he claimed that ERWs threatened prospects for detente.[83] Facing mounting political and diplomatic headwinds, neither the US nor NATO countries therefore wanted to pay the full price of making the unilateral decision on the neutron bomb's manufacture and procurement. Having campaigned on nuclear issues, as well as being personally 'uncomfortable' with advancing the neutron-bomb programme, Carter pressured NATO allies to give explicit approval for ERW deployment before any American procurement decision. European leaders, however, refused to bear the brunt of the ERW decision and insisted that the US had always taken the lead on NATO nuclear decisions.

In early 1978, after a series of tense consultations, a tentative compromise was finally agreed between Washington and its NATO allies: the US would carry the initial burden of authorising ERW procurement, followed by an offer to forgo ERW deployment if the Soviets agreed to shelve their SS-20 programme. Additionally, NATO countries would announce their intent to deploy ERWs in two years in the event that arms-control talks with the Soviets fell apart. Despite a possible way forward through the ERW morass, and against the advice of his closest advisers, Carter abruptly announced in April 1978 that the US would defer indefinitely ERW production. Constrained by his own moral scruples, he 'did not wish the world to think of him as an ogre' and feared that 'his Administration would be stamped forever as the Administration which introduced bombs that kill people but leave buildings intact'.[84]

Carter's decision marked a major setback in US–NATO relations, for several European leaders had invested significant political capital in reaching a satisfactory compromise on the ERW question. Forgoing the weapon without forcing a reciprocal Soviet concession also vindicated Brezhnev's aggressive propaganda and diplomatic offensives, setting a precedent for future Soviet behaviour. More broadly, the ERW episode highlighted the extent to which alliance dynamics, along with domestic politics, shaped US nuclear policy. Public sentiment and moral calculations could guide arms-control and non-proliferation decisions as much as strategic rationale. In its Soviet policy, the US also had to account for the diverse and, at times, divergent interests of its allies – a balancing act that required diplomatic tact and persistent dialogue.

In the end, this confluence of events – a downturn in trans-atlantic relations, intense public fervour and, eventually, the US renunciation of a nuclear capability – helped to decouple the RW initiative from the ERW issue and paved the way for deeper US–Soviet cooperation. Moscow decided to drop ERWs from the scope of the RW convention negotiations and instead pursue 'a separate series of negotiations on the "neutron bomb"' as a stand-alone topic in January 1978.[85] While the US representatives refused to engage in discussions with their Soviet counterparts on a neutron-bomb convention, delinking these issues enabled the bilateral working group on RW to resume its work in February of that year. Although Moscow's campaign against the neutron bomb would soon culminate in the drafting of a Soviet convention on the 'production, stock-piling, deployment and use of nuclear neutron weapons', the independent life that it took on meant that the two sides could engage in substantive exchanges over an RW agreement.

The degree to which the two delegations were able to sepa-rate the increasingly polemical debate over neutron bombs from negotiations on an RW convention is striking. Indeed, on the very day that the Soviet delegation introduced their draft neutron-weapons convention to the CCD, in March 1978, the US delegation transmitted to Washington for approval the 'reformulations of elements 1 and 2 of [the] RW joint initiative' that it proposed to address Soviet concerns.[86] When feedback on the proposals was slow to reach Geneva, the US side cabled the State Department for an immediate response at the behest of their Soviet counterparts, who shared their desire to hold the next meeting on RW as soon as possible.[87] They did so at virtually the same moment that ambassador Fisher, in a statement at the CCD, was accusing the Soviet delegation of 'engaging in a one-sided propaganda exercise' and 'diverting attention from serious attempts to develop arms control agreements that would contribute to international security'.[88] When the revised language on RW was finally approved in May, Likhatchev observed that had they only

> received the US proposals several weeks earlier, the delegations could be raising a glass of champagne to the completion of the agreement rather than sipping mineral water at the end of yet another round of negotiations.[89]

This episode demonstrates that, while negotiations on RW were initially proposed as a way to facilitate the conclusion of SALT II and other, more ambitious arms-control agreements, it was, in fact, their decoupling from other negotiations that enabled them to succeed in their own right.

By the time of the UN Special Session on Disarmament in May 1978, the US delegation had assured its allies that the only issues that remained to be addressed in drafting an agreement on RW were its format and the issue of challenge inspections (procedures that would enable states parties to investigate compliance concerns at the site of their alleged occurrence).[90] While agreeing upon verification provisions for the convention would turn out to be a greater obstacle than the US delegation anticipated, the fifth round of bilateral negotiations, conducted in September 1978, saw near agreement between the two sides on the five key articles of the proposed draft treaty.[91] In spite of this progress, in their analysis of the debate in the First Committee at the 33rd UNGA in December 1978, the US Department of State observed dissatisfaction and frustration 'with the lack of tangible results from the US and USSR in our ongoing negotiations on SALT, CTB, CW and radiological weapons'.[92] Although the report concluded that 'any attempts to undertake multilateral negotiations on priority issues prematurely (i.e. without US/USSR participation) would be exercised in futility',[93] Washington clearly felt increasing international pressure to demonstrate measurable outcomes in these areas.

With this motivation – and having removed the neutron bomb from their discussions – the Soviet and US delegations engaged early in 1979 in their penultimate round of negotiations on an RW treaty. While the two sides quickly reached near-complete agreement on the substance of its provisions at these sessions, including previously contentious issues relating to scope and definitions, it took months to address potential discrepancies in the English and Russian versions of the text during the early part of that year.[94] Eager to report progress to the CCD at its 1979 summer session, however, Fisher and Issraelyan had agreed in April to submit the fruits of their labour for multilateral consideration in June.[95]

By late spring, the last area of disagreement to be resolved by the two delegations was the format in which to table the draft agreement. The Soviet side preferred to introduce the agreement as a complete convention to avoid further multilateral debate. The US side, meanwhile, sought to characterise it as a 'joint initiative' out of respect for the CCD's role as a negotiating body, and to increase the likelihood of adherence.[96] The US side eventually prevailed, and in the period after the conclusion of SALT II, the US–Soviet Joint Initiative on Radiological Weapons was tabled on 10 July 1979.[97] Whether Likhatchev celebrated privately with that long-awaited glass of champagne remains unknown.

Conclusion

The RW proposal that Soviet and US officials hashed out over a series of bilateral talks formed the basis for negotiations at the CD from 1980 to 1992 on a convention prohibiting RW. Over the course of these talks, a congruence of views and a willingness to defend the other's position emerged between the two sides. Having reached shared understandings on RW arms control through persistent consultations in the late 1970s, the two superpowers formed a common front during talks at the CD, drumming up support for their proposal, while at the same time resisting efforts from non-nuclear-weapons states (NNWS) to expand the convention's scope and tie it to broader nuclear issues. This collaboration at the multilateral level, born out of the frequent bilateral discussions between high-level Soviet and US officials, proved to be pivotal, for the two delegations often found themselves pushed into a corner at the CD. Like many disarmament and non-proliferation negotiations, the RW talks at the CD did not form along ideological or geopolitical lines, but rather around nuclear-weapons status.

These political dynamics at the CD acted as a strong centripetal force on US–Soviet R\V cooperation, as growing demands from NNWS often compelled the two countries to assume defensive stances together in CD talks. Along with their respective allies, the Soviet Union and the US strove to preserve the original scope of their draft RW convention, insisting that prohibitions should only cover weapons designed to disseminate radioactive materials.[98] Many NNWS, primarily from the Non-Aligned Movement, sought to expand the scope of the proscriptions in the US–Soviet proposal to cover all weapons that released radiation. A narrowly defined prohibition that ignored the radiological effects of nuclear weapons, they argued, would amount to a legal pardon for nuclear-weapons use and undercut broader nuclear-disarmament efforts.[99] They also worked to introduce more detailed language outlawing radiological warfare, including attacks on nuclear-power stations and other nuclear facilities.[100]

In multilateral debate at the CD, Soviet and US delegates stood firm against the various proposals tabled by NNWS and together endeavoured to preserve their conception of an RW convention. They resisted commitments that fell outside the boundaries of an RW prohibition, while adhering closely to a more circumscribed definition of RW. Strikingly, Soviet and US statements at these CD sessions not only often mirrored each other, but delegates from both countries were quick to reaffirm the other's position in debate. The convergence of views between the two superpowers, however, was not enough to push the RWC proposal through the CD. Disagreements over scope, along with ones related to safeguards, compliance and verification, persisted in the multilateral forum until 1992, when more pressing disarmament matters, such as the CTBT and CWC, outpaced RW talks and took precedence for multilateral negotiations. Although the US–Soviet joint initiative on RW never truly gained traction at the CD, it nevertheless marked a significant achievement for superpower cooperation on nuclear issues. Through sustained dialogue and an openness to compromise, the two countries surmounted obstacles and developed a shared position on RW arms control.

This example of US–Soviet non-proliferation cooperation offers valuable insights into the motivations and criteria for successful joint work on WMD issues. The first of these insights relates to the fundamental importance of the US president in determining and directing policy, despite the influence of other domestic actors in Washington. Upon taking office in 1977, President Carter made it a policy priority to conclude a major arms-control agreement with the USSR early in his first term in office.[101] To this end, he sent Secretary of State Vance to Moscow in March 1977 in an effort to make progress on SALT II and, when these meetings did not achieve the desired outcome, embraced bilateral discussions on RW instead. While decision-making on nuclear issues in the US generally was less centralised than in the Soviet Union, negotiations on controlling RW show that presidential buy-in was nevertheless a critical criterion for successful non-proliferation cooperation with Moscow. Given that US negotiators characterised the likelihood of pursuit of an RW capability by any nuclear-weapons state as 'remote',[102] it is unlikely that the threat of RW alone would have motivated the US to pursue cooperation on this issue without presidential interest.

The second insight concerns the centrality of issue linkages in the negotiating strategies, and in the arms-control and non-proliferation policies, of the Soviet Union and the US. Policymakers on both sides treated the RWC proposal as a means to advance other strategic interests and improve the broader bilateral environment. Initially, Soviet officials did not allow RWC negotiations to proceed without parallel progress in talks to ban neutron bombs, which was a strategic priority for Moscow but a non-starter for Washington. By impeding progress in one arms-control sphere because of difficulties in another, the Soviet Union hoped to extract greater concessions from the US. For Washington, however, linkage could work in reverse. US representatives to the CCD observed that the conclusion of an RW agreement would carry 'potential utility' for other initiatives, such as the ongoing SALT II talks.[103] In addition to banning an entire class of weapons, it would carry

214 | Once and Future Partners: The United States, Russia and Nuclear Non-proliferation

significant political weight as a treaty that would help preserve detente and improve the conditions for more consequential arms-control agreements. For the US, linkage therefore served as a way to jump-start progress across a broad range of issues; success in one set of negotiations could lead to success in another.

In many ways, the RWC and related non-proliferation initiatives served as vehicles for achieving other goals, rather than representing priorities in and of themselves. As a result, the pursuit of short-term political gains often shaped US and Soviet non-proliferation policy as much as the pursuit of strategic or concrete arms-control benefits. For instance, the Soviet Union launched its WMD-ban initiative in an effort to claim the moral high ground in the disarmament community and recast the US as an obstructionist nuclear power. Political expediency rather than the desire to reach a meaningful non-proliferation agreement therefore largely motivated Soviet proposals at the UNGA and CCD. The same logic guided early US thinking on RW arms control. Sensing an opportunity to jockey for political position as multilateral support waned for the Soviet WMD initiative, US officials hatched their RWC idea. The political benefits of the proposal would be twofold for the US: it could represent not only a more viable alternative to the Soviet proposal, but also an early foreign-policy coup for the Carter administration. Yet the quest for immediate political victories could only sustain non-proliferation initiatives for so long. Progress on the RWC slowed to a halt once the political expediency for reaching an agreement subsided.

A corresponding insight that can be derived from the details of this case is that Soviet and US interest in concluding an RW convention was insufficient to attract multilateral support for it. Following the introduction of the RW initiative to the CD in 1979, for example, Winfried Lang, Austria's chargé d'affaires, relayed to the US mission in Geneva a number of concerns raised by the Group of 21 non-aligned states at the CD pertaining to the draft agreement. Among these was the criticism that 'the RW initiative is insubstantial and a "showcase" item designed to divert attention from more meaningful arms control areas'.[104] Other states were similarly unable to accept the treaty unless its scope was enlarged to include a prohibition on nuclear weapons or attacks on nuclear facilities.

This reaction reflects the view of these states that the RWC would do little to address their most pressing threat perceptions. In fact, both the Soviet Union and the US had pursued state-level RW programmes before starting negotiations on the RWC. However, the existence of these programmes did not enter public discourse until long after the draft RWC was taken off the CD's agenda in 1992.[105] The fact that neither country openly discussed their interest in developing RW in the context of their efforts to ban them likely heightened the perception that RW were not a real threat and that the RWC had minimal practical utility. The removal of the draft RWC from the CD's agenda further illustrates that, while US–Soviet cooperation may have been a necessary prerequisite for negotiating 'priority issues',[106] it alone was not a guarantee of success. This observation has significant implications for Moscow and Washington today, as practitioners in both capitals struggle to find ways to re-engage in the nuclear sphere.

The history of US–Soviet negotiations on a convention to prohibit RW represents an unusual example of bilateral cooperation on non-proliferation between the two superpowers. Born more from an effort to find areas for collaboration rather than to mitigate a looming threat, this case provides a valuable window onto the numerous domestic and international pressures that facilitated successful joint work by Moscow and Washington on nuclear issues. It also illustrates how linkages to other arms-control initiatives can both impede and encourage productive non-proliferation cooperation between the two nuclear rivals. The intrusion of the neutron bomb into negotiations on RW likewise underscores the importance of maintaining alliance relationships, while demonstrating the flexibility necessary for superpower cooperation on nuclear issues. Russian and US policymakers would do well to review these observations in evaluating prospects for resuming non-proliferation cooperation in the current political environment.

CHAPTER EIGHT

Lessons for the future

William C. Potter and Sarah Bidgood

It is important not to overstate the similarities between the political environment during the Cold War and the current crisis in bilateral relations between Russia and the United States. In some ways, tensions between the two countries are higher now than they were before the disintegration of the USSR. At that time, for example, high-level interaction between Soviet and US practitioners and policymakers was both frequent and sustained. Today, with the exception of occasional discussions on strategic stability and narrowly focused hotline communications between Russian and US officials at air-operation centres supporting combatants in Syria, there is virtually no regular interaction between senior members of the countries' national-security establishments. Nor are there indications that this bleak situation will change any time soon.

Fortunately, the highly institutionalised and multilateral non-proliferation regime has helped to preserve a modicum of US–Russia cooperation on nuclear non-proliferation matters, especially those of a more routine and technical nature. However, the precipitous erosion of trust in US–Russia relations and an overall climate of enmity now threatens to contaminate even this domain, which has long been largely insulated from the general turbulence of bilateral relations. Indeed, senior government officials with responsibilities for non-proliferation privately acknowledge the possibility that Moscow and Washington may soon find it difficult to cooperate on even relatively mundane matters in the Treaty on the Non-Proliferation of Nuclear Weapons (Non-Proliferation Treaty, or NPT) review process, much less on more politicised issues involving Iran and North Korea.[1]

Reversing this negative trend in relations undoubtedly will be difficult, and there are no guarantees that common sense and rational calculations of costs and benefits will prevail. This gloomy general prognosis applies also to nuclear non-proliferation, where Russian and US interests would appear to remain largely convergent. As observed during the latter days of the Cold War, slowing the spread of nuclear weapons might have looked like an easy issue area for US–Soviet cooperation. Yet while the two countries shared an interest in preserving their nuclear-weapons preponderance, non-proliferation cooperation was still a mixed-motive game with elements of both cooperation and competition.[2] In other words, a common interest is not equivalent to a symmetrical one, and agreement about the desirability of cooperation in principle may break down or prove very difficult to implement in specific instances, especially where pursuit of a non-proliferation objective is regarded as having asymmetrical political costs.[3] That was the case, for example, with respect to dealing with the 'German problem' in the 1960s, the 'Indian problem' in the 1970s and the 'Israeli problem' for the entire period since the entry into force of the NPT.[4]

In light of this phenomenon – a common but often asymmetrical interest – the significant degree of US–Soviet cooperation on non-proliferation during much of the Cold War is especially noteworthy. It also raises the question: what enabled cooperation in this important but relatively narrow domain to emerge, persist and prosper at a time when there was little bilateral cooperation in other areas? Moreover, what means did Soviet and US policymakers employ to narrow and eventually overcome policy differences, and how did they neutralise or otherwise circumvent domestic, bureaucratic-political and external obstacles in their path? In addition, and perhaps most importantly, to what extent can one extrapolate lessons from these past instances of cooperation on non-proliferation to the present, a time when the non-proliferation regime is under severe stress and much in need of active and cooperative engagement by the Russian Federation and the US?

This concluding chapter provides at least partial answers to these important, albeit very complex, questions. It begins by distilling a number of key lessons from the comparative case studies, identifies several near-term proliferation challenges that would benefit from enhanced US–Russia cooperation and suggests how knowledge from the comparative analyses might be practically applied today. Rather than detail every non-proliferation issue in which such cooperation would be desirable, several opportunities for re-engagement that appear to be feasible, even in a very difficult political environment, are pinpointed. It also is informed by the view that cooperation begets cooperation – an insight supported by the chapters in this book and one that holds out the promise that it may yet prove possible to restore the trust and confidence that once characterised relations between Moscow and Washington in the non-proliferation sphere.

Lesson 1: Non-proliferation cooperation was most likely to occur when Soviet and US leaders attached high importance to non-proliferation objectives, and perceived convergent

national interests in this domain to be best served by collaborative action.

In a number of the cases reviewed, Soviet and US leaders demonstrated an awareness of their convergent non-proliferation interests, even when these interests did not coincide perfectly and entailed asymmetrical costs. This sophisticated approach toward cooperation was perhaps most clearly illustrated in the case of coordinated Soviet and US efforts to forestall a South African nuclear test in 1977. Although at the time the two superpowers were actively engaged in proxy conflict with one another in southern Africa, policymakers in both Moscow and Washington recognised that a South African test would be detrimental to their long-term security interests. They understood that the emergence of a new nuclear-weapons possessor would diminish the appeal of the NPT, make it more difficult to attract additional treaty members and encourage other states to pursue a nuclear-weapons option.

Adopting a coordinated approach to this challenge enabled both countries to achieve outcomes that otherwise would have been more difficult, if not impossible, to accomplish unilaterally. Policymakers in Washington, for example, hoped to dispel the perception that US civil nuclear assistance to South Africa had contributed to its nuclear-weapons programme. From this standpoint, collaborating with Moscow to prevent South Africa from conducting a nuclear test lent greater credibility to the Carter administration's stated interest in preventing the spread of nuclear weapons. For its part, the Soviet Union, lacking diplomatic relations with the apartheid regime, sought assistance from the US – a trading partner and supplier of nuclear material to South Africa – to apply direct pressure on Pretoria. In both the Soviet Union and the US, policymakers were prepared to acknowledge that cooperating to meet this proliferation challenge would be more effective than working alone, and they took the necessary steps to engage one another. In short, notwithstanding very different calculations about the specific foreign-policy costs and benefits of joint action, a shared commitment to non-proliferation ultimately trumped other domestic and foreign-policy considerations.

Similarly, during the negotiation of the Limited Test-Ban Treaty (LTBT), Soviet and US policymakers recognised that working together to regulate peaceful nuclear explosions (PNEs) could facilitate the conclusion of a non-proliferation treaty. Even though the political posturing that came with Cold War geopolitics often coloured delegate statements on the PNE issue in multilateral fora, such as the Eighteen-Nation Disarmament Committee (ENDC), Soviet and US diplomats were able to work together bilaterally to reconcile differences in their positions. While the US initially viewed its domestic PNE programme, Project Plowshare, as a lucrative business opportunity, it eventually opted to forgo this potential commercial avenue in favour of cooperating with the Soviet Union to pursue an international PNE service. Both Moscow and Washington quickly recognised that making PNEs available to non-nuclear-weapons states, while preventing them from developing indigenous PNE capabilities, was crucial to preventing the spread of nuclear weapons. Furthermore, they understood that agreeing to provide these services to third countries would increase the likelihood of gaining adherence to the NPT from some influential states that forcefully opposed any attempts to curtail access to peaceful nuclear energy. Both Moscow and Washington viewed these objectives as superseding the unilateral gains they could have derived as commercial PNE providers. The outcome of superpower engagement on this issue ultimately led to the drafting of Article V of the NPT.

Nowhere was the importance of shared objectives and common interests more evident than in the successful negotiation of the NPT, and subsequent bilateral cooperation in its review and implementation. This achievement is all the more remarkable given the prior history of stormy US–Soviet relations and the gulf that separated the two divergent social, economic and political systems. As the staunch Cold Warrior Walt Rostow tellingly observed, 'the NPT discussion is fascinating because it shows how intimately the US [and] the USSR can work when they have isolated an issue in which both countries feel they have a substantial national interest'.[5] A similar assessment was rendered by Soviet Premier Alexei Kosygin at the NPT signing ceremony in 1968. He observed a 'broad concurrence of views' with respect to the NPT between the two superpowers and ideological rivals, and praised US–Soviet cooperation in this sphere as 'convincing evidence that states [with different social systems] are capable of finding mutually acceptable solutions to complex international problems'.[6]

Lesson 2: When Soviet and US policymakers perceived that cooperation was in their mutual interest, both sides exhibited flexibility and a willingness to compromise to advance their shared objectives.

Policymakers in the Soviet Union and the US exhibited considerable flexibility in accommodating one another's positions when cooperation served their individual and shared objectives. A striking example of this phenomenon can be seen in the process leading to the formation of the Nuclear Suppliers Group (NSG, then called the London Club) in 1974–75 and the negotiation of its first multilateral list of export guidelines. Following India's 'peaceful nuclear explosion' in 1974, Washington undertook an international effort to strengthen and better coordinate nuclear-export policies among major suppliers, including both NPT members and non-member states (and especially France). It placed a premium on securing Moscow's support for strengthened export controls, in part because of the USSR's increasing importance as a nuclear supplier, and also to avoid undermining US competitiveness by strengthening export-control policies unilaterally.

In spite of the parallels in Soviet and US nuclear-export policies at the time, Moscow was initially reluctant to participate in the small conference of nuclear exporters proposed by Washington as it included US allies as prospective participants. Anticipating this difficulty, the US Arms Control and Disarmament Agency (ACDA) expressed its willingness to communicate the Soviet position at the conference and conduct separate consultations on a bilateral basis if Moscow chose not to participate. This approach was not unprecedented and had been used during the Zangger Committee negotiations, which involved determining which nuclear items should trigger International Atomic Energy Agency (IAEA) safeguards. The Soviet Union had not been invited to participate in these negotiations, and the US delegation had represented Soviet views at the negotiating table to increase the likelihood of Moscow's adherence to the committee's guidelines.

Moscow also was willing to exhibit flexibility when it viewed US support as necessary for achieving its non-proliferation objectives. In seeking to prevent South Africa from conducting a nuclear test, for example, the USSR faced the risk of exposing an intelligence source by sharing information with the US about Pretoria's test preparations. While there is no evidence that Soviet officials revealed the identity or existence of this source, US policymakers would have been likely to speculate about why a Soviet satellite had photographed the remote part of the Kalahari where the test site was located. The fact that Moscow shared this sensitive intelligence information with Washington underscores the importance the USSR placed on securing US support on this particular proliferation danger.

Further, because the USSR did not engage in diplomatic or trade relations with the South African government, the Soviet leadership had to rely upon the US to act as an intermediary in pressing Pretoria to abandon its nuclear ambitions. Moscow had to trust its American counterparts when they reported progress in these negotiations, a particularly difficult obligation when Soviet satellites showed little change to the test site itself. Although Moscow felt pressure from Non-Aligned Movement states to support harsh sanctions against South Africa, they resisted in order to avoid hampering Washington's ability to negotiate with Pretoria.[7] Their restrained behaviour under these circumstances is further evidence of the importance the Soviet leadership placed on cooperation with the US in realising its non-proliferation goals.

Lesson 3: Personal relationships between Soviet and US policymakers and negotiators contributed to the process of overcoming differences and reaching common positions on non-proliferation issues.

Many of the same Soviet and US diplomats and officials participated in different non-proliferation negotiations over the years, and they established close working relations with their counterparts in the other capital. Ambassador Roland Timerbaev, for example, was part of a bilateral US–Soviet working group that negotiated Articles I and II of the NPT in 1966, nearly a decade before he engaged with US diplomats to reach an agreement on Soviet participation in the London Club in autumn 1974. He then went on to serve as part of the Soviet delegation to the 1985 NPT Review Conference, where he and his US counterparts cooperated closely to reach a consensus final document. On the US side, there are parallel examples of individuals whose personal experience with their Soviet interlocutors in one setting facilitated successful

cooperation elsewhere. For example, ACDA Director William
Foster engaged with Soviet Minister of Foreign Affairs Andrei
Gromyko and ambassador Anatoly Dobrynin in the mid-1960s
on controlling PNEs while, at virtually the same time, serving
in Geneva as the chief US negotiator on safeguards. Similarly,
US ambassador Adrian Fisher, who served in the ENDC as the
chief negotiator on the issue of PNEs, went on to serve as the
US representative to the bilateral working group established to
negotiate a radiological-weapons convention in 1977.

To be sure, representatives from both sides sought to
advance their own country's national interests in these interactions. But the trust established between the individuals who
worked over extended periods of time on these non-proliferation matters made it more likely for diplomats to take risks
in staking out creative positions that bridged gaps between
the delegations, even if these positions were not necessarily
favoured by their superiors in the two capitals. In particular,
this prolonged contact contributed to the confidence both sides
had in the other's genuine commitment to non-proliferation,
which facilitated successful cooperation in many of the cases
examined. This shared interest in preventing the spread of
nuclear weapons also served as the foundation for strong relationships between key Soviet and US players. As Timerbaev
observed in his moving remembrance of his long-time US
counterpart ambassador George Bunn, 'we deeply believed in
the vital need to stop the proliferation of nuclear weapons, and
we did our utmost to achieve that goal. This was the inherent
basis of our close personal friendship that lasted more than 50
years.'[8]

The frequency of high-level US–Soviet non-proliferation
interactions during the Ford and Carter administrations facilitated the development and reinforcement of professional and
personal relationships. For example, during the mid- to late

1970s Soviet and US representatives routinely consulted in the context of the NPT Review Conference, the UN General Assembly and UN First Committee, a joint committee established by the US–Soviet Agreement for Cooperation in Atomic Energy, the Scientific Advisory Committee of the Director General of the IAEA, the IAEA General Conference, the IAEA Board of Governors, the International Nuclear Fuel Cycle Evaluation programme, the London Club and the Zangger Committee.[9] These years of shared experiences begat further cooperation on nuclear issues, even during very challenging political moments. As senior US official Charles van Doren observed, the US enjoyed 'frequent consultations with the Soviets on IAEA matters … with an excellent record of cooperation and mutual support in this field'.[10] It was partly on this basis that the US State Department decided to approach their Soviet counterparts to cooperate on strengthening nuclear-export controls following India's nuclear test in 1974.

Frequent and routine consultations on nuclear non-proliferation issues also helped Soviet and US practitioners to develop institutional/bureaucratic advocates for cooperation, as well as an institutional memory that enhanced subsequent interactions. For example, in the initial bilateral negotiations between Soviet and US representatives preceding the London Club meetings, Igor Morokhov proposed to his US counterpart, Walter Stoessel, that the chairmanship for these discussions should rotate. This model was one they successfully employed during the Threshold Test-Ban Treaty (TTBT) and Peaceful Nuclear Explosions Treaty (PNET) negotiations, which were being conducted at roughly the same time. Both sides agreed to conduct these confidential bilateral meetings in Moscow at the Ministry of Medium Machine Building, which supervised the Soviet nuclear industry and also hosted the TTBT and PNET negotiations.[11] While far from determining the successful outcome of these deliberations, knowledge of how, where and with whom to negotiate facilitated the negotiating process and contributed to an environment of shared objectives and interests.

Although beyond the time frame of this study, one also can point to a number of instances in which personal relationships initiated during US–Soviet cooperation for non-proliferation carried over into the post-Cold War period. For example, many of the same players who were integral in negotiating the denuclearisation of Belarus, Kazakhstan and Ukraine had worked together previously on other non-proliferation and arms-control efforts during the Soviet period.[12] Similarly, more recent US–Russia cooperation to remove chemical weapons in Syria during a period of very strained bilateral relations was possible, in part, due to the fact that a small cadre of policy-makers in Moscow and Washington knew and respected one another from their much earlier collaboration on chemi-cal-weapons elimination activities under the Nunn–Lugar Cooperative Threat Reduction programme.

Lesson 4: Cooperation was fostered by the presence in both countries of strong institutional advocates for non-proliferation.

In both the Soviet Union and the US, there were institu-tions and individuals who sought to ensure that cooperation on nuclear issues continued even under difficult political circumstances. This situation often pitted government agencies and actors against one another, a dynamic that was evident throughout the NPT negotiations. In Washington, for example, ACDA, established at the outset of the Kennedy administration in 1961, consistently supported the negotiation of the NPT as an important barrier to the spread of nuclear weapons. This posi-tion often put it at odds with a number of senior Department of State officials, who attached greater priority to alliance relations and the development of a Multilateral Nuclear Force.

As in the US, there were important individual and institutional advocates for non-proliferation cooperation in the Soviet Union. One of the most persistent and influential Soviet advocates was Timerbaev, who worked tirelessly with Bunn, his primary US interlocutor, in both formal and informal settings to draft the NPT. Timerbaev brought a similar determination to technical discussions with the US on safeguards, facilitating an agreement between the two sides on this critical element of the non-proliferation regime. In a number of instances when the nascent regime was put to the test, Timerbaev and his superiors in the foreign ministry worked to reinforce it, including by promoting stringent export guidelines. For example, following the negotiation and adoption of the London Club guidelines, the Soviet Union was approached by Libya for assistance in developing a complete nuclear-fuel cycle. According to Timerbaev, 'opinions within the Soviet government varied' about how to respond to this request, but the Ministry of Foreign Affairs lobbied against the deal owing to its proliferation risks, and eventually won the bureaucratic battle.[13] In the light of US concern over Libya's nuclear aspirations, Soviet restraint helped to ensure that the US and USSR could continue to work closely on non-proliferation issues, including, specifically, nuclear-export controls.[14]

The tasks for institutional champions of non-proliferation obviously are made easier when national policies are clear and reflect inter-agency agreement – or at least the absence of overt opposition. For example, US–Soviet cooperation in the context of the London Club was precipitated by National Security Decision Memorandum 255, issued on 3 June 1974. This memorandum explicitly called for consultations with other countries on coordinating their conditions of nuclear supply and provided guidelines for the scope and format these should take.[15] With these clear-cut directives in hand, US representatives were able to engage their Soviet counterparts in negotiations that led with relative expediency to the first multilateral meeting of what would become the NSG. Similarly, US–Soviet cooperation to negotiate a radiological-weapons convention was immediately preceded by the adoption in 1976 of a new US nuclear-energy policy. Among other objectives, this policy sought to mitigate the proliferation risks posed by separated plutonium and spent reactor fuel and called for more rigorous protection of sensitive nuclear material and equipment. To this end, Ford announced that he had directed the secretary of state to 'address vigorously the problem of physical security at both bilateral and multilateral levels, including exploration of a possible international convention'.[16] In announcing this new policy, the US delegation to the 1976 meeting of the UN First Committee proposed consideration of 'an agreement prohibiting use of radioactive materials as radiological weapons', to be undertaken without 'adversely affecting ongoing efforts to pursue a physical security convention for nuclear fuel materials'.[17] This concrete articulation of policy simultaneously enabled ACDA Director Fred Ikle to inform his Soviet counterpart of this new arms-control initiative and seek Soviet input on its implementation.[18]

Conversely, it is possible to observe how cooperation was hampered when disagreement among domestic actors prevented the articulation of cohesive and clear policies with respect to US–Soviet efforts to regulate PNEs. When Project Plowshare was launched by the US Atomic Energy Commission (AEC) in 1957, a split emerged between those US officials who touted the industrial applications of PNEs and those who feared its proliferation implications. During the NPT negotiations, ACDA representatives proposed a restrictive definition of nuclear weapons that would have prohibited the application of PNEs for peaceful purposes under Articles I and II of the NPT. This position placed the agency at odds with the AEC, which advocated the inclusion of a provision that would have permitted the nuclear-weapons states to conduct PNEs for other countries. Over the course of the negotiations, the US adopted a unified stance most similar to that advocated by the AEC, and it supported the establishment of an international PNE service with the USSR. While these plans were abandoned following the conclusion of the PNET in 1976, they enabled Soviet and US representatives to arrive at a common front on PNEs, culminating in the drafting of Article V and the conclusion of the NPT. This outcome evidences how important institutions and individuals could be in enabling non-proliferation cooperation when they had clear and coherent policies to represent.

Lesson 5: Policymakers on both the Soviet and US sides appreciated the importance of one another's buy-in in achieving important non-proliferation objectives.

The Soviet Union and the US recognised that as superpowers and alliance leaders, obtaining one another's support for key non-proliferation objectives would greatly increase the prospects for their realisation. For this reason, officials from both countries would frequently undertake bilateral consultations on a particular issue in advance of their consideration at multilateral meetings. This approach can be observed in the negotiation of the NPT. In these negotiations, a working group comprising equal numbers of American and Russian policymakers undertook bilateral consultations to draft the language that would appear in Articles I and II of that treaty. The work of this group enabled the two sides to table identical draft treaties in the ENDC in 1967.[19]

Subsequent US–Soviet negotiations on safeguards agreements also exemplify this practice. In this matter, the Soviet Union sought the agreement of the US on each detail before entering into negotiations with other delegations. They employed this approach in order to ensure that other countries would have to contend with a united US–Soviet front should they favour other positions. The US similarly sought Soviet agreement on issues relating to strengthened export controls before presenting its positions at the inaugural multilateral meeting of the group that became known as the London Club. Through bilateral negotiations, US policymakers hoped to reach 'agreement both on the outline of a multilateral safeguards approach and on the desirability of a conference of key suppliers', support they viewed as fundamental to the success of any effort to coordinate export-supplier policy.[20] Similarly, during the period 1977–79, both sides relied on bilateral consultations to reach an agreement on the scope of a radiological-weapons convention before taking negotiations to the multilateral Conference on Disarmament negotiating forum in 1980. This practice reflected the importance both sides placed on securing the support of the other on critical non-proliferation issues.

Lesson 6: Soviet and US policymakers recognised that their countries' international images typically were enhanced when they were seen to cooperate. In these instances, non-proliferation cooperation was viewed as a goal worthy of significant effort and investment.

Although US–Soviet cooperation on non-proliferation prospered when it served both countries' national interests, policymakers in both countries on occasion also pursued it as an objective in and of itself. For example, US Undersecretary of State George Ball favoured cooperating with the USSR to provide PNE services to third parties because these negotiations could initiate 'a useful dialogue' with Soviet counterparts 'based on our mutual interest in deterring proliferation and in sponsoring peaceful nuclear applications'.[21] He viewed this process – and the discussions it would foster – as valuable, irrespective of the more tangible outcomes they could yield.[22]

A perception of the inherent importance of non-proliferation cooperation also is evident in Moscow and Washington's joint efforts to pressure South Africa not to conduct a nuclear test in summer 1977. The talking points prepared for US Secretary of State Cyrus Vance to use in a meeting with Soviet Minister of Foreign Affairs Gromyko included reference to the view that 'the quiet cooperation in which we have been engaged will be … a significant development in its own right'.[23] Soviet diplomat Victor Issraelyan appeared to reach the same conclusion, with US diplomats observing that he 'would like to do better than just avoid confrontation with the US on non-proliferation, including the South African case – he would like to cooperate'.[24]

The significance of this instance of cooperation between two nuclear rivals was recognised at the time by some US journalists. A *Washington Post* article by Murrey Marder and Don Oberdorfer from 28 August 1977 hailed the joint US–Soviet collaboration on non-proliferation as precedent-setting, suggesting that, 'if this cooperation can be buttressed and extended … what happened without much public notice in these past weeks may set a pattern of historic importance'.[25] Not all observers took such a positive view of cooperation for cooperation's sake, however. According to a 1977 diplomatic cable from the US secretary of state to the US mission in Geneva, conservative syndicated columnists Rowland Evans and Robert Novak expressed a much more cynical view, and reportedly suggested that the US had agreed to help the USSR in pressuring South Africa not to conduct a nuclear test solely in the hope that 'cooperation on South African matter [sic] might rekindle what in early August seemed [like] dying embers of détente'.[26] From the columnists' perspective, the absence of hard evidence that a test was planned meant that the August 1977 'reports of major diplomatic triumph now seem greatly exaggerated'.[27] In other words, an assessment of the value of the pursuit of US–Soviet cooperation on non-proliferation for its own sake may depend on a variety of factors, including the importance attached to both non-proliferation and the desirability of good US–Russia relations.

While the Soviet Union and the US often found it very useful to consult on and coordinate their non-proliferation approaches in advance of multilateral deliberations, they also had to be prepared for charges that they were engaged in superpower collusion. US policymakers, in particular, were sensitive about this perception. In the context of nuclear export-control policy, for example, Washington hoped to encourage the Soviet Union to embrace multilateral negotiations in order to minimise 'signs of US–Soviet condominium in light of relations with our allies and the Chinese'.[28] The US also sought to move away from bilateral meetings with the Soviet Union on PNE cooperation, as policymakers in Washington feared that too close an embrace of PNEs would unintentionally encourage other countries to develop them.[29]

While policymakers in Moscow were less concerned about the need to obtain support from the Soviet bloc for their positions, they were nevertheless aware of the optics surrounding cooperation with Washington and its allies.[30] For example, in advance of a conference of nuclear suppliers to coordinate export policies, Roland Timerbaev asked his US counterpart ambassador Walter Stoessel to invite the German Democratic Republic (East Germany) to take part in the negotiations, to avoid the appearance that Moscow and Washington were engaged in efforts to restrict other states' access to nuclear energy.[31] While Secretary of State Henry Kissinger declined this request, the Soviet approach to Stoessel is indicative of how US–Soviet non-proliferation cooperation could be viewed both positively and negatively by other states, depending on their own policy preferences and the importance they attached to non-proliferation.

Lesson 7: Non-proliferation cooperation was usually easier on purely technical issues.

Cooperation between Soviet and US scientists on technical matters often preceded successful diplomatic cooperation for non-proliferation. By the early 1970s, 11 intergovernmental agreements on areas including peaceful uses of atomic energy had been concluded between the Soviet Union and the US. These exchanges were marked by extensive interactions, enabling leading US scientists, such as AEC Chairman Glenn Seaborg, to travel to closed Soviet nuclear facilities. In his memoirs of these exchanges, Seaborg notes that 'the warmth of the welcome accorded to us was too clearly genuine to be credited to policy or protocol'.[32] He was even made a foreign member of the USSR Academy of Sciences, underscoring the mutual respect and admiration that the scientific communities in the two countries shared for one another.

This relationship between Soviet and US scientists helped to facilitate the negotiation of agreements such as PNET, which required the development of sophisticated monitoring capabilities and exchanges of sensitive information. Between 1969 and 1971, technical experts from both countries held a series of discussions on PNEs aimed at determining what the impact of radioactive fallout would be from these types of explosions. In a summary of their discussions on this issue, ambassador Robert Ingersoll noted that this exchange of views had 'extended mutual understanding of the problems associated with the use of peaceful nuclear explosions and will facilitate more successful work in this field of atomic energy uses'.[33] Technical meetings continued in 1974, where both sides sought to address prospects for the international monitoring of PNEs. The US delegation in particular sought to determine the types of information, including 'geography, geology and other factors descriptive of PNE operations', that would need to be exchanged in order to verify the peaceful nature of these explosions.[34] During the course of these discussions, and briefings on different PNE activities, the Soviet delegation – headed by Igor Morokhov – revealed in confidence that the Soviet programme was several years behind that of the US, indicating that American cooperation would be helpful 'for technical as well as political reasons'.[35]

Although beyond the scope of this study, the history of detente also is a history of extensive and diverse scientific cooperation in the nuclear sector between the United States and Soviet Union (and later Russia). As Seaborg himself observed of a trip to the USSR in August 1971, this experience 'represented a high point in the development of US–Soviet cooperation in peaceful nuclear applications'.[36] There can be little doubt that the trust, face-to-face contacts and scientific advances enabled by these experiences had positive implications for broader US–Soviet cooperation on non-proliferation during this period.

Near-term proliferation challenges requiring US–Russia collaboration

A number of pressing proliferation problems were identified in the introduction to this book. Most of them would benefit from enhanced US–Russia non-proliferation consultations, coordination and collaboration, although such cooperation in and of itself would not ensure their resolution. At least three challenges, however, are unlikely to be dealt with effectively in the absence of much improved US–Russia cooperation. They pertain to: the risks of nuclear accidents, mistakes and miscalculations leading to nuclear-weapons use; the threat of nuclear terrorism; and the continued relevance and integrity of the NPT as the cornerstone of the international non-proliferation regime.

Reducing the risks of inadvertent nuclear use

The current civilian and military leadership in Russia and the US, as well as in the other nuclear-weapons possessors, are far too cavalier regarding the risks of nuclear-weapons use due to miscalculations, misperceptions and accidents. As demonstrated by a very rich scholarly and popular literature on nuclear mishaps and cases of near nuclear use, it would appear that luck and the illusion of weapons safety and secure command and control, as much as anything, account for the fact that nuclear weapons have not yet been used inadvertently.[37] But continued illusions and the pursuit of more luck are hardly sound policy prescriptions, especially in light of the long and growing list of accidents involving nuclear weapons and close calls involving their potential use, and beg the question: what must be done to promote nuclear-risk reduction in an age of reduced warning time, high alert rates, new disruptive technologies, increased command-and-control vulnerabilities and nuclear-doctrinal changes that provide incentives for early use of nuclear weapons? It is not at all evident that the Russian Federation, the US or other members of the international community will display the political will and acumen to tackle these very complex and challenging issues, but unless they acknowledge their existence it probably is only a matter of time before a lapse in human judgement, misunderstanding aggravated by lack of communication, or mechanical or human error involving nuclear weapons results in catastrophe.

Combatting nuclear terrorism

Luck also appears to play a prominent role in accounting for the relatively small number of incidents involving nuclear terrorism. To date, among the multiple ways in which non-state actors might be able to inflict or precipitate nuclear violence, the only form to have been demonstrated in practice involves attacks on and the sabotage of nuclear facilities, and even these instances are very limited.[38] Although non-state actors are known to have expressed interest in acquiring nuclear weapons, and in at least two cases actively sought to secure weapons-usable material, terrorists have yet to succeed in that quest, despite the huge number of nuclear weapons in arsenals around the world, and the even larger global stocks of highly enriched uranium and plutonium.[39] Progress has been made in recent years in reducing the vulnerability of this material to theft and diversion – in part through the work of the Cooperative Threat Reduction Program and the actions taken during the Nuclear Security Summit process – but much more remains to be done in terms of enhancing and sustaining the physical protection, material control and accounting of this material. Perhaps most surprising is the absence of incidents involving terrorist use of radiological weapons, more commonly known as 'dirty bombs'. This form of nuclear violence, while far less lethal than the detonation of even a crude, improvised nuclear weapon, is much easier to achieve as it entails little technical know-how, and potential radiological sources are abundant and often poorly protected.[40]

Although rarely the focus of attention, until recently, a fifth form of nuclear terrorism may be one of greatest potential risks, possibly involving an existential threat. That is the possibility that non-state actors might be able to precipitate a nuclear-weapons exchange among existing nuclear-weapons possessors – including Russia and the US – without actually acquiring nuclear-weapons material or detonating a nuclear device themselves. This situation could arise through successful spoofing, in which a third party deceives a nuclear-weapons possessor into believing that it is under nuclear attack and thereby precipitates a retaliatory/pre-emptive strike. Spoofing could take the form of a cyber attack on command-and-control communications, but also might rely on less technically sophisticated actions, such as the launch of multiple scientific rockets whose characteristics resemble submarine-launched ballistic missiles (SLBMs) or a Mumbai-like terrorist attack on a high-value target of a nuclear-weapons possessor. Indicative of the danger of spoofing is the 'too close for comfort' episode in January 1995, when the launch of a single four-stage research rocket off the coast of Norway was misidentified by Russian early-warning systems as a US *Trident* II SLBM.[41] The Norwegian scientific-rocket incident is illustrative of how a number of mistakes and misperceptions came close to precipitating a Russian nuclear response. It did not progress beyond a 'close call' due, in part, to the fact that it involved a single rocket, but also because it occurred at a time when Russia and the US enjoyed a relatively cordial relationship. However, what would happen were the episode to be repeated today, this time perhaps involving multiple scientific rockets and/or instigated by a doomsday cult or militant terrorist organisation aligned against both Russia and the US?

Strengthening the NPT

The views of experts and diplomats diverge over the degree to which the NPT is at risk today, and what must be done to strengthen what has long been the foundation of the international non-proliferation regime. What is not in dispute is the severe challenge the treaty faces due to growing polarisation between nuclear-weapons states and their allies and non-nuclear-weapons states, a condition aggravated by the tendency of both to cherry-pick those NPT obligations, principles and objectives they choose to emphasise or discount. In addition, more so than at any other time in its nearly 50-year history, there are no obvious political or regional groupings positioned to serve as effective bridge-builders across the growing divide. Perhaps most disconcerting, as the 25th anniversary of the indefinite extension of the NPT approaches, is the very possible disappearance of even any pretence of cooperation between Moscow and Washington in securing a successful outcome at an NPT Review Conference. As noted previously, about the only issue on which the two major architects of the NPT currently agree is the damage allegedly done to the legitimacy and efficacy of the treaty by the nuclear-prohibition treaty. If Lewis Dunn is correct that it is increasingly important for Russia and the US – along with other nuclear-weapons states – to identify and pursue cooperatively new approaches to regain the nuclear-disarmament initiative, it is difficult to imagine this occurring unless the two largest nuclear-weapons states resume some form of regular consultation about the NPT and nuclear disarmament.

What is to be done?

It is, of course, much easier to identify problems than to recommend practical means to remedy them, and this applies very much in the case of current US–Russia relations. Nevertheless, the seven lessons derived from a comparative analysis of past cases of US–Soviet cooperation on non-proliferation point to a number of concrete and practical steps that might usefully be undertaken.

The first recommendation – that Russia and the US undertake parallel nuclear-proliferation threat assessments – is informed by historical knowledge that cooperation is easier when threat perceptions and non-proliferation interests correspond, and there is prima facie evidence that there is still a convergence of such perceptions and interests today in a number of areas. Ideally, a joint threat-assessment exercise would be undertaken by government experts to corroborate this point and to identify more precisely those areas in which perspectives about threats and interests converge and diverge. If it proved difficult to organise a joint proliferation assessment or a set of parallel assessments at the government–government level, it would still be useful to pursue the exercise in a Track 1.5 or even Track 2 format. One method would be to make use of the Russian and US academies of sciences, which have previously conducted collaborative scientific research on non-proliferation issues, to conduct a joint study on the topic. Alternatively, a number of Russian and US non-governmental organisations (NGOs), think tanks and academic-research centres might sponsor the project.[42] (The editors of this book, for example, are part of several ongoing Track 1.5 nuclear dialogues involving Russian and US officials and NGO experts.) Regardless of the method that is employed, the findings of the assessments would be helpful in identifying areas in which it might be possible to fashion new or reinvigorated non-proliferation collaboration.

A second recommendation, the specificity of which might be sharpened following a joint assessment of national interests in the non-proliferation sphere, is to initiate collaborative technical projects in the realm of peaceful nuclear use, disarmament and non-proliferation verification, and possibly also best practices in nuclear security and countering nuclear terrorism. All of these areas have significant technical components in which the Russian Federation and the US have cooperated in the past, and to some degree continue to do, especially in multilateral fora such as the IAEA and the NSG. The idea underpinning this recommendation is to identify less politically sensitive areas in the non-proliferation domain where scientific and technical interactions can be encouraged, and which may have some spillover effect into other areas. At the moment, for example, the NSG is exploring the potential proliferation impact of evolving 'disruptive technologies' such as additive manufacturing (i.e. 3D printing) on nuclear commerce, and Russian and US technical know-how in this sphere could be helpful to the work of the group. Although, to date, Russia has been reluctant to participate actively in the work of the International Partnership for Nuclear Disarmament Verification (IPNDV), there is growing international support for the initiative. As both Russia and the US have found it difficult to gain support from most non-nuclear-weapons states for their disarmament positions in the NPT context, future cooperation in the IPNDV may prove to be one of the relatively few unthreatening areas in which the two largest nuclear-weapons states can engage in a multilateral disarmament initiative.

As has been noted before, the impact of personal relationships in non-proliferation diplomacy cannot be underestimated.[43] Yet without more opportunities for regular interactions between both senior policymakers and working-level experts from both countries, it is very difficult to imagine how these relationships will be forged or sustained. Although there is little reason to believe that major changes in the current insular state of US–Russia bilateral relations are on the horizon, it could prove feasible to initiate more routine meetings that address the shared proliferation problems identified in the aforementioned parallel threat assessments. Relatively easy issues to address relate to the NPT review process, threats posed by nuclear terrorism (including cyber threats to civil nuclear facilities), non-proliferation education and training, and promoting peaceful nuclear-energy use in a fashion that minimises proliferation risks. One forum in which these and other nuclear-proliferation issues could be addressed is the currently dormant US–Russia Bilateral Presidential Commission.[44] Among the 13 working groups that were established as part of this were those on Nuclear Energy and Nuclear Security, Arms Control and International Security, and Military-to-Military Relations. If it proved too difficult politically to resume the work of the commission, some of the same benefits could be achieved were it possible to secure participation by appropriate Russian and US government officials in Track 1.5 dialogues on different non-proliferation topics. While Russian officials have been willing to participate in recent hybrid workshops, it has proved more difficult to attract their US counterparts. One possible means to secure greater US engagement is to imbed US–Russia interaction within a slightly larger framework, such as nuclear deliberations among the five permanent members of the UN Security Council, the so-called P5.

A potentially attractive subject for P5 discussion would be revisiting the draft US–Soviet treaty prohibiting radiological weapons. The topic has the virtue of being consistent with most of the current stated positions of the NPT-recognised nuclear-weapons states. In addition, at a time when these states are especially on the defensive about the role played by nuclear weapons in their security postures, a common P5 position on a radiological-weapons-prohibition treaty might be of assistance in burnishing their images in the NPT context and therefore have considerable political appeal.

Many of the case studies emphasise the importance of empathy in identifying and promoting compromises that were seen as serving, or at least compatible with, the national interests of both sides. This ability typically was born of first-hand experiences – both good and bad – that were accumulated over an extended period of bilateral interactions and negotiations. This capacity and knowledge base often resided in those organisations that also served as institutional advocates for non-proliferation cooperation. Regrettably, many of these individuals, as well as some of their organisations, are no longer active today, contributing to the growing loss of memory about non-proliferation successes and their determinants. If this institutional deficit is to be overcome, it is necessary for both Russia and the US to nurture and sustain a new generation of non-proliferation experts familiar with both the history and practice of non-proliferation diplomacy. The process of refreshing and restoring collective memories will take time and will be more difficult the longer the pause in bilateral nuclear-arms-control negotiations and the less frequent the consultations between Russian and US officials on non-proliferation issues. It is imperative, however, to accelerate the process of rebuilding US–Russia non-proliferation expertise and to do so while there remains a modicum of cooperation in this policy sector.[45]

Despite profound disagreement in many areas during the Cold War, policymakers in the Soviet Union and the US recognised that non-proliferation cooperation served each country's own interests. As documented here, this recognition did not occur immediately or without significant costs, and it followed a number of false steps and crises, including, most famously, the Cuban Missile Crisis. It would be tragic if this earlier learning experience was ignored and today's policymakers had to meet comparable challenges, perhaps with less sanguine outcomes, before they too recognise the necessity of reviving nuclear non-proliferation cooperation.

NOTES

Introduction

1   Richard Haass, *A World in Disarray: American Foreign Policy and the Crisis of the Old Order* (New York: Penguin Press, 2017).

2   Among prominent national-security figures making this case are Alexei Arbatov, Igor Ivanov, William Perry and Sam Nunn.

3   'Russia to Drop Cooperative Threat Reduction Deal with U.S.: Report', *Nuclear Threat Initiative*, 10 October 2012, http://www.nti.org/gsn/article/russia-drop-cooperative-threat-reduction-deal-us-report/.

4   Ernest Moniz and Sam Nunn, 'Three Steps to Avert an Accidental Nuclear War', *Bloomberg View*, 1 February 2018, https://www.bloomberg.com/view/articles/2018-02-01/three-steps-to-avert-an-accidental-nuclear-war.

Chapter One

1   The author is grateful to Jeffrey Lewis for the many useful suggestions he made about relevant Chinese source materials. He also wishes to thank Sarah Bidgood and Paul Warnke for their assistance in scouring for new sources.

2   Roland Timerbaev, 'The Nuclear Nonproliferation Treaty Has Largely Achieved Its Goals', *Arms Control Today*, September 2017, p. 41; Joseph Nye, Jr, 'US–Soviet Cooperation in a Nonproliferation Regime', in Alexander George, Philip Farley and Alexander Dallin (eds), *US–Soviet Security Cooperation: Achievements, Failures, Lessons* (New York: Oxford University Press, 1988), p. 341.

3   This section draws upon the framework and analysis first elaborated by the author 35 years ago: see William C. Potter, 'Nuclear Export Policy: A Soviet–American Comparison', in Charles Kegley, Jr and Pat McGowan (eds), *Foreign Policy: USA/USSR* (Beverly Hills, CA: Sage Publications, 1982), pp. 291–313. It has been substantially revised to take

account of new archival material and analyses, particularly with respect to Soviet nuclear non-proliferation and export policy. A similar but more differentiated set of phases is suggested by Nye in 'US–Soviet Cooperation in a Nonproliferation Regime', p. 338. Peter R. Lavoy also employs a very similar periodisation framework in his study of 'Learning and the Evolution of Cooperation in U.S. and Soviet Nuclear Nonproliferation Activities', in George W. Breslauer and Philip E. Tetlock (eds), *Learning in U.S. and Soviet Foreign Policy* (Boulder, CO: Westview Press, 1991), pp. 735–83.

4   These generally dominant tendencies occasionally were reinforced by, but also subordinated to, other considerations, usually political in nature.

5   'The Baruch Plan: Statement by the United States Representative (Baruch) to the United Nations Atomic Energy Commission, 14 June 1946', in *Documents on Disarmament, 1945–1959* (Washington DC: Department of State, 1960), pp. 7–11, http://unoda-web.s3-accelerate.amazonaws.com/wp-content/uploads/assets/publications/documents_on_disarmament/1945-1956/DoD_1945-1959_VOL_I.pdf.

6   Michael A. Guhin, *Nuclear Paradox: Security Risks of the Peaceful Atom* (Washington DC: American Enterprise Institute, 1976), p. 10, http://www.aei.org/wp-content/uploads/2017/07/Nuclear-Paradox-text.pdf.

7   Joseph Nogee, 'Soviet Nuclear Proliferation Policy: Dilemmas and Contradictions', *Orbis*, vol. 24, 1981, pp. 751–69.

8   The first Soviet nuclear-weapons test did not occur until 1949.

9   Guhin, *Nuclear Paradox: Security Risks of the Peaceful Atom*, p. 11.

10 Harold Nieburg, *Nuclear Secrecy and Foreign Policy* (Washington DC: Public Affairs Press, 1964), p. 89.

11 Bertrand Goldschmidt, 'A Historical Survey of Nonproliferation Policies', *International Security*, vol. 2, 1977, p. 73.

12 William Bader, *The United States and the Spread of Nuclear Weapons* (New York: Pegasus, 1968), as cited by Nye in 'U.S.–Soviet Cooperation in a Nonproliferation Regime', p. 339.

13 Shane Maddock, 'The Fourth Country Problem: Eisenhower's Nuclear Nonproliferation Policy', *Presidential Studies Quarterly*, vol. 28, no. 3, 1998, p. 558. Maddock (p. 553) also argues compellingly that a combination of Cold War suspicions, bureaucratic politics and presidential impotence made it impossible for the Eisenhower administration to divorce arms-control and non-proliferation policy from the anti-Soviet thrust of its foreign policy. As such, non-proliferation objectives were subordinated to other foreign-policy goals and important opportunities were lost to fashion policies that might have served the interests of both countries.

14 Nye, 'US–Soviet Cooperation in a Nonproliferation Regime', pp. 341–42. Although the general trend was toward greater support of non-proliferation, the direction sometimes was not straightforward, as in the case of nuclear sharing via a Multilateral Force as a means to head off independent nuclear-weapons programmes, especially in West Germany. The first Chinese nuclear test in 1964 also altered US calculations about the likely course of proliferation and contributed to a revision in US non-proliferation policy.

15 Ironically, one manifestation of this phenomenon was the reduced priority given to non-proliferation in both the Soviet Union and the US once the NPT entered into force and the German issue was resolved. This phenomenon could be seen with respect to the failure to act decisively to curtail the Indian nuclear-weapons programme. On this point, see Nye, 'US–Soviet Cooperation in a Nonproliferation Regime', p. 344.

16 David Holloway, 'The Soviet Union and the Creation of the International Atomic Energy Agency', Cold War History, vol. 16, no. 2, 2016, p. 182. See also Roland Timerbaev, Rossiya i yadernoe nerasprostranenie [Russia and Nuclear Non-proliferation, 1945–1968] (Moscow: Nauka, 1999). Timerbaev (p. 86) suggests that an indication of the Soviet attitude toward Eisenhower's speech was the fact that it was published in a huge circulation in 1954.

17 'A Conversation with Roland Timerbaev', conducted by Rich Hooper and Jenni Rissanen, 14 June 2007, https://cgs.pnnl.gov/fois/doclib/Timerbaev(transcript)2.pdf.

18 Izvestia, 18 January 1955.

19 Nieburg, Nuclear Secrecy and Foreign Policy, p. 93. A 92-page English-language booklet with illustrations of the newly available nuclear technologies was distributed at the Geneva conference. See 'USSR Scientific & Technical Exhibition', Geneva, 1955.

20 Gloria Duffy, 'Soviet Nuclear Exports', International Security, vol. 3, 1978, p. 85; J.G. Polach, 'Nuclear Energy in Czechoslovakia: A Study in Frustration', Orbis, vol. 12, 1968, pp. 832–33; Polach, 'Nuclear Power in Eastern Europe', East Europe, May 1968, pp. 4–6; J. Wilcznski, 'Atomic Energy for Peaceful Purposes in the Warsaw Pact Countries', Soviet Studies, vol. 26, October 1974, pp. 584–85.

21 Duffy, 'Soviet Nuclear Exports', p. 84; Polach, 'Nuclear Power in Eastern Europe', p. 4.

22 L. Fox, 'L'énergie nucléaire en U.R.S.S. et dans les pay de l'Est', in Memoire pour le Diplome d'Etudes Approfondies d'economie Publique (Paris: University of Paris, 1980), p. 89; Arnold Kramish, Atomic Energy in the Soviet Union (Stanford, CA: Stanford University Press, 1959), pp. 188–89; E. Knorre, 'Dubna, City of Physicists', New Times, no. 14, 1976, pp. 14–15.

23 Nieburg, Nuclear Secrecy and Foreign Policy, pp. 113–14.

24 The latter explanation is consistent with the failure of Moscow to insist on safeguards on nuclear exports during this period, even to countries outside of the bloc.

25 Duffy, 'Soviet Nuclear Exports', pp. 84–85.

26 Khrushchev's first discussion with Mao about nuclear assistance appears to have taken place in October 1954 during his visit to China. Mao reportedly expressed interest in both atomic energy and nuclear weapons, but Khrushchev only offered to assist in building a small research reactor. Zhihua Shen and Yafeng Xia, 'Between Aid and Restriction: Changing Soviet Policies toward China's Nuclear Weapons Program: 1954–1960', Nuclear Proliferation International History Project Working Paper 2, May 2012, p. 6; Viktor Gobarev, 'Soviet Policy Toward China: Developiong Nuclear Weapons 1949–1969', Journal of Slavic Military Studies, vol. 12, no. 4, December 1999, pp. 1–53.

27 Arnold Kramish, 'The Great Chinese Bomb Puzzle – and a Solution',

Fortune, vol. 63, June 1966, pp. 246–48; John Wilson Lewis and Xue Litai, *China Builds the Bomb* (Stanford, CA: Stanford University Press, 1988); Roland Timerbaev, 'How the Soviet Union Helped China Develop the A-Bomb', *Yaderny Kontrol* [*Nuclear Control*], Digest, no. 8, 1998, pp. 44–49; Timerbaev, *Russia and Nuclear Non-proliferation, 1945–1968*; Evgeny A. Negin and Yuri N. Smirnov, 'Did the USSR Share Atomic Secrets with China?', Parallel History Project on Cooperative Security, 2002, http://www.php.isn.ethz.ch/lory1.ethz.ch/collections/coll_china_wapa/negin_smirnov_englf409.html?navinfo=16034.

28 Nikita Khrushchev, *Khrushchev Remembers: The Last Testament* (New York: Little Brown & Company, 1974), pp. 268–69.

29 According to Timerbaev in *Yaderny Kontrol*, a prototype model of the bomb and other equipment and instruction manuals were loaded on railway cars in Arzamas-16, a closed nuclear city now known as Sarov. Citing the former director of Arzamas (Lt-Gen. Evgeny Negin) and another Arzamas colleague (Yuri Smirnov), he suggests that the 'cars stood idle for about half a year before orders came from the Central Committee of the CPSU to destroy everything – both the prototype bomb and the blueprints'. See also Lt-Gen. Evgeny Negin and Yuri Smirnov, 'Did the USSR Reveal Its Nuclear Secrets to China?', report at the Intenational Symposium in Dubna, 14–18 May 1996, in *Science and Society: History of Soviet Nuclear Project (1950–60s)*, vol. 1, 1997, pp. 306–9.

30 Nie Rongzhen, *Nie Rongzhen Juiyilu* [*Memoirs of Nie Rongzhen*] (Beijing:

1984), p. 639; Lewis and Litai, *China Builds the Bomb*, pp. 61–62.

31 Shen and Xia, 'Between Aid and Restriction: Changing Soviet Policies toward China's Nuclear Weapons Program: 1954–1960', p. 19.

32 Lewis and Litai, *China Builds the Bomb*, p. 61. Shen and Xia, 'Between Aid and Restriction: Changing Soviet Policies toward China's Nuclear Weapons Program: 1954–1960', p. 32, suggest that the final Soviet decision occurred later, and that Khrushchev initially only intended 'to temporarily suspend' the delivery. Lewis and Litai (p. 61) indicate that the Soviet reversal was not fully appreciated by China until mid-1959. See also 'The Strange Story of Russia and China's Cold War Nuclear Weapons Break-Up', *National Interest*, 27 November 2016.

33 See Shen and Xia, 'Between Aid and Restriction: Changing Soviet Policies toward China's Nuclear Weapons Program: 1954–1960', pp. 28–33.

34 'Letter from the Communist Party of the Soviet Union Central Committee to the Chinese Communist Party Central Committee on the Temporary Halt in Nuclear Assistance', 20 June 1959, Wilson Center Digital Archive, http://digitalarchive.wilsoncenter.org/document/114346; Lewis and Litai, *China Builds the Bomb*, p. 64; 'Letter from Nikita Khrushchev to Zhou Enlai on the Prohibition of Nuclear Testing', 4 April 1958, Wilson Center Digital Archive, http://digitalarchive.wilsoncenter.org/document/114343.

35 Department of State, Office of the Historian, '52. Paper Prepared by an Interagency Working Group: Implications of the Indian Test', 30 May 1974, Foreign Relations of the United States, 1969–76, vol. E-14, part 2, Documents on Arms

Control and Nonproliferation, 1973–76, https://history.state.gov/historical documents/frus1969-76ve14p2/d52.

36 Department of State, Office of the Historian, '57. Paper Prepared by the NSC Under Secretaries Committee, 21 June 1974, Foreign Relations of the United States, 1969–76, vol. E-14, part 2, Documents on Arms Control and Nonproliferation, 1973–76, https://history.state.gov/historicaldocuments/frus1969-76ve14p2/d57.

37 Todd Perry, 'The Origins and Implementation of the 1992 Nuclear Suppliers Group (NSG) Agreement', PhD dissertation, University of Maryland, 2002, http://proxy.miis.edu/login?url=https://search.proquest.com/docview/305524424?accountid=12457.

38 Office of Technology Assessment, *Nuclear Proliferation and Safeguards* (Washington DC: US Government Printing Office, 1977), p. 221.

39 President Gerald Ford, 'Statement on Nuclear Policy', 28 October 1976, American Presidency Project, University of California Santa Barbara, http://www.presidency.ucsb.edu/ws/?pid=6561. Plutonium 'recycling' is its re-use as reactor fuel following a chemical conversion process.

40 US Government Publishing Office, 'Public Law 94–242: Nuclear Non-Proliferation Act of 1978', 10 March 1978, https://www.gpo.gov/fdsys/pkg/STATUTE-92/pdf/STATUTE-92-Pg120.pdf.

41 Gloria Duffy, 'Soviet Nuclear Energy: Domestic and International Policies', RAND Corporation, 1979, p. 7, https://www.rand.org/pubs/reports/R2362.html.

42 Karel Docek, 'Czechoslovak Uranium and the USSR', Radio Liberty Dispatch, 9 July 1974, p. 3.

43 Christer Jonsson, *Soviet Bargain Behavior: The Nuclear Test Ban Case* (New York: Columbia University Press, 1979); Glenn Seaborg, *Kennedy, Khrushchev, and the Test Ban* (Berkeley, CA: University of California Press, 1981); and George Bunn, *Arms Control by Committee: Managing Negotiations with the Russians* (Stanford, CA: Stanford University Press, 1992).

44 Gerhard Wetting, 'Soviet Policy on the Nonproliferation of Nuclear Weapons, 1966–1968', *Orbis*, vol. 13, pp. 1,058–84; Dane Eugene Swango, *The Nuclear Nonproliferation Treaty: Constrainer, Screener, or Enabler* (Los Angeles, CA: University of California Press, 2009), pp. 22–75; Hal Brands, 'Non-Proliferation and the Dynamics of the Middle Cold War: The Superpowers, the MLF, and the NPT', *Cold War History*, vol. 7, no. 3, August 2007, pp. 389–423.

45 US Arms Control and Disarmament Agency, *Documents on Disarmament, 1965* (Washington DC: US Government Printing Office, 1966), pp. 443–46. Although the Soviet Union initially sought to conclude a separate non-proliferation accord limited to the two Germanys, by late 1962 the US was persuaded 'that Moscow was amenable to supporting a general agreement on nuclear nonproliferation'; see 'Document 10: Secretary of State to the President, Agreement on Non-Diffusion of Nuclear Weapons', 27 November 1962, https://nsarchive.gwu.edu/briefing-book/nuclear-vault/2018-02-02/german-nuclear-question-nonproliferation-treaty.

46 Brands, 'Non-Proliferation and the Dynamics of the Middle Cold War', p. 403.

47 'Report by A.A. Gromyko in Answer to Inquiries by USSR Supreme Soviet

Deputies', 10 December 1965, in *Current Digest of the Soviet Press*, vol. 17, no. 51, p. 3.

48 As an example, Hal Brands cites a 15 February 1967 article in *Pravda* that warns how nuclear-weapons spread would increase the risk of regional confrontations and the prospects of a thermonuclear exchange. See Brands, 'Non-Proliferation and the Dynamics of the Middle Cold War', p. 403.

49 George Quester, *The Politics of Nuclear Proliferation* (Baltimore, MD: Johns Hopkins University Press, 1973), p. 23.

50 'TASS Daily Report, 18 May 1974', Soviet Union Foreign Broadcast Information Service, 20 May 1974, p. J-1.

51 F.I. Kozhenivikov and V.A. Mazov, 'Scientific and Technical Progress and Certain Problems of International Law', *Voprosy istorii*, January 1975, pp. 58–74.

52 'Memorandum, Hungarian Foreign Ministry, on India's Policy on Nuclear Disarmament', 31 October 1974, Wilson Center Digital Archive, http://digitalarchive.wilsoncenter.org/document/112879.

53 The first 50 tonnes of heavy water shipped to India by the Soviet Union were not preceded by a formal safeguards agreement, although some analysts suggest that Moscow may have obtained assurances from Delhi before any heavy water was shipped that it would not be used for military purposes. See William C. Potter, 'The Soviet Union and Nuclear Proliferation', *Slavic Review*, vol. 44, no. 3, 1985, p. 476.

54 Ashok Kapur, *International Nuclear Proliferation* (New York: Praeger, 1979), pp. 72, 82; Duffy, *Soviet Nuclear Energy*, p. 23.

55 The Soviet Union had endorsed the principle of full-scope safeguards at the discussions of the London Group but indicated they would not apply them unilaterally.

56 Duffy, *Soviet Nuclear Energy*, pp. 108–18. The agreement specified that safeguards be applied to 'any nuclear material, including subsequent generations of produced special fissional material, produced, processed or used in the [Rajasthan Atomic Power] Station' and 'any nuclear material, including subsequent generations of produced special fissionable material, produced, processed, or used ... by the use of the heavy water' supplied by the Soviet Union to India. The agreement also specified that the heavy water not be used for the manufacture of any nuclear weapon or to further any other military purpose. These same conditions appear to have applied in 1980 when the Soviet Union shipped an additional 250 tonnes of heavy water to India.

57 'The text of the Agreement of 17 November 1977 Between the Agency and India for the Application of Safeguards in Connection with the Supply of Heavy Water from the Soviet Union', IAEA Information Circular, 260, July 1978; Potter, 'The Soviet Union and Nuclear Proliferation', p. 476.

58 Potter, 'The Soviet Union and Nuclear Proliferation', pp. 468–89.

59 Balazs Szalontai, 'The Elephant in the Room: The Soviet Union and India's Nuclear Program, 1967–1989', Nuclear Proliferation International History Project Working Paper 1, November 2011, Wilson Center Digital Archive, https://www.wilsoncenter.org/sites/default/files/indian_nuclear_history_and_soviet_relations_-_ver_2.pdf.

60 'Memorandum, Hungarian Foreign Ministry, 31 October 1974'.

61 Author interviews in Delhi in autumn 1983.

62 A.L. Hammond, 'Brazil's Nuclear Program: Carter's Nonproliferation Policy Backfires', *Science*, vol. 195, no. 4,279, 18 February 1977, pp. 657–59.

63 Article VI specifies that each of the parties to the NPT 'undertakes to pursue negotiations in good faith on effective measures relating to cessation of the nuclear arms race at an early date and to nuclear disarmament, and on a treaty on general and complete disarmament under strict and effective international control'.

64 William Potter, 'India and the New Look of US Nonproliferation Policy', *Nonproliferation Review*, vol. 12, no. 2, 2005, pp. 343–54.

65 Gerhard Wettig, 'Soviet Policy on the Nonproliferation of Nuclear Weapons, 1966–1968', *Orbis*, vol. 13, 1969, pp. 1,058–84.

66 William Burr, 'The Nuclear Nonproliferation Treaty and the German Nuclear Question, Part 1, 1954–1964', 2 February 2018.

67 Joseph Nye, 'Nonproliferation: A Long-Term Strategy', *Foreign Affairs*, April 1978, p. 615.

68 International Atomic Energy Agency, 'International Nuclear Cycle Evaluation summary volume', 1980, https://inis.iaea.org/search/searchsinglerecord.aspx?recordsFor=SingleRecord&RN=11555701.

69 Joseph Nye cites the more general aphorism related to him by a French official, who said 'each nation makes one big mistake before it learns its interest in non-proliferation: the Soviet lesson was China, the French lesson was Israel, and the American lesson was India'; see Nye, 'US–Soviet Cooperation in a Nonproliferation Regime', p. 338.

Chapter Two

1 Zondi Masiza, 'A Chronology of South Africa's Nuclear Program', *Nonproliferation Review*, Fall 1993, https://www.nonproliferation.org/wp-content/uploads/npr/masiza11.pdf.

2 Jo-Ansie van Wyk and Anna-Mart van Wyk, 'From the Nuclear Laager to the Non-Proliferation Club: South Africa and the NPT', *South African Historical Journal*, vol. 67, no. 1, 2015, http://dx.doi.org/10.1080/02582473.2014.977337.

3 Nic von Wiellgh and Lydia von Wiellgh-Steyn, *The Bomb: South Africa's Nuclear Weapons Programme* (Litera Publications: Pretoria, 2015), pp. 136–49; Jeffrey Richelson, *Spying on the Bomb: American Nuclear Intelligence from Nazi Germany to Iran and North Korea* (New York: W.W. Norton and Co., 2006), pp. 277–82.

4 The earliest example can be found in William Potter, 'The Soviet Union and Nuclear Nonproliferation', *Slavic Review*, vol. 44, no. 3, Autumn 1985, p. 472. See also Murrey Marder and Don Oberdorfer, 'How West, Soviets Acted to Defuse S. African A-Test', *Washington Post*, 28 August 1977, https://www.washingtonpost.com/archive/politics/1977/08/28/how-west-soviets-acted-to-defuse-s-african-a-test/eada5bcc-7727-

4c32-b8e2-f21d55a9d4c3/?utm_term=.2e79115d315f.

5   Richardt van der Walt, Hannes Steyn and Jan van Loggerenberg, *Armament and Disarmament: South Africa's Nuclear Experience* (Lincoln, NE: iUniverse, 2005), p. 30.

6   Masiza, 'A Chronology of South Africa's Nuclear Program'.

7   South African Department of Foreign Affairs, 'Letter Informing the United States of South Africa's Intent to Request Nuclear Materials', 30 March 1960, Wilson Center Digital Archive, http://digitalarchive.wilsoncenter.org/document/116042.

8   This reactor was downgraded to 5 MWe in 1977 after the US export of fuel elements to South Africa was halted in 1976. See von Wielligh and von Wielligh-Steyn, *The Bomb: South Africa's Nuclear Weapons Programme*, p. 107.

9   Jean du Preez and Thomas Maettig, 'From Pariah to Nuclear Poster Boy', in William C. Potter with Gaukhar Mukhatzhanova (eds), *Forecasting Nuclear Proliferation in the 21st Century: A Comparative Perspective*, vol. 2 (Stanford, CA: Stanford University Press, 2010), p. 309.

10 David Albright and Andrea Stricker, *South Africa's Nuclear Weapons Program: Its History, Dismantlement, and Lessons for Today* (Washington DC: Institute for Science and International Security Press, 2016), p. 11.

11 *Ibid.*, p. 23.

12 Waldo Stumpf, 'South Africa's Nuclear Weapons Program: From Deterrence to Dismantlement', *Arms Control Today*, December 1995/January 1996.

13 Arms Control Association, 'The Nuclear Suppliers Group (NSG) at a Glance', 16 August 2017, https://www.armscontrol.org/factsheets/NSG.

14 Von Wielligh and von Wielligh-Steyn, *The Bomb: South Africa's Nuclear Weapons Programme*, p. 120.

15 Masiza, 'A Chronology of South Africa's Nuclear Program'.

16 Waldo Stumpf, 'Birth and Death of the South African Nuclear Weapons Programme', conference presentation given at '50 Years After Hiroshima', 28 September–2 October 1995, http://fas.org/nuke/guide/rsa/nuke/stumpf.htm.

17 Von Wielligh and von Wielligh-Steyn, *The Bomb: South Africa's Nuclear Weapons Programme*, p. 128.

18 Van Wyk and van Wyk, 'From the Nuclear Laager to the Non-Proliferation Club: South Africa and the NPT', p. 42.

19 Masiza, 'A Chronology of South Africa's Nuclear Program'.

20 Stumpf, 'South Africa's Nuclear Weapons Program: From Deterrence to Dismantlement'.

21 Or Rabinowitz, *Bargaining on Nuclear Tests: Washington and its Cold War Deals* (Oxford: Oxford University Press, 2014), p. 113.

22 David Albright et al., 'Rendering Useless South Africa's Nuclear Test Shafts in the Kalahari Desert', Institute for Science and International Security, 30 November 2011, http://isis-online.org/uploads/isis-reports/documents/Vastrap_30November2011.pdf; Jeffrey Lewis, 'Geolocating the Kalahari Test Site', *Arms Control Wonk*, 21 May 2015, http://www.armscontrolwonk.com/archive/207666/geolocating-the-kalahari-test-site.

23 Albright and Stricker, 'Revisiting South Africa's Nuclear Weapons Program: Its History, Dismantlement, and Lessons for Today', p. 13; Van Wyk and van Wyk, 'From the Nuclear Laager to the

Non-Proliferation Club: South Africa and the NPT', p. 42.

24 Van der Walt, Steyn and van Loggerenberg, *Armament and Disarmament: South Africa's Nuclear Experience*, p. 5.

25 Lawrence Livermore National Laboratory, Special Projects Division, 'South Africa: Motivations and Capabilities for Nuclear Proliferation', September 1977, Wilson Center Digital Archive, http://digitalarchive. wilsoncenter.org/document/119212.

26 Van der Walt, Steyn and van Loggerenberg, *Armament and Disarmament: South Africa's Nuclear Experience*, p. 3; United States Department of State, Office of the Historian, '181. Report Prepared by the Working Group on Angola', 20 February 1976, Foreign Relations of the United States, 1969–76, vol. 28, Southern Africa, https://history. state.gov/historicaldocuments/ frus1969-76v28/d181.

27 Lawrence Livermore National Laboratory, Special Projects Division, 'South Africa: Motivations and Capabilities for Nuclear Proliferation', p. 4.

28 The Soviet Union's involvement in southern Africa and its impact on Pretoria's threat perception are detailed by Anna-Mart van Wyk in 'South African Nuclear Development in the 1970s: A Non-Proliferation Conundrum?', *International History Review*, February 2018, p. 10. See also Stumpf, 'South Africa's Nuclear Weapons Program: From Deterrence to Dismantlement'; Lawrence Livermore National Laboratory, Special Projects Division, 'South Africa: Motivations and Capabilities for Nuclear Proliferation'.

29 Lawrence Livermore National Laboratory, Special Projects Division, 'South Africa: Motivations and Capabilities for Nuclear Proliferation'.

30 Van der Walt, Steyn and van Loggerenberg, *Armament and Disarmament: South Africa's Nuclear Experience*, p. 3.

31 Described as 'catalytic deterrence' by some scholars, South Africa's nuclear posture relied on the 'use, or threat of use, of a nuclear explosive device – as a goad to force other nations to intervene' (see Frank Pabian, 'South Africa's Nuclear Weapon Program: Lessons for US Nonproliferation Policy', *Nonproliferation Review*, vol. 3, no. 1, 1995, p. 7). See also Donald Goodson, 'Catalytic Deterrence? Apartheid South Africa's Nuclear Weapons Strategy', *Politikon*, vol. 39, no. 2, 2012.

32 Sources provide conflicting information: for sources indicating 1975, see Masiza, 'A Chronology of South Africa's Nuclear Program'; for a source indicating 1976, see von Wielligh and von Wielligh-Steyn, *The Bomb: South Africa's Nuclear Weapons Programme*, p. 128.

33 Von Wielligh and von Wielligh-Steyn, *The Bomb: South Africa's Nuclear Weapons Programme*, p. 137.

34 Sasha Polakow-Suransky, *The Unspoken Alliance: Israel's Secret Relationship with Apartheid South Africa* (New York: Pantheon Books, 2010), p. 112.

35 Richelson, *Spying on the Bomb: American Nuclear Intelligence from Nazi Germany to Iran and North Korea*, pp. 277–87.

36 Marder and Oberdorfer, 'How West, Soviets Acted to Defuse S. African A-Test'.

37 Richelson, *Spying on the Bomb: American Nuclear Intelligence from Nazi Germany to Iran and North Korea*, pp. 277–87.

38 Communiqué from Brezhnev to Carter, 'Soviet Demarche on South African Nuclear Program', August 1977, US National Archives, https://aad.archives.gov/aad/createpdf?rid=181956&dt=2532&dl=1629.

39 Ibid.

40 Cable from US Ambassador to Germany to Secretary of State Cyrus Vance, 'South African Nuclear Test Site', August 1977, US National Archives, https://aad.archives.gov/aad/createpdf?rid=188788&dt=2532&dl=1629.

41 Communiqué from Brezhnev to Carter, 'Soviet Demarche on South African Nuclear Program'.

42 Ibid.

43 'Letter, Warren Christopher to William Hyland, Response to Soviet Message on South Africa', 10 August 1977, Wilson Center Digital Archive, http://digitalarchive.wilsoncenter.org/document/119249.

44 Ibid.

45 Von Wielligh and von Wielligh-Steyn, *The Bomb: South Africa's Nuclear Weapons Programme*, p. 137; Richelson, *Spying on the Bomb: American Nuclear Intelligence from Nazi Germany to Iran and North Korea*, p. 279.

46 Richelson, *Spying on the Bomb: American Nuclear Intelligence from Nazi Germany to Iran and North Korea*, p. 279.

47 Director of Central Intelligence, 'Memorandum for: Representative of the National Foreign Intelligence Board', 12 August 1977, https://www.cia.gov/library/readingroom/docs/CIA-RDP79R00603A002900120003-8.pdf.

48 Marder and Oberdorfer, 'How West, Soviets Acted to Defuse S. African A-Bomb'.

49 World Conference for Action Against Apartheid, Lagos, 'Supplement to Brief No. A7 (Nuclear Questions): Soviet Allegations About South African Nuclear Weapons Development', 22 August 1977, Wilson Center Digital Archive, http://digitalarchive.wilsoncenter.org/document/116615.

50 Ibid.

51 'Letter, US Secretary of State Vance to South African Foreign Minister Botha', 19 August 1977, Wilson Center Digital Archive, http://digitalarchive.wilsoncenter.org/document/114153.

52 Ibid.

53 'Telegram from South African Embassy in the US on President Carter's Press Conference on the Kalahari Nuclear Test Site', 23 August 1977, Wilson Center Digital Archive, http://digitalarchive/wilsoncenter/org/document/116609.

54 David Albright, 'South Africa and the Affordable Bomb', *Bulletin of the Atomic Scientists*, vol. 50, no. 3, July/August 1994, p. 41; van der Walt, Steyn and van Loggerenberg, *Armament and Disarmament: South Africa's Nuclear Experience*, p. 41.

55 Van der Walt, Steyn and van Loggerenberg, *Armament and Disarmament: South Africa's Nuclear Experience*, pp. 40–41; von Wielligh and von Weilligh-Steyn, *The Bomb: South Africa's Nuclear Weapons Programme*, p. 138.

56 Cable transcription detailing Warren Christopher statement to Soviet Ambassador Dobrynin, 'South African Nuclear Problem', August 1977, US National Archives, https://aad.archives.gov/aad/createpdf?rid=194647&dt=2532&dl=1629.

57 Jimmy Carter, 'The President's News Conference', American Presidency Project, University of California Santa Barbara, 23 August 1977, http://www.presidency.ucsb.edu/ws/index.php?pi

d=7987&st=south+africa&st1=.

58 Cable, South African Department of Foreign Affairs, 'South Africa: Nuclear Bomb Charges', 26 August 1977, Wilson Center Digital Archive, http://digitalarchive.wilsoncenter.org/document/114180.

59 'Extract from Speech by the South African Prime Minister at Congress of the National Party of Cape Province', 24 August 1977, Wilson Center Digital Archive, http://digitalarchive.wilsoncenter.org/document/116617.

60 Ibid. In a 2012 article, Donald Goodson points out that this type of 'calculated ambiguity', whereby South African officials would 'neither confirm nor deny whether [they] possessed a nuclear weapon' in order to compel the US to assist in an attack on the country, was part of Pretoria's official deterrence strategy; see Donald Goodson, 'Catalytic Deterrence? Apartheid South Africa's Nuclear Weapons Strategy'.

61 'Cable from South African Embassy in the US to the South African Secretary for Foreign Affairs on South Africa and the Bomb', 31 August 1977, Wilson Center Digital Archive, http://digitalarchive.wilsoncenter.org/document/114181.

62 Ibid.

63 UN Security Council Resolution 418, 'South Africa', S/RES/418 (1977), 4 November 1977, http://www.un.org/en/ga/search/view_doc.asp?symbol=S/RES/418(1977).

64 Von Wielligh and von Weilligh-Steyn, The Bomb: South Africa's Nuclear Weapons Programme, p. 178.

65 US Department of State, Office of the Historian, 'Memorandum From the President's Assistant for National Security Affairs (Brzezinski) to Secretary of State Vance and Secretary of Commerce Kreps', 28 November 1977, 'Foreign Relations of the United States Vol. XVI, Southern Africa', https://history.state.gov/historicaldocuments/frus1977-80v16/d324.

66 Albright, 'South Africa and the Affordable Bomb', p. 42.

67 Some former members of South Africa's nuclear leadership have speculated that the US may have learned about the South African test site before being alerted by the Soviets through an individual named Robert Clyde Ivy, an affiliate of Kentron, the division of Armscor that built South Africa's nuclear weapons. Their accounts suggest that Ivy had connections to the US intelligence community, and that he had likely informed the US government about preparations for the cold test before Vasev delivered his démarche in 1977. See von Wielligh and von Weilligh-Steyn, The Bomb: South Africa's Nuclear Weapons Programme, p. 146; van der Walt, Steyn and van Loggerenberg, Armament and Disarmament: South Africa's Nuclear Experience, p. 93.

68 Leonard Spector with Jacqueline Smith, Nuclear Ambitions: The Spread of Nuclear Weapons 1989–1990 (Boulder, CO: Westview Press, 1990), p. 271.

69 Lawrence Livermore National Laboratory, Special Projects Division, 'South Africa: Motivations and Capabilities for Nuclear Proliferation'.

70 Central Intelligence Agency, 'South Africa Again Rumored To Be Working on Nuclear Weapons', Weekly Surveyor, 13 September 1976, http://nsarchive.gwu.edu/NSAEBB/NSAEBB181/sa14.pdf.

71 Director of Central Intelligence, 'Memorandum: Subject: Analytical Resources on Sub-Saharan Africa',

6 May 1977, p. 2, https://www.cia.gov/library/readingroom/document/cia-rdp83m00171r001200110001-2.

[72] William Lowther, 'The SOB of the CIA', *MacLean's Magazine*, 6 March 1978, https://www.cia.gov/library/readingroom/docs/CIA-RDP81M00980R001700080057-4.pdf.

[73] Cable transcription from US Embassy in Pretoria to US State Department, 'Press Leaks on US–South Africa Nuclear Talks', August 1978, https://aad.archives.gov/aad/createpdf?rid=20 2716&dt=2694&dl=2009.

[74] Frank Barnaby, 'Nuclear South Africa', *New Scientist*, 19 October 1978, p. 168; Richelson, *Spying on the Bomb: American Nuclear Intelligence from Nazi Germany to Iran and North Korea*, p. 279.

[75] James G. Hershberg, '"Seventeen Days (or Fifteen, Sixteen, or Eighteen, But Who's Counting?)": The South African Nuclear Crisis (or Was It?) of August 1977', paper presented at the conference The Historical Dimensions of South Africa's Nuclear Program, 10–12 December 2012, p. 14.

[76] The USSR – and the rest of the world – learned about the *Big Bird* 1977-56A KH-11's ability to 'transmit directly from space the pictures it took to US ground stations' in 1978 when a CIA employee sold a stolen copy of its manual to Soviet officials. See George C. Wilson, 'Soviets Learned of Spy Satellite from US Manual', *Washington Post*, 23 November 1978; 'The CIA: Mission Impossible?', *Time*, 7 February 1978.

[77] Lowther, 'The SOB of the CIA'.

[78] Hershberg, '"Seventeen Days (or Fifteen, Sixteen, or Eighteen, But Who's Counting?)": The South African Nuclear Crisis (or Was It?) of August 1977', p. 14. This characterisation of

events was corroborated through interviews conducted by CNS staff with former US officials.

[79] Richard Burt, 'Aides to Carter Find Unsettled Questions in Intelligence Plan', *New York Times*, 24 December 1977.

[80] Kenneth Adelman and Albion Knight, 'Can South Africa Go Nuclear?', *Orbis*, vol. 23, Fall 1979, p. 646.

[81] Jeffrey Lewis, director of the East Asia Nonproliferation Program at the James Martin Center for Nonproliferation Studies, points to the surprisingly lax security at the site in a blog post he published on the topic, noting that 'the South Africans apparently didn't even bother to close the airspace over the test site'. See Lewis, 'Geolocating the Kalahari Test Site'.

[82] Lawrence Livermore National Laboratory, Special Projects Division, 'South Africa: Motivations and Capabilities for Nuclear Proliferation'.

[83] Letter from H.M.S. Reid to Mr Mallaby, 'South African Nuclear Intentions: the Kalahari Facility', 22 September 1977, Wilson Center Digital Archive, http://digitalarchive.wilsoncenter.org/document/116628.

[84] 'Soviet Demarche on South African Nuclear Program', August 1977, US National Archives, https://aad.archives.gov/aad/createpdf?rid=18195 6&dt=2532&dl=1629.

[85] 'US/Soviet Consultations on the Special Session on Disarmament', September 1977, US National Archives, https://aad.archives.gov/aad/createpdf?rid=20 6162&dt=2532&dl=1629.

[86] Von Wielligh and von Wielligh-Steyn, *The Bomb: South Africa's Nuclear Weapons Programme*, p. 143; Cable from Deputy Secretary of State to US Embassy Lagos, US Embassy Tel

Aviv, and US Permanent Mission New York, 'Israeli Participation in Lagos Conference', August 1977, US National Archives, https://aad.archives.gov/aad/createpdf?rid=184112&dt=2532&dl=1629.

87   Central Intelligence Agency, 'National Intelligence Daily Cable', 17 August 1977, https://www.cia.gov/library/readingroom/docs/CIA-RDP79T00975A030300010012-1.pdf.

88   'Non-Proliferation Issues at the 32nd UNGA; South Africa Nuclear Issues', October 1977, US National Archives, https://aad.archives.gov/aad/createpdf?rid=232436&dt=2532&dl=1629.

89   Von Wielligh and von Weilligh-Steyn, *The Bomb: South Africa's Nuclear Weapons Programme*, p. 145.

90   *Ibid.*

91   Cable from Secretary of State to US Embassy Vienna, 'Soviet Demarche on Nuclear Weapons Development by SAG', August 1977, US National Archives, https://aad.archives.gov/aad/createpdf?rid=184751&dt=2532&dl=1629.

92   National Security Council, 'Memorandum: South African Nuclear Fuel Agreement', 19 November 1971, Wilson Center Digital Archive, http://digitalarchive.wilsoncenter.org/document/114144.

93   'Soviet Demarche on Nuclear Weapons Development by SAG', August 1977, US National Archives, https://aad.archives.gov/aad/createpdf?rid=184751&dt=2532&dl=1629; Cable from US Mission to UN, New York, to Secretary of State, 'Non-proliferation Issues at the 32nd UNGA; South Africa Nuclear Issues', October 1977, US National Archives, https://aad.archives.gov/aad/createpdf?rid=232436&dt=2532&dl=1629.

94   The United States faced criticism domestically and internationally for its export-control policies. See 'Soviet Demarche on Nuclear Weapons Development by SAG'.

95   National Security Council, 'South Africa: Memorandum for the Secretary of State and the Secretary of Defense', 25 October 1977, p. 2, https://www.cia.gov/library/readingroom/docs/CIA-RDP80M00165A000400350006-7.pdf.

96   In an October 1976 memorandum of conversation, Henry Kissinger states that Soviet involvement in Africa is 'pure mischief. They don't really stand to gain much from this gang and they have no permanent interests there. They can only be doing it to weaken and humiliate us …' See US Department of State, Office of the Historian, '294. Memorandum of Conversation', 3 October 1976, Foreign Relations of the United States, 1969–76, vol. 16, https://history.state.gov/historicaldocuments/frus1969-76v16/d294; United States Department of State, Office of the Historian, '181. Report Prepared by the Working Group on Angola', 20 February 1976, Foreign Relations of the United States, 1969–76, vol. 28, Southern Africa, https://history.state.gov/historicaldocuments/frus1969-76v28/d181.

97   Joseph S. Nye, Jr, 'US–Soviet Cooperation in a Nonproliferation Regime', in Alexander George, Philip Farley and Alexander Dallin (eds), *US–Soviet Security Cooperation: Achievements, Failures, Lessons* (New York: Oxford University Press, 1988), p. 346.

98   'Non-Proliferation Issues at the 32nd UNGA; South Africa Nuclear Issues'.

99   Cable from US Embassy London to Secretary of State, 'Soviet–US Bilateral

on Non-Proliferation', September 1977, US National Archives, https://aad. archives.gov/aad/createpdf?rid=21806 7&dt=2532&dl=1629.

100 *Ibid.*

101 US Department of State, 'Your Meeting with Gromyko: South African Nuclear Issue', 1977, http://proxy.miis.edu/ login?url=http://search.proquest.com/ docview/1679140216?accountid=12457.

102 Cable transcription from US Secretary of State, 'South African [sic] and the NPT: Cooperation with USSR', September 1977, https://aad.archives. gov/aad/createpdf?rid=220735&dt=253 2&dl=1629.

103 'On US Dealings with the Soviet Union', *New York Times*, 11 January 1977, http://www.nytimes.com/1977/01/11/ archives/on-us-dealings-with-the-soviet-union.html.

104 A 1978 non-paper drafted by the US for the Soviet Union on the South African nuclear-weapons programme

welcomed 'any additional information you have that the South African Government may be working on a second test range and building a reactor dedicated to plutonium production'. See 'Non-Paper to Dobrynin on South African Nuclear Test Site', March 1978, US National Archives, https://aad. archives.gov/aad/createpdf?rid=64690 &dt=2694&dl=2009.

105 Sarah Bidgood and William Potter, 'Cold War Lessons for Contemporary US–Russian Nonproliferation Cooperation: The South African Case', Nuclear Threat Initiative, 17 October 2016, http://www.nti.org/analysis/articles/ cold-war-lessons-contemporary-us-russian-nonproliferation-cooperation-south-african-case.

106 Cable from State Department to Secretary of State, 'Press Material', August 1977, US National Archives, https://aad.archives.gov/aad/createpdf ?rid=193634&dt=2532&dl=1629.

Chapter Three

1 Scott Kaufman, *Project Plowshare: The Peaceful Use of Nuclear Explosives in Cold War America* (Ithaca, NY: Cornell University Press, 2013), p. 2.

2 Trevor Findlay, *Nuclear Dynamite: The Peaceful Nuclear Explosion Fiasco* (New York: Pergamon Books, 1990), p. 2.

3 Iris D. Borg, 'Nuclear Explosions for Peaceful Purposes', in Jozef Goldblat and David Cox (eds), *Nuclear Weapon Tests: Prohibition or Limitation?* (Oxford: Oxford University Press, 1988), pp. 68–69.

4 Milo D. Nordyke, *The Soviet Program for Peaceful Uses of Nuclear Explosions* (Springfield, VA: National Technical Information Service, 2000), p. 73.

5 Findlay, *Nuclear Dynamite: The Peaceful Nuclear Explosions Fiasco*, pp. 2–5.

6 *Ibid.*, p. 10.

7 Ralph Sanders, *Project Plowshare: The Development of the Peaceful Uses of Nuclear Explosions* (Washington DC: Public Affairs Press, 1962), p. 183.

8 *Ibid.*

9 Glenn T. Seaborg and Benjamin S. Loeb, *Stemming the Tide: Arms Control in the Johnson Years* (Lexington, MA: Lexington Books, 1987), p. 316.

10 US Department of State, Office of the Historian, '294. Memorandum of Conversation: Nuclear Test Ban Treaty', 14 June 1963, Foreign Relations of the

United States, 1961–63, vol. 7, Arms Control and Disarmament, https://history.state.gov/historicaldocuments/frus1961-63v07/d294.

11 Harold K. Jacobson and Eric Stein, *Diplomats, Scientists, and Politicians: The United States and the Nuclear Test Ban Negotiations* (Ann Arbor, MI: University of Michigan Press, 1966), p. 456.

12 US Department of State, Office of the Historian, '328. Telegram From the Embassy in the Soviet Union to the Department of State', 16 July 1963, Foreign Relations of the United States, 1961–63, vol. 7, Arms Control and Disarmament, https://history.state.gov/historicaldocuments/frus1961-63v07/d328.

13 Findlay, *Nuclear Dynamite*, p. 52; US Department of State, Office of the Historian, '328. Telegram From the Embassy in the Soviet Union to the Department of State', 16 July 1963.

14 US Department of State, Office of the Historian, '328. Telegram From the Embassy in the Soviet Union to the Department of State', 16 July 1963.

15 US Department of State, Office of the Historian, '337. Memorandum for the Record: Test Ban Treaty', 22 July 1963, Foreign Relations of the United States, 1961–63, vol. 7, Arms Control and Disarmament, https://history.state.gov/historicaldocuments/frus1961-63v07/d337.

16 US Department of State, 'Treaty Banning Nuclear Weapon Tests in the Atmosphere, in Outer Space and Under Water', 10 October 1963, https://www.state.gov/t/isn/4797.htm#treaty.

17 Glenn T. Seaborg and Benjamin S. Loeb, *Kennedy, Khrushchev and the Test Ban* (Berkeley, CA: University of California

Press, 1981), p. 246; US Department of State, Office of the Historian, '332. Telegram from the Department of State to the Embassy in the Soviet Union', 18 July 1963, Foreign Relations of the United States, 1961–63, vol. 7, Arms Control and Disarmament, https://history.state.gov/historicaldocuments/frus1961-63v07/d332.

18 US Department of State, Office of the Historian, '338. Telegram from the Embassy in the Soviet Union to the Department of State', 22 July 1963, Foreign Relations of the United States, 1961–63, vol. 7, Arms Control and Disarmament, https://history.state.gov/historicaldocuments/frus1961-63v07/d338.

19 'Letter to Senate Leaders Restating the Administration's Views on the Nuclear Test Ban Treaty', 11 September 1963, *Public Papers of the Presidents of the United States, 1963*: 670–71, https://quod.lib.umich.edu/p/ppotpus/4730928.1963.001/727?page=root;rgn=full+text;size=100;view=image.

20 Findlay, *Nuclear Dynamite*, p. 82.

21 William Epstein, *The Last Chance: Nuclear Proliferation and Arms Control* (New York: The Free Press, 1976), p. 173; Seaborg and Loeb, *Stemming the Tide: Arms Control in the Johnson Years*, p. 321.

22 Seaborg and Loeb, *Stemming the Tide: Arms Control in the Johnson Years*.

23 *Ibid.*

24 *Ibid.*, pp. 321–22.

25 US Department of State, Office of the Historian, '123. Memorandum of Conversation: Peaceful Uses of Atomic Energy', 18 March 1966, Foreign Relations of the United States, 1964–68, vol. 11, https://history.state.gov/historicaldocuments/frus1964-68v11/d123.

26   Ibid.; Findlay, *Nuclear Dynamite*, p. 68; Seaborg and Loeb, *Stemming the Tide: Arms Control in the Johnson Years*, p. 322.

27   Seaborg and Loeb, *Stemming the Tide: Arms Control in the Johnson Years*, p. 355.

28   United Nations Department of Political and Security Council Affairs, *The United Nations and Disarmament 1945–1970* (New York: United Nations Publications, 1970), pp. 270–80, https://unoda-web.s3-accelerate.amazonaws.com/wp-content/uploads/assets/publications/yearbook/en/EN-YB-VOL-00-1945-1970.pdf.

29   Seaborg and Loeb, *Stemming the Tide: Arms Control in the Johnson Years*, p. 364.

30   Findlay, *Nuclear Dynamite*, p. 115.

31   Seaborg and Loeb, *Stemming the Tide: Arms Control in the Johnson Years*, p. 364.

32   Epstein, *The Last Chance: Nuclear Proliferation and Arms Control*, pp. 65–70.

33   US Department of State, Office of the Historian, '144. Memorandum from the Under Secretary of State (Ball) to President Johnson', 8 August 1966, Foreign Relations of the United States, 1964–68, vol. 11, https://history.state.gov/historicaldocuments/frus1964-68v11/d144.

34   Ibid.

35   Ibid.

36   Ibid.

37   Ibid.

38   'Final verbatim record of the two hundred and eightieth meeting', Conference of the United Nations Eighteen-Nation Committee on Disarmament, Geneva, 9 August 1966, p. 14, https://quod.lib.umich.edu/e/endc/4918260.0280.001/14.

39   Ibid., p. 14.

40   Ibid., p. 15.

41   Ibid., p. 15.

42   Mohammed I. Shaker, *The Nuclear Non-Proliferation Treaty: Origin and Imple-mentation 1959–1979*, vol. 1 (London: Oceana Publications, 1980), p. 380; Seaborg and Loeb, *Stemming the Tide: Arms Control in the Johnson Years*, p. 365.

43   'Final verbatim record of the two hundred and eighty-fourth meeting', Conference of the United Nations Eighteen-Nation Committee on Disarmament, Geneva, 23 August 1966, p. 22, https://quod.lib.umich.edu/e/endc/4918260.0284.001/22.

44   US Department of State, Office of the Historian, '160. Memorandum of Conversation', 10 October 1966, Foreign Relations of the United States, 1964–68, vol. 11, https://history.state.gov/historicaldocuments/frus1964-68v11/d160.

45   Nordyke, *The Soviet Program for Peaceful Uses of Nuclear Explosions*, pp. 33–34.

46   US Department of State, Office of the Historian, '165. Memorandum from the Acting Director of the Arms Control and Disarmament Agency (Fisher) to Secretary of State Rusk', 22 November 1966, Foreign Relations of the United States, 1964–68, vol. 11, https://history.state.gov/historicaldocuments/frus1964-68v11/d165.

47   'Final verbatim record of the two hundred and ninety-eighth meeting', Conference of the United Nations Eighteen-Nation Committee on Disarmament, Geneva, 23 May 1967, p. 12, https://quod.lib.umich.edu/e/endc/4918260.0298.001/12.

48   US Department of State, Office of the Historian, '166. Memorandum from Secretary of State Rusk to President Johnson', undated, Foreign Relations of the United States, 1964–68, vol. 11, https://history.state.gov/historicaldocuments/frus1964-68v11/d166.

49   US Department of State, Office of the Historian, '175. Memorandum of

Conversation: US–Soviet Technical Discussions on Nuclear Explosions', 18 January 1967, Foreign Relations of the United States, 1964–68, vol. 11, https://history.state.gov/historicaldocuments/frus1964-68v11/d175.

50 *Ibid.*

51 'Final verbatim record of the two hundred and eighty-seventh meeting', Conference of the United Nations Eighteen-Nation Committee on Disarmament, Geneva, 21 February 1967, p. 11, https://quod.lib.umich.edu/e/endc/4918260.0287.001/11.

52 'Final verbatim record of the two hundred and ninety-third meeting', Conference of the United Nations Eighteen-Nation Committee on Disarmament, Geneva, 14 March 1967, pp. 13, 15, https://quod.lib.umich.edu/e/endc/4918260.0293.001?rgn=main;view=fulltext; 'Final verbatim record of the two hundred and ninety-eighth meeting', Conference of the United Nations Eighteen-Nation Committee on Disarmament, p. 12.

53 'Final verbatim record of the two hundred and eighty-eighth meeting', Conference of the United Nations Eighteen-Nation Committee on Disarmament, Geneva, 23 February 1967, pp. 13–15, https://quod.lib.umich.edu/e/endc/4918260.0288.001?rgn=main;view=fulltext.

54 'Final verbatim record of the two hundred and eighty-seventh meeting', Conference of the United Nations Eighteen-Nation Committee on Disarmament, Geneva, pp. 19–29, https://quod.lib.umich.edu/e/endc/4918260.0287.001?rgn=main;view=fulltext.

55 'Final verbatim record of the two hundred and ninety-third meeting', Conference of the United Nations Eighteen-Nation Committee on Disarmament, Geneva, 14 March 1967, p. 23, https://quod.lib.umich.edu/e/endc/4918260.0293.001/23.

56 US Department of State, Office of the Historian, '239. Memorandum of Conversation: Nonproliferation Treaty', 17 May 1968, Foreign Relations of the United States, 1964–68, vol. 11, Arms Control and Disarmament, https://history.state.gov/historicaldocuments/frus1964-68v11/d239.

57 'Final verbatim record of the two hundred and ninety-third meeting', Conference of the United Nations Eighteen-Nation Committee on Disarmament, Geneva, 14 March 1967, p. 23.

58 'Final verbatim record of the two hundred and ninety-fifth meeting', Conference of the United Nations Eighteen-Nation Committee on Disarmament, Geneva, 21 March 1967, pp. 23–26, https://quod.lib.umich.edu/e/endc/4918260.0295.001?rgn=main;view=fulltext.

59 Shaker, *The Nuclear Non-Proliferation Treaty: Origin and Implementation 1959–1979*, vol. 1, p. 380; 'Final verbatim record of the two hundred and ninety-seventh meeting', Conference of the United Nations Eighteen-Nation Committee on Disarmament, Geneva, 18 May 1967, pp. 8–9, https://quod.lib.umich.edu/e/endc/4918260.0297.001?rgn=main;view=fulltext.

60 Seaborg and Loeb, *Stemming the Tide: Arms Control in the Johnson Years*, p. 365.

61 Epstein, *The Last Chance: Nuclear Proliferation and Arms Control*, pp. 69–71.

62 'Final verbatim record of the three hundred and thirtieth meeting', Conference of the United Nations Eighteen-Nation Committee on Disarmament, Geneva, 14 September

1967, p. 8, https://quod.lib.umich.
edu/e/endc/4918260.0330.001/8.

63 'Final verbatim record of the three
hundred and thirty-ninth meeting',
Conference of the United Nations
Eighteen-Nation Committee on
Disarmament, Geneva, 17 October
1967, pp. 6–8, https://quod.lib.umich.
edu/e/endc/4918260.0339.001?rgn=mai
n;view=fulltext.

64 United States Arms Control and
Disarmament Agency, 'Documents
on Disarmament, 1967' (Washington
DC: US Government Printing Office,
1968), no. 46, pp. 398–400, http://
unoda-web.s3-accelerate.amazonaws.
com/wp-content/uploads/assets/
publications/documents_on_
disarmament/1967/DoD_1967.pdf.

65 US Department of State, Office of the
Historian, '212. Memorandum of Conversation: Non-Proliferation Treaty,
ABMs', 4 October 1967, Foreign Relations of the United States, 1964–68, vol.
11, https://history.state.gov/historical
documents/frus1964-68v11/d212.

66 'Final verbatim record of the three
hundred and thirty-eighth meeting',
Conference of the United Nations
Eighteen-Nation Committee on
Disarmament, Geneva, 12 October
1967, p. 8, https://quod.lib.umich.
edu/e/endc/4918260.0338.001/8.

67 Seaborg and Loeb, *Stemming the Tide:
Arms Control in the Johnson Years*, p. 365.

68 Epstein, *The Last Chance: Nuclear
Proliferation and Arms Control*, p. 71.

69 US Department of State, Office of
the Historian, '224. Memorandum
of Conversation: Reconvening of
the ENDC', 26 December 1967,
Foreign Relations of the United
States, 1964–68, vol. 11, https://
history.state.gov/historicaldocuments/
frus1964-68v11/d224.

70 'Final verbatim record of the three
hundred and fifty-seventh meeting',
Conference of the United Nations
Eighteen-Nation Committee on
Disarmament, Geneva, 18 January
1968, p. 19, https://quod.lib.umich.
edu/e/endc/4918260.0357.001/19.

71 *Ibid.*, pp. 10–11.

72 'Final verbatim record of the three
hundred and fifty-ninth meeting',
Conference of the United Nations
Eighteen-Nation Committee on
Disarmament, Geneva, 25 January
1968, p. 11, https://quod.lib.umich.
edu/e/endc/4918260.0359.001/11.

73 'Final verbatim record of the three
hundred and sixty-sixth meeting',
Conference of the United Nations
Eighteen-Nation Committee on
Disarmament, Geneva, 16 February
1968, p. 9, https://quod.lib.umich.
edu/e/endc/4918260.0366.001/9.

74 'Final verbatim record of the three
hundred and seventy-third meeting',
Conference of the United Nations
Eighteen-Nation Committee on Disarmament, Geneva, 5 March 1968, pp.
6–8, https://quod.lib.umich.edu/e/endc
/4918260.0373.001?rgn=main;view=full
text.

75 Seaborg and Loeb, *Stemming the Tide:
Arms Control in the Johnson Years*, p. 366.

76 Shaker, *The Nuclear Non-Proliferation
Treaty: Origin and Implementation 1959–
1979*, vol. 1, p. 448.

77 'Final verbatim record of the three
hundred and sixty-ninth meeting',
Conference of the United Nations
Eighteen-Nation Committee on
Disarmament, Geneva, 22 February
1968, https://quod.lib.umich.edu/e/end
c/4918260.0369.001?rgn=main;view=ful
ltext.

78 'Final verbatim record of the three
hundred and seventieth meeting',

Conference of the United Nations Eighteen-Nation Committee on Disarmament, Geneva, 27 February 1968, https://quod.lib.umich.edu/e/endc/491 8260.0370.001?rgn=main;view=fulltext.

79 Seaborg and Loeb, *Stemming the Tide: Arms Control in the Johnson Years*, p. 366.

80 '1571st Plenary meeting of the First Committee', United Nations Office for Disarmament Affairs, 20 May 1968, http://undocs.org/A/C.1/PV.1571.

81 US Department of State, Office of the Historian, '239. Memorandum of Conversation: Non-proliferation Treaty', 17 May 1968, Foreign Relations of the United States, 1964–68, vol. 11, https://history.state.gov/ historicaldocuments/frus1964-68v11/ d239.

82 Epstein, *The Last Chance: Nuclear Proliferation and Arms Control*, p. 119.

83 United Nations Department of Political and Security Council Affairs, *The United Nations and Disarmament 1945–1970*, p. 296.

84 '1577th Plenary meeting of the First Committee', United Nations Office for Disarmament Affairs, 31 May 1968, pp. 13–19, http://undocs.org/A/C.1/ PV.1577.

85 United Nations Department of Political and Security Council Affairs, *The United Nations and Disarmament 1945–1970*, p. 299.

Chapter Four

1   This chapter sets aside discussion of the many elements of continuing NPT cooperation between Moscow and Washington in the immediate post-Soviet period, particularly at the 1995 NPT Review and Extension Conference.

2   Lewis A. Dunn, 'Redefining the U.S. Agenda for Nuclear Disarmament: Analysis and Reflections', *Livermore Papers on Global Security*, no. 1, October 2016, Center for Global Security Research, pp. 57–61, https://cgsr. llnl.gov/content/assets/docs/CGSR_ Document_LLNL-TR-701463_103116. pdf.

3   See George Bunn and John B. Rhinelander, 'Looking Back: The Nuclear Nonproliferation Treaty Then and Now', *Arms Control Today*, 7 August 2008, https://armscontrol.org/ act/2008_07-08/lookingback.asp#bio; George Bunn, 'Brief History of NPT Safeguards Article', 6 February 2006, Center for Global Security, Pacific Northwest National Laboratory, https://cgs.pnnl.gov/fois/doclib/ NPTNegHist.Art.III.6%20Feb.06. pdf; George Bunn, 'The Nuclear Nonproliferation Treaty: History and Current Problems', *Arms Control Today*, 1 December 2003, https://www. armscontrol.org/act/2003_12/Bunn; 'The Impulse towards a Safer World: 40th Anniversary of the Nuclear Nonproliferation Treaty', National Security Archive, George Washington University, https://nsarchive2.gwu. edu/nukevault/ebb253/index.htm; Rich Hooper and Jenni Rissanen, 'Transcript of Interview with Ambassador Roland Timerbaev', Vienna, Austria, 14 June 2007, Center for Global Security, Pacific Northwest National Laboratory, https://cgs.pnnl.gov/fois/ doclib/Timerbaev(transcript)2.pdf;

Roland Timerbaev, 'In Memoriam: George Bunn (1925–2013)', *Arms Control Today*, 3 June 2013, https://www.armscontrol.org/act/2013_06/In-Memoriam-George-Bunn.

4   Hooper and Rissanen, 'Transcript of Interview with Ambassador Roland Timerbaev', p. 6.

5   'War and peace in the nuclear age; Carter's New World; interview with Roland Timerbaev', *Openvault*, 26 November 1986, http://openvault.wgbh.org/catalog/V_ED432881A740475493E7664F1DD93816.

6   'War and Peace in the Nuclear Age; Haves and Have-nots; interview with George Bunn', *Openvault*, 30 October 1986, http://openvault.wgbh.org/catalog/V_0F767B2E981F4131A728F6FA05A9CB29.

7   Article I states in part that: 'Each nuclear-weapon State Party to the Treaty undertakes not to transfer to any recipient whatsoever nuclear weapons or other nuclear explosive devices or control over such weapons or explosive devices directly, or indirectly.'

8   Article II states in part that: 'Each non-nuclear-weapon State Party to the Treaty undertakes not to receive the transfer from any transferor whatsoever of nuclear weapons or other nuclear explosive devices or of control over such weapons or explosive devices directly, or indirectly.'

9   Bunn and Rhinelander, 'Looking Back: The Nuclear Nonproliferation Treaty Then and Now'; Timerbaev, 'In Memoriam: George Bunn (1925–2013)'; Hooper and Rissanen, 'Transcript of Interview with Ambassador Roland Timerbaev'.

10 Bunn, 'Brief History of NPT Safeguards Article'; Hooper and Rissanen, 'Transcript of Interview with Ambassador Roland Timerbaev'; Timerbaev, 'In Memoriam: George Bunn (1925–2013)'.

11 International Atomic Energy Agency, 'Treaty on the Non-Proliferation of Nuclear Weapons', Notification of the entry into force, 22 April 1970, https://www.iaea.org/sites/default/files/publications/documents/infcircs/1970/infcirc140.pdf.

12 Bunn, 'Brief History of NPT Safeguards Article'; Hooper and Rissanen, 'Transcript of Interview with Ambassador Roland Timerbaev'; Timerbaev, 'In Memoriam: George Bunn (1925–2013)'.

13 George Bunn and Roland M. Timerbaev, 'Security Assurances to Non-Nuclear-Weapon States', *Nonproliferation Review*, Fall 1993, pp. 12–13, https://www.nonproliferation.org/wp-content/uploads/npr/buntim11.pdf.

14 Mohamed Shaker, *The Nuclear Non-Proliferation Treaty: Origin and Implementation, 1959–1979*, vol. II (London: Oceana Publications, 1980), pp. 558–59, http://www.nonproliferation.org/wp-content/uploads/2016/01/mohamed_shaker_npt_vol_2.pdf.

15 Cable from State Department to US Mission to the UN, New York, 'NPT: Mexican Amendments', 10 May 1968, National Security Archive, George Washington University, https://nsarchive2.gwu.edu/nukevault/ebb253/doc23a.pdf; Cable from State Department to US Mission to the UN, New York, 'Mexican Amendments to NPT', 11 May 1968, National Security Archive, George Washington University, https://nsarchive2.gwu.edu/nukevault/ebb253/doc23b.pdf.

16 Hooper and Rissanen, 'Transcript of Interview with Ambassador Roland Timerbaev', p. 10.

17 At the same time, as noted, the US continued to consult closely with its European allies on NPT issues.

18 The following discussion draws on the author's role as US ambassador to the 1985 NPT Review Conference.

19 'National Intelligence Estimate, NIE-4-82, Nuclear Proliferation Trends Through 1987', July 1982, Wilson Center Digital Archive, http://digitalarchive.wilsoncenter.org/document/116894.pdf?v=41ddf717816 89548f17de72de809cb51.

20 Ibid.

21 Information on consultations on changing the committee structure is based on the author's role in heading US preparations for the 1985 Review Conference.

22 'Final Document of the Third Review Conference of the Parties to the Treaty on the Non-Proliferation of Nuclear Weapons', 1985, p. 112, https://unoda-web.s3-accelerate.amazonaws.com/wp-content/uploads/assets/WMD/Nuclear/pdf/finaldocs/1985%20-%20 Geneva%20-%20NPT%20Review%20 Conference%20-%20Final%20 Document%20Part%20I.pdf.

23 United Nations Office for Disarmament Affairs, 'Memorandum of Conversation', 31 July 1985, National Security Archive, George Washington University, p. 11, https://nsarchive2. gwu.edu/NSAEBB/NSAEBB481/docs/ Document%203.pdf.

24 The existence of two Soviet speeches was made known to the author by a former Soviet diplomat some years later.

25 United Nations Office for Disarmament Affairs, 'Final Document of the Third Review Conference of the Parties to the Treaty on the Non-Proliferation of Nuclear Weapons', 1985, p. 14.

26 Hooper and Rissanen, 'Transcript of Interview with Ambassador Roland Timerbaev'.

27 Timerbaev, 'In Memoriam: George Bunn (1925–2013)'.

28 'Department of State: Memorandum of Conversation – Nonproliferation Treaty', 17 May 1968, National Security Archive, George Washington University, https://nsarchive2.gwu. edu/nukevault/ebb253/doc24.pdf.

29 The First Preparatory Committee Meeting for the 1985 Review Conference took place on 2–6 April 1984 and the Second Preparatory Committee Meeting took place on 1–11 October 1984.

30 Timerbaev, 'In Memoriam: George Bunn (1925–2013)'.

31 Once China and France joined the NPT in the early 1990s, this unique NPT-derived institutional US–Soviet dimension and dynamic first faded and then eventually ceased to exist. It has been suggested that this change made it more complicated and ultimately harder to cooperate closely with Moscow in the new configuration of five NPT nuclear-weapons states, of which two were close US allies.

32 A similar proposal also has been made by Robert Einhorn in 'Prospects for U.S.–Russian nonproliferation cooperation', Brookings Institution, 26 February 2016, https://www.brookings. edu/research/prospects-for-u-s-russian-nonproliferation-cooperation; see also Dunn, 'Redefining the U.S. Agenda for Nuclear Disarmament', pp. 60–61.

33 On such actions by the five NPT nuclear-weapons states – either bilaterally, as with Russia and the

US, or as a grouping – to address the concerns raised by the humanitarian movement about the risk of use

of nuclear weapons, see Dunn, 'Redefining the U.S. Agenda for Nuclear Disarmament', pp. 71–72.

Chapter Five

[1]   The author wishes to thank Mr Louis Nosenzo for reading earlier drafts of this chapter and providing many useful comments, recollections and insights.

[2]   Todd Perry, 'The Origins and Implementation of the 1992 Nuclear Suppliers Group (NSG) Agreement', PhD dissertation, University of Maryland, 2002, p. 80.

[3]   The domestic actors and foreign-policy considerations that formed the US posture on nuclear exports in the mid-1950s are analysed in Mara Drogan, 'The Nuclear Imperative: Atoms for Peace and the Development of US Policy on Exporting Nuclear Power 1953–55', *Diplomatic History*, vol. 40, no. 5, 1 November 2016, p. 972.

[4]   Leonard Weiss, 'Atoms for Peace', *Bulletin of the Atomic Scientists*, vol. 59, no. 6, 1 November 2003, pp. 40–41; Peter Lavoy, 'The Enduring Effects of Atoms for Peace', *Arms Control Today*, 1 December 2003, https://www.armscontrol.org/act/2003_12/Lavoy.

[5]   Mark Hibbs, 'A More Geopoliticized Nuclear Suppliers Group', *Strategic Trade Review*, vol. 3, no. 5, Autumn 2017, pp. 5–24, https://strategictraderesearch.org/wp-content/uploads/2018/01/Strategic-Trade-Review-Autumn-2017.pdf.

[6]   William Potter, 'Nuclear Export Policy: A Soviet–American Comparison', in Charles W. Kegley, Jr and Pat McGowan (eds), *Foreign Policy: USA/USSR*, Sage International Yearbook of Foreign Policy Studies (Beverly Hills, CA: Sage Publications, 1982), p. 297.

[7]   *Ibid.*, p. 297. Their pursuit of this objective led the US to engage large numbers of Indian scientists on nuclear-energy projects and was behind the Soviet establishment of the Joint Institute for Nuclear Research in Dubna, where Chinese scientists were able to train. It prompted the US to sell a research reactor and highly enriched uranium to South Africa and the USSR to conclude a nuclear-cooperation agreement with Yugoslavia.

[8]   Alfred Goldberg, 'The McNamara Ascendancy 1961–65: History of the Office of the Secretary of Defense volume V' (Washington DC: US Government Printing Office, 1984), p. 419, http://history.defense.gov/Portals/70/Documents/secretaryofdefense/OSDSeries_Vol5.pdf.

[9]   Fritz W. Schmidt, 'The Zangger Committee: Its History and Future Role', *Nonproliferation Review*, vol. 2, no. 1, Fall 1994, p. 38.

[10] US Department of State, Office of the Historian, '52: Paper Prepared by an Interagency Working Group: Implications of the Indian Test', 30 May 1974, Foreign Relations of the United States, 1969–76, vol. E-14, part 2, https://history.state.gov/historicaldocuments/frus1969-76ve14p2/d52.

[11] *Ibid.*

12 *Ibid.*

13 Or Rabinowitz and Jayita Sarkar, 'It isn't over until the fuel cell sings: a reassessment of the US and French pledges of nuclear assistance in the 1970s', *Journal of Strategic Studies*, vol. 41, no. 1–2, 2017, pp. 275–300.

14 Joseph Nye, 'US–Soviet Cooperation in a Nonproliferation Regime', in Alexander L. George, Philip J. Farley and Alexander Dalling (eds), *US–Soviet Security Cooperation: Achievements, Failures, Lessons* (New York: Oxford University Press, 1988), p. 344; US Department of State, Office of the Historian, '31. Paper Prepared by the National Security Council Under Secretaries Committee: Action Plan for Implementing National Security Decision Memorandum 235', 1 March 1974, Foreign Relations of the United States, 1969–76, vol. E-14, part 2, Documents on Arms Control and Nonproliferation, 1973–76, https://history.state.gov/historicaldocuments/frus1969-76ve14p2/d31.

15 Jaclyn Tandler, 'French Nuclear Diplomacy: Grand Failure?', *Nonproliferation Review*, vol. 21, no. 2, 2014.

16 US Department of State, Office of the Historian, '45. Memorandum From Michael Guhin of the National Security Council Staff to Secretary of State Kissinger', 16 May 1974, Foreign Relations of the United States, 1969–76, vol. E-14, part 2, Documents on Arms Control and Nonproliferation, 1973–76, https://history.state.gov/historicaldocuments/frus1969-76ve14p2/d45.

17 US Department of State, Office of the Historian, '53. National Security Decision Memorandum 255: Security and Other Aspects of the Growth and Dissemination of Nuclear Power Industries', 3 June 1974, Foreign Relations of the United States, 1969–76, vol. E-14, part 2, Documents on Arms Control and Nonproliferation, 1973–76, https://history.state.gov/historicaldocuments/frus1969-76ve14p2/d53.

18 US Department of State, Office of the Historian, '65. Minutes of Secretary of State Kissinger's Analytical Staff Meeting', 12 July 1974, Foreign Relations of the United States, 1969–76, vol. E-14, part 2, Documents on Arms Control and Nonproliferation, 1973–76, https://history.state.gov/historicaldocuments/frus1969-76ve14p2/d65.

19 US Department of State, Office of the Historian, '57. Paper Prepared by the NSC Under Secretaries Committee: US Nonproliferation Policy', 21 June 1974, Foreign Relations of the United States, 1969–76, vol. E-14, part 2, Documents on Arms Control and Nonproliferation, 1973–76, https://history.state.gov/historicaldocuments/frus1969-76ve14p2/d57.

20 US Department of State, Office of the Historian, '65. Minutes of Secretary of State Kissinger's Analytical Staff Meeting', 12 July 1974.

21 'US Department of State: The Secretary's Analytical Staff Meeting on Nonproliferation, 2 August 1974', 8 August 1974, National Security Archive, George Washington University, https://nsarchive2.gwu.edu/nukevault/ebb467/docs/doc%20 7%208-2-74%20staff%20meeting.pdf.

22 *Ibid.*

23 This experience is detailed in Chapter One. See also 'US Department of State: Consultations with the Soviets on Non-proliferation Strategy', 18 September 1974, National Security Archive, George Washington

University, http://nsarchive2.gwu.edu//nukevault/ebb467/docs/doc%20 9A%209-18-74%20consultations%20 with%20Sovs.pdf.

24 US Department of State, Office of the Historian, '65. Minutes of Secretary of State Kissinger's Analytical Staff Meeting', 12 July 1974.

25 US Department of State, Office of the Historian, '57. Paper Prepared by the NSC Under Secretaries Committee: US Nonproliferation Policy', 21 June 1974.

26 Cable from US mission UN New York to Secretary of State, 'Talk with Soviet MFA official on NPT review conference and non-proliferation at UNGA', 17 December 1974, US National Archives, https://aad.archives.gov/aad/createpdf?rid=28243 9&dt=2474&dl=1345; US Department of State, Office of the Historian, '41. Statement by the United States Representative to the Conference of the Committee on Disarmament (Martin)', 16 April 1974, Foreign Relations of the United States, 1969–76, vol. E-14, part 2, Documents on Arms Control and Nonproliferation, 1973–76, https://history.state.gov/historicaldocuments/frus1969-76ve14p2/d41.

27 US Department of State, Office of the Historian, '58. Memorandum of Conversation: ABM; Test Ban', 28 June 1974, Foreign Relations of the United States, 1969–76, vol. E-14, part 2, Documents on Arms Control and Nonproliferation, 1973–76, https://history.state.gov/historicaldocuments/frus1969-76ve14p2/d58.

28 US Department of State, Office of the Historian, '72. Action Memorandum From the Director of the Arms Control and Disarmament Agency (Iklé) and the Director of the Policy Planning Staff (Lord) to Secretary of State Kissinger',

26 August 1974, Foreign Relations of the United States, 1969–76, vol. E-14, part 2, Documents on Arms Control and Nonproliferation, 1973–76, https://history.state.gov/historicaldocuments/frus1969-76ve14p2/d72.

29 Ibid.

30 'US Department of State: The Secretary's Analytical Staff Meeting on Nonproliferation, 2 August 1974', 8 August 1974.

31 Ibid., p. 15.

32 Ibid., p. 35.

33 US Department of State, Office of the Historian, '40. Memorandum of Conversation', 21 September 1974, Foreign Relations of the United States, 1969–76, vol. 16, Soviet Union, August 1974–December 1976, https://history.state.gov/historicaldocuments/frus1969-76v16/d40.

34 Ibid.

35 Ibid.

36 Cable from Secretary of State to US Embassy Moscow, 'Nuclear safeguards consultation', 17 October 1974, US National Archives, https://aad.archives.gov/aad/createpdf?rid=23 4399&dt=2474&dl=1345.

37 Ibid.

38 Cable from US Embassy Moscow to Secretary of State, 'Nuclear safeguards consultation, second meeting', 23 October 1974, US National Archives, https://aad.archives.gov/aad/createpdf ?rid=234754&dt=2474&dl=1345.

39 Cable from US Mission IAEA Vienna to Secretary of State, 'Negotiation of Argentine safeguards agreement with IAEA', 14 August 1974, US National Archives, https://aad.archives.gov/aad/createpdf?rid=182049&dt=2474 &dl=1345.

40 Cable from US Mission IAEA Vienna to Secretary of State, 'NPT exporters

committee – Soviet position', 29 July 1974, US National Archives, https://aad.archives.gov/aad/createpdf?rid=159036&dt=2474&dl=1345.

41 Cable from US Embassy Moscow to Secretary of State, 'Nuclear safeguards consultations first plenary session, message number one', 22 October 1974, US National Archives, https://aad.archives.gov/aad/createpdf?rid=234695&dt=2474&dl=1345.

42 'US Department of State: Consultations with the Soviets on Non-proliferation Strategy', 18 September 1974'.

43 Cable from US Embassy Moscow to Secretary of State, 'Nuclear safeguards consultations first plenary session, message number one', 22 October 1974.

44 *Ibid.*

45 *Ibid.*

46 *Ibid.*

47 Cable from Secretary of State to US Embassy Moscow, 'Nuclear safeguards consultations', 26 October 1974, US National Archives, https://aad.archives.gov/aad/createpdf?rid=232924&dt=2474&dl=1345.

48 *Ibid.*

49 Cable from Secretary of State to US Embassy Moscow, 'Nuclear safeguards consultations', 5 November 1975, US National Archives, https://aad.archives.gov/aad/createpdf?rid=260293&dt=2474&dl=1345.

50 Cable from Secretary of State to US Embassy Moscow, 'Nuclear safeguards consultations', 26 October 1974.

51 Cable from US Embassy Moscow to Secretary of State, 'Nuclear Safeguards Consultations – Verbatim Of Third Plenary October 29, Message Number 3', 30 October 1974, US National Archives, https://aad.archives.gov/aad/createpdf?rid=233499&dt=2474&dl=1345.

52 *Ibid.*

53 Cable from Secretary of State to US Embassy Moscow, 'Nuclear Safeguards Consultations', 26 October 1974.

54 Cable from US Embassy Moscow to Secretary of State, 'Nuclear Safeguards Consultations, Second Meeting', 23 October 1974.

55 Cable from Secretary of State to US Embassy Moscow, 'Nuclear Safeguards Consultations', 26 October 1974.

56 Cable from US Embassy Moscow to Secretary of State, 'Nuclear Safeguards Consultations – Verbatim Of Third Plenary October 29, Message Number 3', 30 October 1974.

57 *Ibid.*

58 Cable from US Embassy Moscow to Secretary of State, 'Nuclear Safeguards Consultations – Verbatim Report of Nov 5 Plenary, Message Number Eight', 6 November 1974, US National Archives, https://aad.archives.gov/aad/createpdf?rid=260329&dt=2474&dl=1345.

59 *Ibid.*

60 Cable from US Embassy Moscow to Secretary of State, 'Nuclear Safeguards Consultations – Summary of Nov. 5 Plenary', 5 November 1974, US National Archives, https://aad.archives.gov/aad/createpdf?rid=260273&dt=2474&dl=1345.

61 Cable from US Embassy Moscow to Secretary of State, 'Soviets Again Propose General Bilateral Review Of Nuclear Matters', 29 November 1974, US National Archives, https://aad.archives.gov/aad/createpdf?rid=260692&dt=2474&dl=1345.

62 Cable from Secretary of State to US Embassy Moscow, 'Nuclear Safeguards Consultations', 9 December

1974, US National Archives, https://aad.archives.gov/aad/createpdf?rid=28
2188&dt=2474&dl=1345.

63 Cable from US Embassy Moscow to Secretary of State, 'Nuclear Questions', 20 December 1974, US National Archives, https://aad.archives.gov/aad/createpdf?rid=282523&dt=2474&dl=1345; Cable from US Embassy Moscow to Secretary of State, 'Bilateral Technical PNE Consultations with USSR', 7 January 1975, US National Archives, https://aad.archives.gov/aad/createpdf?rid=124884&dt=2476&dl=1345.

64 While the USSR was interested in conducting bilateral consultations with the US on export controls and other issues, the US was adamant about the need to include other countries in these negotiations. See paragraph F in cable from Secretary of State to US Embassy Moscow, 'Nuclear Safeguards Consultations', 26 October 1974.

65 Cable from Secretary of State to US Mission IAEA Vienna, 'Coordination of Nuclear Export Policy: Soviet CIEWS [sic]', 30 November 1974, US National Archives, https://aad.archives.gov/aad/createpdf?rid=260876&dt=2474&dl=1345.

66 Ibid.

67 Cable from Secretary of State to US Embassy Moscow, 'Nuclear Suppliers' Conference', 10 April 1975, US National Archives, https://aad.archives.gov/aad/createpdf?rid=14890&dt=2476&dl=1345.

68 Cable from Secretary of State to US Embassy Moscow, 'Nuclear Safeguards Consultations', 9 December 1974, US National Archives, https://aad.archives.gov/aad/createpdf?rid=282188&dt=2474&dl=1345.

69 'US Department of State: Nuclear Suppliers Conference/French Participation', 26 March 1975, National Security Archive, George Washington University, https://nsarchive2.gwu.edu/nukevault/ebb467/docs/doc%2013D%203-26-75%20background%20on%20French%20participation.pdf.

70 Ibid.

71 US Department of State, Office of the Historian, '105: Memorandum of Conversation: European Unity; Nuclear Proliferation', 16 December 1974, Foreign Relations of the United States, 1969–76, vol. E-14, part 2, Documents on Arms Control and Nonproliferation, 1973–76, https://history.state.gov/historicaldocuments/frus1969-76ve14p2/d105.

72 William Burr, 'A Scheme of "Control": The United States and the Origins of the Nuclear Suppliers' Group, 1974–76', International History Review, vol. 36, no. 2, 2014, p. 263.

73 US Department of State, Office of the Historian, '138: Minutes of a Verification Panel Meeting: Nuclear Non-Proliferation', 19 April 1975, Foreign Relations of the United States, 1969–76, vol. E-14, part 2, Documents on Arms Control and Nonproliferation, 1973–76, https://history.state.gov/historicaldocuments/frus1969-76ve14p2/d138.

74 Cable from Secretary of State to US Embassy Paris, 'Exploratory Meeting of Nuclear Suppliers', 19 April 1975, US National Archives, https://aad.archives.gov/aad/createpdf?rid=18798&dt=2476&dl=1345.

75 'US Department of State: Nuclear Suppliers Conference/French Participation', 26 March 1975.

76 Cable from Secretary of State to US Embassy Tripoli, 'Morokhov Comments on Soviet–Libyan Nuclear Cooperation; FRG–Brazil Nuclear Coopera-

tion; Nuclear Suppliers Conference', 3 July 1975, US National Archives, https://aad.archives.gov/aad/createpdf?rid=148170&dt=2476&dl=1345.

77 Cable from US Embassy London to Secretary of State, 'Nuclear Suppliers Conference: Bilateral with Soviets', 18 June 1975, US National Archives, https://aad.archives.gov/aad/createpdf?rid=177515&dt=2476&dl=1345.

78 US Department of State, Office of the Historian, '160. Memorandum From David Elliott and Jan Lodal of the National Security Council Staff to Secretary of State Kissinger', 6 September 1975, Foreign Relations of the United States, 1969–76, vol. E-14, part 2, Documents on Arms Control and Nonproliferation, 1973–76, https://history.state.gov/historicaldocuments/frus1969-76ve14p2/d160.

79 Ibid.

80 Cable from Secretary of State to US Mission Geneva, 'US/French Talks on Nuclear Export Matters', 30 May 1975, US National Archives, https://aad.archives.gov/aad/createpdf?rid=236732&dt=2476&dl=1345.

81 'National Security Council: National Security Decision Memorandum 261: Nuclear Sales to the PRC', 22 July 1974, Richard Nixon Presidential Library and Museum, https://www.nixonlibrary.gov/virtuallibrary/documents/nsdm/nsdm_261.pdf.

82 Cable from US Embassy Bonn to Secretary of State, 'COCOM-Sale of Nuclear Power Plant to USSR', 21 October 1974, US National Archives, https://aad.archives.gov/aad/createpdf?rid=234590&dt=2474&dl=1345.

83 Cable from Secretary of State to US Mission Geneva, 'US/French Talks on Nuclear Export Matters', 30 May 1975.

84 US Department of State, Office of the Historian, '160. Memorandum From David Elliott and Jan Lodal of the National Security Council Staff to Secretary of State Kissinger'.

85 Cable from US Embassy Paris to Secretary of State, 'French Bilateral Requests', 11 September 1975, US National Archives, https://aad.archives.gov/aad/createpdf?rid=324331&dt=2476&dl=1345.

86 Cable from Secretary of State to US Mission IAEA Vienna, 'French/Soviet Accord on Nuclear Exports', 11 November 1975, US National Archives, https://aad.archives.gov/aad/createpdf?rid=262953&dt=2476&dl=1345.

87 'Assistant Secretary of State for Politico-Military Affairs George S. Vest to the Secretary of State: September 16–17 Nuclear Suppliers' Meeting', 23 September 1975, National Security Archive, George Washington University, http://nsarchive.gwu.edu/nukevault/ebb467/docs/doc%2015A%209-23-75%20status%20of%20nsg.pdf.

88 Ibid.

89 Cable from US Mission IAEA Vienna to Secretary of State, 'Soviet Views on IAE Safeguards and Non-Proliferation', 23 September 1975, US National Archives, https://aad.archives.gov/aad/createpdf?rid=323110&dt=2476&dl=1345.

90 Ibid.

91 Ibid.

92 Ibid.

93 Cable from US Embassy London to Secretary of State, 'Nuclear Suppliers Conference – Multilateral Proceedings, November 4–5', 6 November 1975, US National Archives, https://aad.archives.gov/aad/createpdf?rid=262390&dt=2476&dl=1345.

94 Cable from US Embassy Ottawa to Secretary of State, 'Nuclear Suppliers

Guidelines Implementation', 4 February 1976, US National Archives, https://aad.archives.gov/aad/createpdf?rid=86360&dt=2082&dl=1345.

95 'US Department of State: Action Memorandum: Department Position on White House Nuclear Policy Review, from Robinson to Secretary', 4 September 1976, Princeton University, US State Department Cables Event Exploration, http://www.princeton.edu/~achaney/capsule/doc/1976STATE220666.

96 Dani K. Nedal and Tatiana Coutto, 'Brazil's 1975 Nuclear Agreement with West Germany', Wilson Center Nuclear Proliferation International History Project, 13 August 2013, https://www.wilsoncenter.org/publication/brazils-1975-nuclear-agreement-west-germany.

97 Cable from Secretary of State to US Embassy Bonn, 'FRG Nuclear Exports; Ref: (A) Bonn 07964, (B) State', 7 June 1975, US National Archives, https://aad.archives.gov/aad/createpdf?rid=177358&dt=2476&dl=1345.

98 Cable from US Mission IAEA Vienna to Secretary of State, 'US/USSR Informal Consultations', 25 July 1975, US National Archives, https://aad.archives.gov/aad/createpdf?rid=151997&dt=2476&dl=1345.

99 William Glenn Gray, 'Commercial Liberties and Nuclear Anxieties: The US–German Feud over Brazil, 1975–7', *International History Review*, vol. 34, no. 3, p. 459.

100 *Ibid.*, p. 455.

101 Cable from US Mission IAEA Vienna to Secretary of State, 'FRG/IAEA/Brazil Trilateral Safeguards Agreement', 13 February 1976, US National Archives, https://aad.archives.gov/aad/createpdf?rid=86410&dt=2082&dl=1345; Cable from US Mission IAEA Vienna to

Secretary of State, 'FRG/IAEA/Brazil Trilateral Safeguards Agreement', 17 February 1976, US National Archives, https://aad.archives.gov/aad/createpdf?rid=93185&dt=2082&dl=1345.

102 Cable from US Embassy Moscow to Secretary of State, 'Nuclear Suppliers Agreement at IAEA: Soviet Comments', 19 February 1976, US National Archives, https://aad.archives.gov/aad/createpdf?rid=93173&dt=2082&dl=1345.

103 Cable from Secretary of State to US Embassy Dacca [Dhaka], 'FRG/Brazil/IAEA Safeguards Agreement', 12 March 1976, US National Archives, https://aad.archives.gov/aad/createpdf?rid=228025&dt=2082&dl=1345.

104 Cable from Secretary of State to US Del Secretary, 'Memorandum of Conversation between Mr. Ingersoll and German Ambassador Von Staden', 18 February 1976, US National Archives, https://aad.archives.gov/aad/createpdf?rid=86473&dt=2082&dl=1345.

105 Cable from US Embassy Moscow to Secretary of State, 'Nuclear Suppliers Agreement at IAEA: Soviet Comments', 19 February 1976.

106 Cable from Secretary of State to US Embassy Dacca [Dhaka], 'FRG/BRAZIL/IAEA Safeguards Agreement', 12 March 1976.

107 Cable from US Mission IAEA Vienna to Secretary of State, 'FRG/Brazil/IAEA Safeguards Agreement', 20 February 1976, US National Archives, https://aad.archives.gov/aad/createpdf?rid=93213&dt=2082&dl=1345.

108 *Ibid.*

109 Cable from Secretary of State to US Embassy Dacca [Dhaka], 'FRG/BRAZIL/IAEA Safeguards Agreement', 12 March 1976.

110 *Ibid.*

111 *Ibid.*

112 'US Department of State: Consultations with the Soviets on Non-proliferation Strategy', 18 September 1974'.

113 Cable from US Embassy Paris to Secretary of State, 'French Reaction to INFCE and September London Suppliers Meeting', 14 September 1977, US National Archives, https://aad.archives.gov/aad/createpdf?rid=21 1157&dt=2532&dl=1629.

114 Cable from US Embassy London to Secretary of State, 'Soviet–US Bilateral on Non-Proliferation', 21 September 1977, US National Archives, https://aad.archives.gov/aad/createpdf?rid=21 8067&dt=2532&dl=1629.

115 *Ibid.*

116 Cable from Secretary of State to US Embassy London, 'Nuclear Suppliers Meeting – Assessment', 23 September 1977, US National Archives, https:// aad.archives.gov/aad/createpdf?rid=22 1426&dt=2532&dl=1629.

117 'US Department of State: The Secretary's Analytical Staff Meeting on Non-Proliferation, Friday, August 2, 1974', 8 August 1974, National Security Archive, George Washington University, p. 41, https://nsarchive2. gwu.edu/nukevault/ebb467/docs/ doc%207%208-2-74%20staff%20 meeting.pdf.

118 Cable from US Mission IAEA Vienna to Secretary of State, 'NPT Exporters Committee – Soviet Position', 29 July 1974, US National Archives, https:// aad.archives.gov/aad/createpdf?rid=15 9036&dt=2474&dl=1345.

119 'US Department of State: Action Memorandum: Department Position on White House Nuclear Policy Review, from Robinson to Secretary', 4 September 1976.

Chapter Six

1 International Atomic Energy Agency, 'Treaty on the Non-Proliferation of Nuclear Weapons', Notification of the entry into force, 22 April 1970, https://www.iaea.org/sites/default/files/publications/documents/infcircs/1970/infcirc140.pdf.

2 One exception to this position occurred in the context of comprehensive test-ban negotiations in the late 1950s, when the Soviet Union reluctantly agreed to a limited number of on-site inspections. When the US proposed increasing this number, however, Moscow backed out of its agreement to the verification measure. This experience only reinforced the negative attitude toward on-site inspections in general displayed by Soviet policymakers.

3 'State Department: Aide-Memoire on the Draft Non-Proliferation Treaty (NPT)', 24 August 1967, National Security Archive, George Washington University, https://nsarchive.gwu.edu/ nukevault/ebb253/doc05b.pdf.

4 John Krige, 'Euratom and the IAEA: The Problem of Self-Inspection', *Cold War History*, vol. 15, no. 3, 2015.

5 'Preoccupation with West Germany's Nuclear Weapons Potential Shaped Kennedy-Era Diplomacy', Briefing Book no. 617, National Security Archive, George Washington University, 2 February 2018, https:// nsarchive.gwu.edu/briefing-book/

nuclear-vault/2018-02-02/german-nuclear-question-nonproliferation-treaty.

6   'Department of State: Memorandum of Conversation: Non-dissemination and the MLF', 10 October 1963, National Security Archive, George Washington University, https://nsarchive2.gwu.edu//dc.html?doc=4364708-Document-25-Memcon-Non-Dissemination-and-the-MLF.

7   'Comments on the Proposed Revision of the Draft Non-Proliferation Treaty, Deputy Under Secretary of State for Political Affairs U. Alexis Johnson to the Secretary of State', 8 July 1966, National Security Archive, George Washington University, https://nsarchive.gwu.edu//dc.html?doc=4415114-Document-13-Deputy-Under-Secretary-of-State-for.

8   'Nonproliferation Treaty, Memorandum for the Secretary of Defense, Joint Chiefs of Staff', 29 June 1966, Digital National Security Archive.

9   United States Arms Control and Disarmament Agency, 'International Negotiations on the Treaty on the Nonproliferation of Nuclear Weapons', 1969, p. 70.

10 George Bunn, 'Brief History of NPT Safeguards Article', 6 February 2006, Center for Global Security, Pacific Northwest National Laboratory, https://cgs.pnnl.gov/fois/doclib/NPTNegHist.Art.III.6%20Feb.06.pdf.

11 'National Intelligence Estimate, NIE 4-66: The Likelihood of Further Nuclear Proliferation', 20 January 1966, Wilson Center Digital Archive, http://digitalarchive.wilsoncenter.org/document/116887.

12 'Report by William C. Foster, Director, US Arms Control and Disarmament Agency, to the President', 29 December 1966, Digital National Security Archive.

13 Ibid.

14 Roland Timerbaev, *Rossiya i Yadernoe Nerasprostranenie* [*Russia and Nuclear Non-proliferation*] (Moscow: Nauka, 1999), p. 287; George Bunn, *Arms Control by Committee* (Stanford, CA: Stanford University Press, 1992), p. 98.

15 The same procedure was used for similar issues and in similar circumstances in the context of arms-control negotiations in the 1980s.

16 International Atomic Energy Agency, 'Treaty on the Non-Proliferation of Nuclear Weapons'.

17 United States Arms Control and Disarmament Agency, 'Memorandum: Basic Issues Regarding NPT and Timing of Ratification', 22 November 1968, National Security Archive, George Washington University, https://nsarchive.gwu.edu/nukevault/ebb253/doc34.pdf.

18 Timerbaev, *Rossiya i Yadernoe Nerasprostranenie* , pp. 296–97.

19 Cable from Secretary of State to US Embassy Moscow, 'Nuclear Safeguards Consultations', 17 October 1974, Wilson Center Digital Archive, http://digitalarchive.wilsoncenter.org/document/119781.

20 Ibid.

21 One exception to this general rule involved Romania, which embarked on a largely independent nuclear-energy programme.

22 Cable from Secretary of State to US Embassy Moscow, 'Nuclear Safeguards Consultations', 17 October 1974.

23 'Department of State Action Memorandum: Talks on Reactor Safeguards and Related Matters with the Soviets on October 15', 5 October

1974, Wilson Center Digital Archive, http://digitalarchive.wilsoncenter.org/document/119780.

24 Cable from Secretary of State to US Embassy New Delhi, 'Soviet Sale of Heavy Water to India', 10 December 1976, US National Archives, https://aad.archives.gov/aad/createpdf?rid=74040&dt=2082&dl=1345.

25 Cable from US Consul Rio de Janeiro to Secretary of State, 'IAEA 20th General Conference: Meeting with USSR Reps, Sept 22, 1976 During IAEA General Conference', 24 September 1976, US National Archives, https://aad.archives.gov/aad/createpdf?rid=344920&dt=2082&dl=1345.

26 'Department of State Action Memorandum: Talks on Reactor Safeguards and Related Matters with the Soviets on October 15', 5 October 1974.

27 Cable from US Mission to IAEA Vienna to Secretary of State, 'Discussions with Professor Morokhov, USSR State Committee on Peaceful Uses of Atomic Energy', 3 March 1976, US National Archives, https://aad.archives.gov/aad/createpdf?rid=228243&dt=2082&dl=1345.

28 *Ibid.*

29 This cooperation was interrupted during the period immediately following the Soviet invasion of Afghanistan in 1979 when prior routine bilateral interactions were suspended in a number of fora.

30 Vladimir Orlov, 'Iran, North Korea, and the Tomorrow of Nonproliferation', *Yadernyi Kontrol [Nuclear Control]*, 2003.

31 'Fact Sheet No. 3: Safeguards Resolution', James Martin Center for Nonproliferation Studies, September 2014, https://www.nonproliferation.org/wp-content/uploads/2014/09/2014_IAEA_GC_QA_Safeguards.pdf. The state-level approach optimised the use of resources available to the IAEA, which was particularly valuable under the principle of zero budget growth and the expanding volume of work in the post-Iraq environment. See Laura Rockwood, 'The IAEA's State-Level Concept and the Law of Unintended Consequences', *Arms Control Today*, September 2014, https://www.armscontrol.org/act/2014_09/Features/The-IAEAs-State-Level-Concept-and-the-Law-of-Unintended-Consequences.

32 Mark Hibbs, 'Russia's Safeguards Problem', *Arms Control Wonk*, 3 December 2012, https://www.armscontrolwonk.com/archive/1101196/russias-safeguards-problem.

33 *Ibid.*

Chapter Seven

1 'Joint Communique Issued by the United States and the Soviet Union on Conclusion of Summit Talks in Vienna', 18 June 1979, in US Arms Control and Disarmament Agency, 'Documents on Disarmament, 1979', p. 229, https://unoda-web.s3-accelerate.amazonaws.com/wp-content/uploads/assets/publications/documents_on_disarmament/1979/DoD_1979.pdf.

2 The authors were surprised by the number of past and present US

diplomats who were unfamiliar with the draft convention.

3   United Nations General Assembly, 'Resolution A/RES/1(I): Establishment of a Commission to Deal with the Problems Raised by the Discovery of Atomic Energy', Para. 5(c), 24 January 1946, https://documents-dds-ny.un.org/doc/RESOLUTION/GEN/NR0/032/52/IMG/NR003252.pdf?OpenElement.

4   'Commission for Conventional Armaments: Resolutions Adopted by the Commission at its Thirteenth Meeting, 12 August 1948, and a Second Progress Report of the Commission', 18 August 1948, p. 2, http://repository.un.org/handle/11176/332321; Jerzy Zaleski, 'New Types and Systems of WMD: Consideration by the CD. UNIDIR', May 2011, p. 1, http://www.unidir.org/files/publications/pdfs/new-types-and-systems-of-wmd-consideration-by-the-cd-374.pdf.

5   'Maltese Draft Resolution Introduced in the First Committee of the General Assembly: Updating of United Nations Disarmament Publication', 1 December 1969, in US Arms Control and Disarmament Agency, 'Documents on Disarmament, 1969', pp. 616, 712, http://unoda-web.s3-accelerate.amazonaws.com/wp-content/uploads/assets/publications/documents_on_disarmament/1969/DoD_1969.pdf.

6   'Statement by the British Representative (Chalfont) to the First Committee of the General Assembly', 9 December 1969, in US Arms Control and Disarmament Agency, 'Documents on Disarmament, 1969', pp. 653–54.

7   'Statement by the United States Representative (Leonard) to the First Committee of the General Assembly', 9 December 1969, in US Arms Control and Disarmament Agency, 'Documents on Disarmament, 1969', p. 659.

8   'Statement by the Soviet Representative (Roshchin) to the First Committee of the General Assembly', 9 December 1969, in US Arms Control and Disarmament Agency, 'Documents on Disarmament, 1969', pp. 616, 712.

9   'Statement by the Soviet Representative (Roshchin) to the Conference of the Committee on Disarmament', 3 September 1970, in US Arms Control and Disarmament Agency, 'Documents on Disarmament, 1970', p. 499, http://unoda-web.s3-accelerate.amazonaws.com/wp-content/uploads/assets/publications/documents_on_disarmament/1970/DoD_1970.pdf.

10   'Netherlands Working Paper Submitted to the Conference of the Committee on Disarmament: Radiological Warfare', 14 July 1970, in US Arms Control and Disarmament Agency, 'Documents on Disarmament, 1970', p. 308–09.

11   'Statement by the Swedish Representative (Myrdal) to the Conference of the Committee on Disarmament', 13 August 1970, in US Arms Control and Disarmament Agency, 'Documents on Disarmament, 1970', p. 418.

12   'Soviet Draft Agreement on the Prohibition of the Development and Manufacture of New Types of Weapons of Mass Destruction and New Systems of Such Weapons', 23 September 1975, in US Arms Control and Disarmament Agency, 'Documents on Disarmament, 1975', pp. 479–82; 'Soviet Draft Resolution Introduced in the First Committee of the General Assembly: Prohibition of the Development and Manufacture

of New Types of Weapons of Mass Destruction and New Systems of Such Weapons', 30 September 1975, in US Arms Control and Disarmament Agency, 'Documents on Disarmament, 1975', p. 495 (see pp. 798–803 for text of the final resolution and draft agreement).

13 Cable from US Embassy Moscow to Secretary of State, 'Brezhnev election speech: first impressions', June 1975, US National Archives, https://aad.archives.gov/aad/createpdf?rid=178262&dt=2476&dl=1345.

14 Christopher S. Wren, 'Brezhnev Calls for Accord Against "Terrifying Arms"', *New York Times*, 14 June 1975, http://www.nytimes.com/1975/06/14/archives/front-page-1-no-title-brezhnev-urges-accord-against-terrifying-arms.html.

15 'Soviet Draft Agreement on the Prohibition of the Development and Manufacture of New Types of Weapons of Mass Destruction and New Systems of Such Weapons' and 'Soviet Draft Resolution Introduced in the First Committee of the General Assembly: Prohibition of the Development and Manufacture of New Types of Weapons of Mass Destruction and New Systems of Such Weapons', in US Arms Control and Disarmament Agency, 'Documents on Disarmament, 1975'.

16 *Ibid.*, p. 799.

17 'Address by Soviet Foreign Minister Gromyko to the General Assembly [Extract]', 23 September 1975, in US Arms Control and Disarmament Agency, 'Documents on Disarmament, 1975', p. 484; 'Letter from Foreign Minister Gromyko to Secretary-General Waldheim: Ban on New Weapons Systems', 23 September 1975, in US Arms Control and Disarmament Agency, 'Documents on Disarmament, 1975', p. 478.

18 'Soviet Draft Agreement on the Prohibition of the Development and Manufacture of New Types of Weapons of Mass Destruction and New Systems of Such Weapons' and 'Soviet Draft Resolution Introduced in the First Committee of the General Assembly: Prohibition of the Development and Manufacture of New Types of Weapons of Mass Destruction and New Systems of Such Weapons', in US Arms Control and Disarmament Agency, 'Documents on Disarmament, 1975', p. 800.

19 Cable from Secretary of State to US Mission to the UN, New York, 'Soviets seek US support for UNGA initiative on mass destruction weapons', October 1975, US National Archives, https://aad.archives.gov/aad/createpdf?rid=290890&dt=2476&dl=1345.

20 Cable from Secretary of State to US Mission to the UN, New York, 'UNGA disarmament: Soviet mass destruction weapons (MDW) proposal', November 1975, US National Archives, https://aad.archives.gov/aad/createpdf?rid=265136&dt=2476&dl=1345.

21 Cable from Secretary of State to US Mission to the UN, New York, 'Soviets seek US support for UNGA initiative on mass destruction weapons', October 1975.

22 *Ibid.*

23 Cable from US Mission to the UN, New York, to Secretary of State,' 'UNGA Disarmament: Consultations with USSR On Soviet Mass Destruction Weapons (MDW) Proposal', 15 November 1975, US National Archives, https://aad.archives.gov/aad/createpdf?rid=266681&dt=2476&dl=1345.

24 *Ibid.*

25 *Ibid.*

26 Authors' interviews with former Soviet and Russian ambassadors, Geneva, Switzerland, December 2016.

27 Cable from US Mission to the UN, New York, to Secretary of State, 'Israelyan and Timerbayev on the Soviet MDW proposal', December 1975, US National Archives, https://aad.archives.gov/aad/createpdf?rid=75785&dt=2476&dl=1345.

28 Cable from Secretary of State to US Mission to the UN, New York, 'UNGA disarmament: Soviet mass destruction weapons (MDW) proposal', 19 November 1975.

29 *Ibid.*

30 'Statement by Soviet Representative (Roshchin) to the First Committee of the General Assembly: Weapons of Mass Destruction and Cessation of Nuclear-Weapon Tests, 2 December 1975', in US Arms Control and Disarmament Agency, 'Documents on Disarmament, 1975', pp. 720, 798–803, http://unoda-web.s3-accelerate.amazonaws.com/wp-content/uploads/assets/publications/documents_on_disarmament/1975/DoD_1975.pdf.

31 'Statement by the Italian Representative (Di Bernardo) to the First Committee of the General Assembly: Weapons of Mass Destruction, December 5, 1975' and 'Statement by the French Representative (Scalabre) to the First Committee of the General Assembly: Weapons of Mass Destruction', 5 December 1975, in US Arms Control and Disarmament Agency, 'Documents on Disarmament, 1975', pp. 734–37, http://unoda-web.s3-accelerate.amazonaws.com/wp-content/uploads/assets/publications/documents_on_disarmament/1975/DoD_1975.pdf.

32 Cable from US Mission to the UN, New York, to Secretary of State, 'UNGA disarmament 1975: review and assessment', December 1975, US National Archives, https://aad.archives.gov/aad/createpdf?rid=75783&dt=2476&dl=1345.

33 Cable from US Embassy Moscow to Secretary of State, 'Israelyan and Timerbayev on the Soviet MDW Proposal', 17 December 1975, US National Archives, https://aad.archives.gov/aad/createpdf?rid=75785&dt=2476&dl=1345.

34 *Ibid.*

35 Cable from Secretary of State to US Embassy Bonn, US Embassy London, US Embassy Paris, 'Soviet requests for bilaterals on mass destruction weapons (MDW)', February 1976, US National Archives, https://aad.archives.gov/aad/createpdf?rid=85030&dt=2082&dl=1345; US Department of State, Office of the Historian, '194. Telegram 3110 From the Mission in Geneva to the Department of State', 23 April 1976, Foreign Relations of the United States, 1969–76, vol. E-14, part 2, Documents on Arms Control and Nonproliferation, 1973–76, https://history.state.gov/historicaldocuments/frus1969-76ve14p2/d194.

36 Cable from US Secretary of State to US Mission Geneva, 'CCD – informal meetings with experts on new mass destruction weapons (MDW)', April 1976, US National Archives, https://aad.archives.gov/aad/createpdf?rid=22413&dt=2082&dl=1345.

37 Cable from US Mission Geneva to Secretary of State, 'CCD: informal meetings on new mass destruction weapons (MDW), April 7–8, 1976', April 1976, para. 10, US National Archives, https://aad.archives.gov/

aad/createpdf?rid=32494&dt=2082
&dl=1345.

38 *Ibid.*, para. 24.

39 *Ibid.*

40 Cable from Secretary of State to
US Embassy Moscow, 'Briefing
memorandum: Dobrynin approach
on MDW', May 1976, US National
Archives, https://aad.archives.gov/
aad/createpdf?rid=256487&dt=2082
&dl=1345.

41 Cable from US Mission Geneva to
Secretary of State, 'CCD – US/USSR
bilateral MDW meetings, August
9, 1976', August 1976, US National
Archives, https://aad.archives.gov/
aad/createpdf?rid=57410&dt=2082
&dl=1345.

42 'Soviet Working Paper Submitted to
the Conference of the Committee on
Disarmament: Definitions of New
Types of Weapons of Mass Destruction
and New Systems of Such Weapons', 10
August 1976, in US Arms Control and
Disarmament Agency, 'Documents
on Disarmament, 1976', pp. 538–41;
'Statement by the Soviet Representative
(Likhatchev) to the Conference of the
Committee on Disarmament: Weapons
of Mass Destruction', 17 August 1976,
p. 556, http://unoda-web.s3-accelerate.
amazonaws.com/wp-content/uploads/
assets/publications/documents_on_
disarmament/1976/DoD_1976.pdf.

43 'Soviet Working Paper Submitted to
the Conference of the Committee on
Disarmament: Definitions of New
Types of Weapons of Mass Destruction
and New Systems of Such Weapons', 10
August 1976, in US Arms Control and
Disarmament Agency, 'Documents on
Disarmament, 1976', p. 539.

44 Cable from US Mission Geneva to
Secretary of State, 'CCD: assessment
of third round of informal meetings

on Soviet proposal on new mass
destruction weapons (MDW)', March
1977, US National Archives, https://
aad.archives.gov/aad/createpdf?rid=61
862&dt=2532&dl=1629

45 'Statement by the United States
Representative (Martin) to the
Conference of the Committee on
Disarmament: Weapons of Mass
Destruction, 17 August 1976', in US
Arms Control and Disarmament
Agency, 'Documents on Disarmament,
1976', pp. 547–50, http://unoda-
web.s3-accelerate.amazonaws.
com/wp-content/uploads/assets/
publications/documents_on_
disarmament/1976/DoD_1976.pdf;
Cable from US Mission Geneva to
Secretary of State, 'CCD – meetings
on Soviet MDW proposal – summary',
August 1976, pp. 18–22, para 11,
https://aad.archives.gov/aad/createpdf
?rid=56165&dt=2082&dl=1345.

46 Cable from US Mission Geneva to
Secretary of State, 'CCD – meetings
on Soviet MDW proposal – summary',
August 1976.

47 *Ibid.*; 'Statement by the Soviet
Representative (Likhatchev) to the
Conference on the Committee on
Disarmament: Weapons of Mass
Destruction', 17 August 1976, in US
Arms Control and Disarmament
Agency, 'Documents on Disarmament,
1976', p. 559.

48 Cable from US Mission Geneva to
Secretary of State, 'CCD: assessment
of third round of informal meetings
on Soviet proposal on new mass
destruction weapons (MDW)', March
1977.

49 *Ibid.*

50 Cable from Secretary of State to US
Embassy Moscow, 'Radiological
warfare initiative', November 1976,

US National Archives, https://aad.archives.gov/aad/createpdf?rid=290924&dt=2082&dl=1345.

51 *Ibid.*

52 'Statement by ACDA Director Ikle to the First Committee of the General Assembly: Nuclear Policy and Radiological Weapons, 18 November 1976', in US Arms Control and Disarmament Agency, 'Documents on Disarmament, 1976', pp. 815–20, http://unoda-web.s3-accelerate.amazonaws.com/wp-content/uploads/assets/publications/documents_on_disarmament/1976/DoD_1976.pdf; Cable from Secretary of State to US Mission to the UN, New York, 'Radiological warfare', November 1976, US National Archives, https://aad.archives.gov/aad/createpdf?rid=286877&dt=2082&dl=1345; Cable from the US Mission to the UN, New York, to Secretary of State, 'Ikle–Kuznetsov Conversation On Disarmament Topics', November 1976, US National Archives, https://aad.archives.gov/aad/createpdf?rid=279047&dt=2082&dl=1345.

53 'Statement by President Ford: Nuclear Policy, October 28, 1976', in US Arms Control and Disarmament Agency, 'Documents on Disarmament, 1976', p. 711, http://unoda-web.s3-accelerate.amazonaws.com/wp-content/uploads/assets/publications/documents_on_disarmament/1976/DoD_1976.pdf.

54 Cable from Secretary of State to US Embassy Moscow, 'Radiological Warfare Initiative', 17 November 1976, US National Archive, https://aad.archives.gov/aad/createpdf?rid=290924&dt=2082&dl=1345.

55 Cable from US Mission Geneva to Secretary of State, 'CCD: assessment of third round of informal meetings on Soviet proposal on new mass destruction weapons (MDW)', March 1977.

56 Cable from US Embassy Moscow to Secretary of State, 'Soviet MFA officials comment on arms control issues', February 1977, US National Archives, https://aad.archives.gov/aad/createpdf?rid=36832&dt=2532&dl=1629.

57 Cable from US Mission to the UN, New York, to Secretary of State, 'Radiological Warfare', 19 November 1976, para. 9. The Soviet Union often referred to its WMD initiative as a ban on mass destruction weapons (MDW). This chapter uses the two terms, WMD and MDW, interchangeably.

58 Cable from Secretary of State to US Mission Geneva and US Mission at NATO, 'US participation in experts meeting on MDW', February 1977, US National Archives, https://aad.archives.gov/aad/createpdf?rid=30779&dt=2532&dl=1629; Cable from Secretary of State to US Embassy Moscow, 'Official – Informal', February 1977, US National Archives, https://aad.archives.gov/aad/createpdf?rid=35026&dt=2532&dl=1629.

59 US Department of State, Office of the Historian, '1. Letter From President Carter to Soviet General Secretary Brezhnev', 26 January 1977, Foreign Relations of the United States, 1977–80, vol. 6, Soviet Union, https://history.state.gov/historicaldocuments/frus1977-80v06/d1.

60 Cable from US Mission Geneva to Secretary of State, 'CCD: third informal meeting with experts on new mass destruction weapons (MDW), March 16, 1977', March 1977, US National Archives, https://aad.archives.gov/aad/createpdf?rid=57624&dt=2532&dl=1629.

61 *Ibid.*; Cable from US Mission Geneva to Secretary of State, 'CCD: fourth informal meeting with experts on new mass destruction weapons (MDW), March 17, 1977', March 1977, US National Archives, https://aad.archives.gov/aad/createpdf?rid=58905&dt=2532&dl=1629; Cable from US Mission Geneva to Secretary of State, 'CCD: assessment of third round of informal meetings on Soviet proposal on new mass destruction weapons (MDW)', March 1977.

62 Cable from US delegation secretary in Moscow to Secretary of State, 'Fourth meeting with Gromyko et al.', March 1977, US National Archives, https://aad.archives.gov/aad/createpdf?rid=69686&dt=2532&dl=1629.

63 'News Conference Remarks by Secretary of State Vance on Negotiations in Moscow [Extract], 30 March 1977', in US Arms Control and Disarmament Agency, 'Documents on Disarmament, 1977', p. 178; Adam Ulam, 'U.S. Soviet Relations: Unhappy Coexistence', *Foreign Policy*, vol. 57, no. 3, America & the World 1978.

64 Cable from Secretary of State to US Mission at NATO, 'NATO disarmament experts, April 21–22: instructions for USDEL', April 1977, US National Archives, https://aad.archives.gov/aad/createpdf?rid=89671&dt=2532&dl=1629; Cable from Secretary of State to US Mission Geneva, 'CMD: US–USSR arms control working group on radiological weapons and new mass destruction weapons (RW/MDW)', January 1978, US National Archives, https://aad.archives.gov/aad/createpdf?rid=22872&dt=2694&dl=2009.

65 Cable from Secretary of State to US Mission Geneva, 'US–USSR working group on RW/MDW, first round', May 1977, US National Archives, https://aad.archives.gov/aad/createpdf?rid=103059&dt=2532&dl=1629.

66 *Ibid.*

67 Cable from Secretary of State to US Mission Geneva, 'CCD 1977 summer session: guidance for US delegation', July 1977, US National Archives, https://aad.archives.gov/aad/createpdf?rid=173611&dt=2532&dl=1629https://aad.archives.gov/aad/createpdf?rid=173611&dt=2532&dl=1629m, April 16, 2018].

68 Cable from Secretary of State to all NATO capitals, 'Discussion paper for May 24–27 APAG meeting', May 1977, US National Archives, https://aad.archives.gov/aad/createpdf?rid=104246&dt=2532&dl=1629; Ulam, 'US–Soviet Relations: Unhappy Coexistence', p. 557.

69 Cable from US Mission Geneva to Secretary of State, 'RW (MDW): RS (MDW) CW/bilaterals with Soviets: Geneva message no. 2', May 1977, US National Archives, https://aad.archives.gov/aad/createpdf?rid=104824&dt=2532&dl=1629.

70 Cable from Secretary of State to US Mission Geneva, 'CCD 1977 summer session: guidance for US delegation', July 1977.

71 Cable from US Mission Geneva to Secretary of State, 'CCD: need for decision concerning RW negotiations, message no. 12', August 1977, US National Archives, https://aad.archives.gov/aad/createpdf?rid=182842&dt=2532&dl=1629.

72 George Kistiakowsky, 'The folly of the neutron bomb', *Bulletin of the Atomic Scientists*, vol. 34, no. 7, 1978, pp. 25–29.

73 Vincent Auger, *The Dynamics of Foreign Policy Analysis: The Carter*

Administration and the Neutron Bomb (Lanham, MD: Rowman & Littlefield, 1976), p. 15.

74 Kistiakowsky, 'The folly of the neutron bomb', p. 26.

75 Walter Pincus, 'Neutron Killer Warhead Buried in ERDA Budget', *Washington Post*, 6 June 1977, https://www.washingtonpost.com/archive/politics/1977/06/06/neutron-killer-warhead-buried-in-erda-budget/161ae957-099f-4c5b-ad19-052699d60f4d/?utm_term=.0ef5531c6c08.

76 Auger, *The Dynamics of Foreign Policy Analysis: The Carter Administration and the Neutron Bomb*, p. 73.

77 'The Heated Debate Over the Neutron Bomb', *Washington Post*, 31 March 1978, https://www.washingtonpost.com/archive/politics/1978/03/31/the-heated-debate-over-the-neutron-bomb/e286ca5a-b1b1-471f-8f00-5ff3556d1ab3/?utm_term=.293d23a02eaf.

78 'Revised Soviet Draft Agreement Submitted to the Conference of the Committee on Disarmament: Prohibition of the Development and Manufacture of New Types of Weapons of Mass Destruction and New Systems of Such Weapons, 8 August 1977', in US Arms Control and Disarmament Agency, 'Documents on Disarmament, 1977', pp. 493–96, http://unoda-web.s3-accelerate.amazonaws.com/wp-content/uploads/assets/publications/documents_on_disarmament/1977/DoD_1977.pdf.

79 Cable from US Mission Geneva to Secretary of State, 'US–USSR Arms Control Working Group on Radiological Weapons and New Weapons of Mass Destruction', September 1977, US National Archives,

https://aad.archives.gov/aad/createpdf?rid=203728&dt=2532&dl=1629.

80 'The Heated Debate Over the Neutron Bomb'.

81 *Ibid.*

82 Kristina Spohr Readman, 'Germany and the Politics of the Neutron Bomb, 1975–1979', *Diplomacy and Statecraft*, vol. 21, no. 3, 2010, p. 268.

83 *Ibid.*, p. 275.

84 Zbigniew Brzezinski, *Power and Principle: Memoirs of the National Security Advisor, 1977–1981* (New York: Farrar, Straus and Giroux, 1983), p. 304.

85 Cable from US Mission Geneva to Secretary of State, 'US–USSR arms control working group on radiological weapons and new weapons of mass destruction', January 1978, US National Archives, https://aad.archives.gov/aad/createpdf?rid=5855&dt=2694&dl=2009.

86 Cable from US Mission Geneva to Secretary of State, 'CCD weekly report, February 17–March 3, 1978', March 1978, US National Archives, https://aad.archives.gov/aad/createpdf?rid=79329&dt=2694&dl=2009; Cable from US Embassy Bonn to Secretary of State, 'Consultations with FRG, UK and France on chemical weapons and radiological weapons', May 1978, US National Archives, https://aad.archives.gov/aad/createpdf?rid=117835&dt=2694&dl=2009; Cable from US Mission Geneva to Secretary of State, 'US–USSR working group on radiological weapons: request for instructions on reformulation of US elements 1 and 2', March 1978, US National Archives, https://aad.archives.gov/aad/createpdf?rid=62520&dt=2694&dl=2009.

87 Cable from US Mission Geneva to Secretary of State, 'US–USSR working

group on radiological weapons: request for instructions on reformulation of US elements 1 and 2', March 1978.

88   Cable from US Mission Geneva to Secretary of State, 'US statement in CCD on reduced-blast enhanced radiation weapon, March 9, 1978', March 1978, US National Archives, https://aad.archives.gov/aad/createpdf?rid=55316&dt=2694&dl=2009.

89   Cable from US Mission Geneva to Secretary of State, 'US–USSR arms control working group on radiological weapons and new weapons of mass destruction, round four: seventh (final) plenary meeting, May 4, 1978', May 1978, US National Archives, https://aad.archives.gov/aad/createpdf?rid=113604&dt=2694&dl=2009.

90   Cable from US Embassy Bonn to Secretary of State, 'Consultations with FRG, UK and France on chemical weapons and radiological weapons', May 1978.

91   Cable from US Mission Geneva to Secretary of State, 'US–USSR arms control working group on RW/MDW, fifth round, ninth and final meeting, September 8, 1978', September 1978, US National Archives, https://aad.archives.gov/aad/createpdf?rid=220479&dt=2694&dl=2009.

92   Cable from Secretary of State to US Embassy London and US Embassy Bonn, 'Disarmament at 33rd UNGA: wrap-up of first committee debate – an overview', December 1978, US National Archives, https://aad.archives.gov/aad/createpdf?rid=324224&dt=2694&dl=2009.

93   Ibid.

94   Cable from US Mission Geneva to Secretary of State, '(U) US-USSR arms control working group on radiological weapons (RW) and new weapons of mass destruction, round six: elements 1–5 of possible joint initiative', February 1979, US National Archives, https://aad.archives.gov/aad/createpdf?rid=90004&dt=2776&dl=2169.

95   Cable from US Mission Geneva to Secretary of State, 'Committee on disarmament (CD): consideration of prospects of further activities in bilateral negotiations and in the CD', April 1979, US National Archives, https://aad.archives.gov/aad/createpdf?rid=15427&dt=2776&dl=2169.

96   Cable from US Mission Geneva to Secretary of State, '(U) US–USSR arms control working group on RW/MDW, round seven: plenary and subordinate meetings, June 22, 1979', June 1979, US National Archives, https://aad.archives.gov/aad/createpdf?rid=175939&dt=2776&dl=2169.

97   Cable from US Embassy Moscow to Secretary of State, '(C) US–USSR arms control working group on RW/MDW: meeting with ambassador Israelyan', June 1979, US National Archives, https://aad.archives.gov/aad/createpdf?rid=158465&dt=2776&dl=2169; Cable from US Mission Geneva to Secretary of State, 'CD: US–Soviet joint initiative on radiological weapons', July 1979, US National Archives, https://aad.archives.gov/aad/createpdf?rid=132703&dt=2776&dl=2169.

98   Chalmers Hardenbergh, 'The other negotiations', Bulletin of the Atomic Scientists, vol. 42, no. 1, January 1986, p. 45.

99   United Nations, 'Report of the Committee on Disarmament, General Assembly, Official records, thirty-fifth session supplement no. 27, (A/35/27)', paras 16–17, http://undocs.org/A/35/27(SUPP).

100 Ibid., para. 16. The question of whether attacks on nuclear power

plants or other facilities that would release radioactivity emerged as a divisive issue in the Conference on Disarmament after Israel destroyed Iraq's Osirak reactor in 1981, as noted by William Potter and Jeffrey Lewis in 'Cheap and Dirty Bombs', *Foreign Policy*, 17 February 2014, http://foreignpolicy.com/2014/02/17/cheap-and-dirty-bombs.

101 US Department of State, Office of the Historian, '148. Memorandum of Conversation', 1 February 1977, Foreign Relations of the United States, 1969–76, vol. 33, SALT II, 1972–80, https://history.state.gov/historicaldocuments/frus1969-76v33/d148.

102 Cable from Secretary of State, for info US Embassy Vienna, 'Polads meeting on US–USSR radiological weapons initiative (C)', July 1979, US National Archives, https://aad.archives.gov/aad/createpdf?rid=143541&dt=2776&dl=2169.

103 Cable from US Mission Geneva to Secretary of State, 'Radiological weapons initiative: discussion with Austrian charge d'affaires in Geneva

(C)', October 1979, US National Archives, https://aad.archives.gov/aad/createpdf?rid=297787&dt=2776&dl=2169.

104 *Ibid.*

105 In the United States, the history of this programme and its scope were documented for the first time in the report of the Advisory Committee on Human Radiation Experiments, convened in 1994 by President Bill Clinton; see https://ehss.energy.gov/ohre/roadmap/achre/summary.html. There has been no formal acknowledgement of the Soviet radiological-weapons programme by the Russian government to date. See also Potter and Lewis, 'Cheap and Dirty Bombs'.

106 Cable from Secretary of State to US Embassy London, 'Disarmament at 33rd UNGA: wrap-up of first committee debate – an overview', December 1978; Cable from Secretary of State to US Embassy London, US Embassy Bonn, 'Disarmament at 33rd UNGA: Wrap-Up Of First Committee Debate – An Overview', December 1978.

Chapter Eight

1 Authors' interviews with Russian and US officials in Track 1.5 nuclear dialogues in Vienna (June 2017), Moscow (October 2017) and Geneva (December 2017).

2 Joseph Nye, 'U.S.–Soviet Cooperation in a Nonproliferation Regime', in Alexander George, Philip J. Farley and Alexander Dallin (eds), *U.S.–Soviet Security Cooperation: Achievements, Failures, Lessons* (New York: Oxford University Press, 1988), p. 337.

3 *Ibid.*

4 The same phenomenon is apparent in the post-Cold War period with respect to cases such as Iran and North Korea.

5 Hal Brands, 'Non-Proliferation and the Dynamics of the Middle Cold War: The Superpowers, the MLF, and the NPT', *Cold War History*, August 2007, p. 409.

6 'Statement of Kosygin Signing of Treaty on Non-Proliferaiton of Nuclear Weapons', 31 June 1968, *Current Digest of the Soviet Press*, vol. 20, no. 27:3, cited

by Brands, 'Non-Proliferation and the Dynamics of the Middle Cold War: The Superpowers, the MLF, and the NPT', p. 409.

7   Nye, 'U.S.–Soviet Cooperation in a Nonproliferation Regime', p. 346.

8   Roland Timerbaev, 'In Memoriam: George Bunn (1925–2013)', Arms Control Association, 3 June 2013, https://www.armscontrol.org/print/5803.

9   William C. Potter, 'Nuclear Nonproliferation: US–Soviet Cooperation', Washington Quarterly, Winter 1985, p. 144.

10 Cable from Secretary of State to US Embassy Moscow, 'Nuclear Safeguards Consultations', October 1974, US National Archives, https://aad.archives.gov/aad/createpdf?rid=234399&dt=2474&dl=1345.

11 Roland Timerbaev, 'The Nuclear Suppliers Group: Why and How It Was Created: 1974–1978', PIR–Center for Policy Studies in Russia, 2000, p. 29, http://www.pircenter.org/media/content/files/9/13464056390.pdf.

12 A prominent example is ambassador James Goodby, who had frequent interactions with Soviet counterparts on a range of non-proliferation issues during the detente period, including the CTB and SALT II, and then served as a leading US negotiator under the Cooperative Threat Reduction Program.

13 Timerbaev, 'The Nuclear Suppliers Group: Why and How It Was Created: 1974–1978', p. 54.

14 Cable from Secretary of State to US Embassy Tripoli, 'US Goals and Objectives Statements', 26 February 1979, US National Archives, https://aad.archives.gov/aad/createpdf?rid=101154&dt=2776&dl=2169. Ironically, when Belgium subsequently sought to provide nuclear assistance to Libya, the European Union and the US both indicated they would prefer Russia to be the supplier, as they believed Moscow would insist on more stringent safegurds.

15 'National Security Decision Memorandum 255, Henry Kissinger to Secretary of Defense et al.: Security and Other Aspects of the Growth and Dissemination of Nuclear Power Industries', 3 June 1974, Wilson Center Digital Archive, http://digitalarchive.wilsoncenter.org/document/119771.pdf?v=a77e2393be96cb3a2ca9933b2287b87c.

16 Gerald R. Ford, 'Statement on Nuclear Policy', 28 October 1976, http://www.presidency.ucsb.edu/ws/?pid=6561.

17 Cable from Secretary of State to US Mission to the UN, New York, 'Radiological Warfare', 12 November 1976, https://aad.archives.gov/aad/createpdf?rid=286877&dt=2082&dl=1345.

18 Cable from Secretary of State to US Embassy Moscow, 'Radiological Warfare Initiatives', 17 November 1976, https://aad.archives.gov/aad/createpdf?rid=290924&dt=2082&dl=1345.

19 See Chapter Four for additional details.

20 Cable from Secretary of State to US Embassy Moscow, 'Nuclear Safeguards Consultations', 26 October 1974, https://aad.archives.gov/aad/createpdf?rid=232924&dt=2474&dl=1345.

21 US Department of State, Office of the Historian, '144. Memorandum from the Under Secretary of State (Ball) to President Johnson', 8 August 1966, Foreign Relations of the United States, 1964–68, vol. 11, Arms Control and Disarmament, https://history.state.gov/historicaldocuments/frus1964-68v11/d144.

22 *Ibid.*

23 US Department of State, 'Action Memorandum: Your Meeting with Gromyko: South African Nuclear Issue (1977)', Digital National Security Archive, http://nsarchive.chadwyck.com.

24 Cable from Secretary of State to US embassies in Bonn, London, Moscow, Paris, Pretoria, Tel Aviv, Vienna, 'South African [sic] and the NPT: Cooperation with USSR', 30 September 1977, https://aad.archives.gov/aad/createpdf?rid=220735&dt=2532&dl=1629.

25 Murrey Marder and Don Oberdorfer, 'How West, Soviets Acted to Defuse S. African A-Test', *Washington Post*, 28 August 1977, https://www.washingtonpost.com/archive/politics/1977/08/28/how-west-soviets-acted-to-defuse-s-african-a-test/eada5bcc-7727-4c32-b8e2-f21d55a9d4c3/?utm_term=.d7c48a54d64a.

26 Cable from Secretary of State to US Mission Geneva, 'Oct. 20 Press Roundup', 21 October 1977, US National Archives, https://aad.archives.gov/aad/createpdf?rid=246254&dt=2532&dl=1629.

27 *Ibid.*

28 US Department of State, 'Action Memorandum: from Fred Ikle (ACDA) to the Secretary of State, Talks on Reactor Safeguards and Related Matters with the Soviets on October 15', 5 October 1974, Wilson Center Digital Archive, http://digitalarchive.wilsoncenter.org/document/119780.

29 US Department of State, Office of the Historian, '82. Report Prepared by an Interagency Study Group of the National Security Council Under Secretaries Committee', 13 September 1974, Foreign Relations of the United States, 1969–76, vol. E-14, part 2, Documents on Arms Control and Nonproliferation, 1973–76, https://history.state.gov/historicaldocuments/frus1969-76ve14p2/d82.

30 The significant impact of alliance politics on Soviet NPT negotiating positions, especially with respect to the issue of the MLF, is highlighted by Hal Brands. He notes that consideration of Soviet-bloc politics directly influenced the non-proliferation behaviour of Khrushchev and Brezhnev, and on occasion led them to take a harder line on NATO nuclear arrangements, even if this complicated deliberations over a non-proliferation treaty. See Brands, 'Non-Proliferation and the Dynamics of the Middle Cold War: The Superpowers, the MLF, and the NPT', p. 404.

31 Cable from Secretary of State to US Mission IAEA Vienna, 'Coordination of Nuclear Export Policy: Soviet CIEWS [sic]', 30 November 1974, US National Archives, https://aad.archives.gov/aad/createpdf?rid=260876&dt=2474&dl=1345.

32 Glenn T. Seaborg, 'Cooperation between the U.S. and the USSR in the Peaceful Uses of Atomic Energy', paper presented at the International Conference 'Fiftieth Anniversary of Nuclear Fission', Leningrad, USSR, 16–20 October 1989, Lawrence Berkeley National Laboratory, University of California, https://pubarchive.lbl.gov/islandora/object/ir%3A92638/datastream/PDF/view.

33 Cable from Secretary of State to US Embassy Moscow, 'TTBT-PNE Negotiations', 10 October 1974, https://aad.archives.gov/aad/createpdf?rid=233951&dt=2474&dl=1345.

34 Cable from Secretary of State to US Embassy Moscow, 'TTBT/

PNE Negotiations: Instructions for Delevation [sic]', 8 October 1974, https://aad.archives.gov/aad/createpdf?rid=220595&dt=2474&dl=1345.

35 Cable from US Embassy Moscow to Secretary of State, 'TTBT/PNE Negotiations – Summary and Analysis of Negotiations to Date', 21 October 1974, https://aad.archives.gov/aad/createpdf?rid=223071&dt=2474&dl=1345.

36 Glenn T. Seaborg, *A Scientist Speaks Out: A Personal Perspective on Science, Society, and Change* (Singapore: World Scientific Publishing Co., 1996), p. 428.

37 Two very important recent studies are Eric Schlosser, *Command and Control: Nuclear Weapons, the Damascus Accident, and the Illusion of Safety* (New York: Penguin Press, 2014) and Patricia Lewis et al., 'Too Close for Comfort: Cases of Near Nuclear Use and Options for Policy', Chatham House Report, April 2014, https://www.chathamhouse.org/sites/files/chathamhouse/field/field_document/20140428TooCloseforComfortNuclearUseLewisWilliamsPelopidasAghlani.pdf. Among many other important studies, see Scott Sagan, *The Limits of Safety: Organizations, Accidents and Nuclear Weapons* (Princeton, NJ: Princeton University Press, 1993); David E. Hoffman, *The Dead Hand: The Untold Story of the Cold War Arms Race and Its Dangerous Legacy* (New York: Doubleday, 2009); Valery E. Yarynich, *C3: Nuclear Command, Control, Cooperation* (Washington DC: Center for Defense Information, 2003); and Bruce Blair, *The Logic of Accidental Nuclear War* (Washington DC: The Brookings Institution, 1993).

38 For an analysis of the different facets or faces of nuclear terrorism, see Charles D. Ferguson and William C. Potter, *The Four Faces of Nuclear Terrorism* (New York: Routledge, 2005).

39 According to the International Panel on Fissile Materials (http://fissilematerials.org), as of January 2017 the global stockpile of highly enriched uranium was estimated to be approximately 1,340 (plus or minus 125) tons; the global stockpile of separated plutonium was estimated to be about 520 tonnes.

40 This danger was accentuated when the Islamic State, also known as ISIS or ISIL, occupied territory in Iraq on which there were known radiological sources.

41 For a discussion of this case, see Lewis et al., 'Too Close for Comfort' and Nikolai Sokov, 'Could Norway Trigger a Nuclear War? Notes on the Russian Command and Control System', PONARS Policy Memo 24, October 1997, PONARS Eurasia, http://www.ponarseurasia.org/sites/default/files/policy-memos-pdf/pm_0024.pdf.

42 Logical Russian organisations would include such NGOs as the PIR Center, the Center for Energy and Security Studies, the Luxembourg Forum and the Institute for World Economy and International Relations. Their US counterparts include the Nuclear Threat Initiative, Harvard University's Belfer Center, the Carnegie Endowment for International Peace and the James Martin Center for Nonproliferation Studies.

43 Although beyond the time frame of this study, one of the most telling examples of the importance of personal relationships involved US–Russia cooperation to remove chemical weapons (CW) in Syria. This unusual example of such cooperation during a period of very strained bilateral relations was made

possible, in part, due to the personal and professional relationships forged by Russian and US officials during work on chemical-weapons elimination as part of the Nunn–Lugar Cooperative Threat Reduction Program. Many of the same policymakers on each side were involved in both CW elimination activities.

[44] The US–Russia Bilateral Presidential Commission was initiated in 2009, but was suspended following Russian intervention in Crimea.

[45] An unusual initiative to replenish Russian and US non-proliferation expertise is the Dual Master Degree in Nonproliferaiton Studies offered by Moscow State Institute of International Studies (MGIMO) and the Middlebury Institute of International Studies at Monterey (MIIS). The MGIMO–MIIS Dual Degree Program, launched in autumn 2016, enables students to spend one semester in Moscow, two semesters in Monterey and one semester at an international non-governmental organisation with a non-proliferation focus. See: https://www.middlebury.edu/institute/academics/degree-programs/nonproliferation-terrorism-studies/overview/dual-degree.

INDEX

⎰IISS ADELPHI BOOKS

ADELPHI 463

Africa's Lost Leader:
South Africa's continental role
since apartheid

James Hamill

ISBN 978-1-138-54965-4

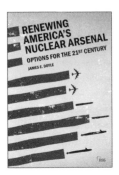

ADELPHI 462

**Renewing America's
Nuclear Arsenal:**
Options for the 21st Century

James E. Doyle

ISBN 978-0-8153-8466-3

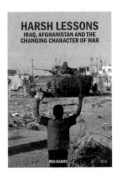

ADELPHI 461

Harsh Lessons: Iraq, Afghanistan
and the changing character
of war

Ben Barry

ISBN 978-1-138-06096-8

ADELPHI 460

Everyone Loses: The Ukraine
crisis and the ruinous contest for
post-Soviet Eurasia

Samuel Charap and Timothy J. Colton

ISBN 978-1-138-63308-7

For credit card orders call **+44 (0) 1264 343 071**
or e-mail **book.orders@tandf.co.uk**
Orders can also be placed at **www.iiss.org**

Adelphi books are published eight times a year by Routledge Journals, an imprint of Taylor & Francis, 4 Park Square, Milton Park, Abingdon, Oxfordshire OX14 4RN, UK.

A subscription to the institution print edition, ISSN 1944-5571, includes free access for any number of concurrent users across a local area network to the online edition, ISSN 1944-558X. Taylor & Francis has a flexible approach to subscriptions enabling us to match individual libraries' requirements. This journal is available via a traditional institutional subscription (either print with free online access, or online-only at a discount) or as part of our libraries, subject collections or archives. For more information on our sales packages please visit www.tandfonline.com/page/librarians.

2018 Annual Adelphi Subscription Rates			
Institution	£719	US$1,262	€1,063
Individual	£254	US$434	€347
Online only	£629	US$1,104	€930

Dollar rates apply to subscribers outside Europe. Euro rates apply to all subscribers in Europe except the UK and the Republic of Ireland where the pound sterling price applies. All subscriptions are payable in advance and all rates include postage. Journals are sent by air to the USA, Canada, Mexico, India, Japan and Australasia. Subscriptions are entered on an annual basis, i.e. January to December. Payment may be made by sterling cheque, dollar cheque, international money order, National Giro, or credit card (Amex, Visa, Mastercard).

For a complete and up-to-date guide to Taylor & Francis journals and books publishing programmes, and details of advertising in our journals, visit our website: http://www.tandfonline.com.

Ordering information:
USA/Canada: Taylor & Francis Inc., Journals Department, 530 Walnut Street, Suite 850, Philadelphia, PA 19106, USA. UK/Europe/Rest of World: Routledge Journals, T&F Customer Services, T&F Informa UK Ltd., Sheepen Place, Colchester, Essex, CO3 3LP, UK.

Advertising enquiries to:
USA/Canada: The Advertising Manager, Taylor & Francis Inc., 530 Walnut Street, Suite 850, Philadelphia, PA 19106, USA. Tel: +1 (800) 354 1420. Fax: +1 (215) 207 0050. UK/Europe/Rest of World: The Advertising Manager, Routledge Journals, Taylor & Francis, 4 Park Square, Milton Park, Abingdon, Oxfordshire OX14 4RN, UK. Tel: +44 (0) 20 7017 6000. Fax: +44 (0) 20 7017 6336.